BEYOND JAPANESE MANAGEMENT
The End of Modern Times?

In memory of

Peter Titherington 1942–92

Convenor

Transport & General Workers Union 6/765
Vauxhall Motors, Ellesmere Port

BEYOND JAPANESE MANAGEMENT

The End of Modern Times?

edited by

PAUL STEWART

FRANK CASS

LONDON • PORTLAND, OR

First published in 1996 in Great Britain by
FRANK CASS AND COMPANY LIMITED
Newbury House, 900 Eastern Avenue, London IG2 7HH, England

and in the United States of America by
FRANK CASS
c/o ISBS, Inc.
5804 N.E. Hassalo Street, Portland, Oregon 97213-3644

Copyright © 1996 Frank Cass & Co. Ltd.

British Library Cataloguing in Publication Data
A catalogue record for this book is available from the British Library.

ISBN 0 7146 4761 6 (hbk)
ISBN 0 7146 4322 X (pbk)

Library of Congress Cataloging-in-Publication Data

Beyond Japanese management: the end of modern times? / edited by
Paul Stewart.
    p.   cm.
    ISBN 0-7146-4761-6. – ISBN 0-7146-4322-X (pbk)
    1. Automobile industry and trade–Japan–Management.
    2. Automobile industry and trade–Management–Case studies.
    3. Comparative management. I. Stewart, Paul
    HD9710.J32B49   1997
    658'.00951–DC20   96-44871
                                             CIP

This group of studies first appeared in a Special Issue of
Asia Pacific Business Review, Vol.2, No.4 (Summer 1996),
[JAPANESE MANAGEMENT: The End of Modern Times?]

Printed in Great Britain by
Redwood Books, Trowbridge, Wiltshire.

Contents

Abstracts

Beyond Japan, beyond Consensus? From Japanese Management to Lean Production *by Paul Stewart*

The author argues that the current hegemonic conceptions of the trajectory of Japanese management at home and abroad allow for only a limited understanding of the broader sociological questions relating to the subordination-insubordination of labour. The Japanese management school in the UK reifies Japanese management by either overplaying its consensual nature or over-estimating its coercive features. In addition, it is suggested that the arguments about 'Japan' in the Japanization school provide the basis, significant differences notwith-standing, for the ideological agenda of the lean production school. A more nuanced account of Japan and Japanese management would draw upon the nature of struggles in the workplace and the wider society. While some of these struggles can be contained within corporatist management and union strategies, others clearly cannot. This suggests that a broader understanding of the unevenness of workplace subordination and quiescence requires an agenda which goes beyond that provided by current hegemonic paradigms.

A Fallen Idol? Japanese Management in the 1990s *by Colin Haslam and Karel Williams, with Sukhdev Johal and John Williams*

The authors argue that the elevation of Japanese manufacturing management in the West rested on the idea that superior performance resulted from new productive techniques and different systems of management. The object of this article is to shift the balance of placing more weight on structural factors and less on management success or failure. Attention is drawn to the fact that Japanese industry operated in a favourable domestic environment. Output expansion at home and a favourable social settlement (wages, hours worked) operated to ensure that exports, sold in markets where quite different social settlements set higher prices, generated a great deal of cash for Japanese producers. It is argued that the erosion, if not disappearance, of these favourable conditions from the mid-1980s onward has contributed substantially to the recent difficulties of Japanese producers.

The Changing Nature of Japanese Production Systems in the 1990s and Issues for Labour Studies *by Koichi Ogasawara and Hirofumi Ueda*

The authors discuss the changing character of production strategies and organizational arrangements at three leading Japanese automotive assemblers against a background of concern with the impact of work regimes upon employees. Innovations in production line organization are compared within and between the companies, and the argument advanced suggests that the attempt to 'humanize' work routines and procedures, by the leading company especially, has met with mixed results. Sometimes more 'efficient' technologies and forms of organization have been inhibited in the pursuit of 'human-centred' forms of work organization. Nevertheless, the article points up the considerable variations which exist both between and within Japanese companies and trade unions with respect to the understanding of the role played by labour.

Working Conditions under Lean Production: A Worker-based Benchmarking Study *by Wayne Lewchuk and David Robertson*

Benchmarking is being used extensively in management's drive to achieve 'world class' levels of performance. The majority of benchmarking studies have little if anything to say about working conditions or the tradeoffs between productivity improvements and the conditions of working life. This article is based on a study which focuses on working conditions as described by workers, raising questions about the tradeoffs between work reorganization and the quality of working life under Lean Production.

The results, based on a survey of 1670 workers at 16 different companies, suggest that work life under Lean Production has not improved. Compared with workers in traditional Fordist style plants, those at Lean companies reported their work load was heavier and faster. They reported work loads were increasing and becoming faster. They reported it was difficult to change things they did not like about their job and that it was becoming more difficult to get time off. While our survey results suggest that working in traditional Fordist plants is far from paradise, they also suggest that working in Lean plants is worse. At a minimum, our results should be viewed as a wake-up call to those who have painted a positive picture of work under Lean Production.

A New Model Ford? *by Steve Babson*

This study compares work organization and labour relations at three assembly plants: the Ford Escort plant in Wayne, Michigan; the Ford Escort-Tracer plant in Hermosillo, Mexico; and the Mazda-Ford joint venture in Flat rock, Michigan. All three plants are commonly understood to be 'team concept' work environments; all three also exhibit a common technical organization derived from the same Mazda-Ford engineering set-up. However, the social organizatin of each plant' s work teams is substantially different. The single most important variable in shaping these contrasting outcomes was the role of the union: aggressively involved in the earliest planning for team production at Wayne, while arriving late at Flat Rock and adopting a passive role. When the UAW local at Flat Rock elected more militant leaders, this evolving dynamic pushed in the direction of worker-centred teams; conversely, when the union in the Ford Hermosillo plant was weakened by company reprisals following a bitter strike, management was free to push in the direction of supervisor-centred teams.

New Manufacturing Strategies and Labour in Latin America
by John Humphrey

Latin American scholars have shown considerable interest in the spread of Japanese methods in the continent and their potential impact on labour. Evidence from case studies shows intensive use of techniques such as multi-tasking, team-working, statistical process control and cellular manufacture. In some cases, firms have invested heavily in education and training in order to make viable new production strategies, and there is some evidence of attempts to stabilize labour forces and establish better plant-level relations with workers. This apparent break with the practices of peripheral Fordism does not appear to be accompanied by improvements in company-union relations. Where unions are strong, management have attempted to undermine union power. Where unions are weak, managements have continued to deny the legitimacy and relevance of union representation. Companies seek the flexibility to make labour work harder as well as smarter, and they are introducing individualized assessment and incentive schemes which tend to be opposed by collective representation.

Volvo–A Force for Fordist Retrenchment or Innovation in the Automobile Industry? *by Kajsa Ellegård*

The article deals with the question: What does the 'Volvo model' stand for? Two car assembly plants within the Volvo Car Corporation are the main exponents of the 'Volvo model', namely the Kalmar and Uddevalla plants, which were innovative and successful. There has been an open atmosphere to new ideas in the company at the top level and innovative ideas were stimulated at Kalmar and Uddevalla. However, simultaneously there was no strategy for spreading the innovations within the company, and resistance to the new ideas within the other operative units was strong. Therefore the diffusion of internal, Volvo-generated innovations was taken on solely by individuals or groups of individuals who were already committed to the ideas. In the Volvo TWR joint venture Autonova AB, the principles of the Reflective Production System, once developed within the Volvo Uddevalla plant, are being further developed. So, Volvo still has a joker left in the pack...

The Competitivity of the Automobile Industry: The French Way
by Jean-Pierre Durand

The French auto industry is now one of the most successful in the world and has developed markets in other European countries and further afield. The intriguing background to this has been that the French manufacturers, Renault and PSA, have developed strategies based largely upon home-grown employment cultures. While the companies have spent considerable time in Japan, the specificity of French employment practices and employee relations have intervened to block or significantly moderate outside practices. Perhaps the most important lesson is that any organizational system cannot be separated from its social, historical and economic context, in which the interests of different actors impact upon the process of innovation.

Reactions to the Crisis – Job Losses, Shortened Working Week, Income Losses and Business Re-engineering in the German Auto Industry by Ulrich Bochum and C. Dörrenbächer

After very successful years in terms of employment and sales in the 1980s the German car industry was hit by a deep economic slump in 1993. German unification had triggered a car boom that concealed serious problems of the German production model. This production model was characterized by high labour costs, high qualification levels, strong trade unions and worker representation and a technology-oriented productivity strategy. In this context work organization was neglected. The introduction of lean production principles was seen as a way of improving work organization and management strategy, but soon it became clear that it was mainly related to job losses and cost-cutting measures. Many approaches to enrich work structures on the shop floor were abandoned in favour of reaching competitive cost structures. Manufacturers' reactions to the crisis varied widely. While Mercedes-Benz and BMW started a strong trend towards internationalizaton of car production, Volkswagen made headlines by introducing the four-day working-week. Above all, adjustment to global competitive challenges is on the agenda of German car companies. Negotiations with unions and works councils over greater flexibility of collective bargaining agreements have led to greater flexibility in capacity utilization.

Taylorism, Lean Production and the Automotive Industry
by Mike Rawlinson and Peter Wells

This article examines the nature of work organization in vehicle assemblers and how new production technology has led to a convergence in organizational structure between all vehicle assemblers. The nature of work under lean production is examined and its origins are traced back directly to Taylorism, in particular the building blocks of the Toyota Production System of Jidoka and SMED. The authors argue that to understand changing skill compositions and work organization in vehicle assemblers it is necessary to look beyond the assembly line. The assembly line demands little skill content from its workers and also only adds a small proportion of value to the end product. The paper examines changes in the higher value added and more skill-demanding manufacturing areas of the press shop. It illustrates how workers are in effect becoming 'multi-purpose, semi-skilled' in so-called lean and other producers.

Beyond Japan, Beyond Consensus? From Japanese Management to Lean Production

PAUL STEWART

INTRODUCTION: BEYOND 'JAPANESE MANAGEMENT'?

The following discussion rests on the contention that the Japanization school in the UK can be understood as a specific moment in the rise of theories of globalization more generally (Stewart and Garrahan, 1997). The Japanization school's approach can be interpreted as a fatalistic response to Japanese foreign direct investment and Japanese social relations, including Japanese management and industrial relations practices. In particular, I argue that the school displays a number of interrelated features which limit its scope as a research agenda for the analysis of the current phase in the internationalization of capitalist social relations:

- the school overplays, through reification, the role of the culture of management;

- the school constitutes an oversocialized view of labour;

- related to this is an unresolved tension between a view of labour as incorporated (consensus-quiescence) and labour as insubordinate despite domination;

- the school provides for a highly institutionalist view of industrial relations; its reified understanding of management practices allows for the underestimation of the barriers to their portability (Boyer and Freyssenet 1996; da Costa and Garanto 1993); and

- it lays the basis, important differences accepted, for the ideological agenda of the lean production school and its imperative of the One Best Way.

Indeed, what links the above projects, in addition to the role played by the Japanization school as a precursor to lean production, is that they promote, in Gramsci's terms, a specific ideological current given legitimacy by researchers and academics who perform the role of 'organic intellectuals' (Gramsci, 1971). The schools propagate a particular ideology about the character of industrial development which has become hegemonic in academic and practitioner discourse, the prodigious efforts of critics notwithstanding (see the work of the Williams–Haslam team below). This

Paul Stewart, University of Wales, Cardiff.

kind of hegemony was important for Gramsci, who considered that one of the key roles of the organic intellectual is to make conventional the non-natural (and unaccepted) by construing as 'natural' what is in reality socially contrived. Both these schools share this transformative relation to the worlds they purport to describe (Stewart and Martinez Lucio, 1996).

In this introduction, I want to provide an overview of what I take to be the key conceptual problems in the debate about the nature of so-called Japanese management practices in the UK. There will be no attempt to discuss the nuts and bolts of 'doing it the Japanese way', an agenda which, outside the assumptions of management teaching, is surely untenable, rooted as it is in an easy assumption about the malleability of distinctly different social formations (see Wood, 1991). Nor am I concerned with the problems *per se* of adaptation of supposedly Japanese management practices to the British (or any other) economy, although it needs to be noted that this concern is still axiomatic for the Japanization school in the UK (Morris and Wilkinson, 1995).

The Japanisation of British Industry (1988) was the point of take off for the school after the elaboration of an earlier idea by Turnbull (1986). The telos was subsequently refined in 1992 in a sequel to the *Japanisation of British Industry*, subtitled, '*New Developments in the 1990s*'. The main thesis was, and remains, that the significant and transformative management practices in Britain today are (or will be) *essentially* Japanese, which is to say that new management practices are either Japanese in fact or Japanese by proxy (*qua* 'functional equivalents' – this concept is also utilized by the lean production school). Japan and Japanese practices are the benchmark by which the efficacy of new practices are to be judged. Indeed, this is the only basis upon which progress, for which read competitiveness, can be assured. The current updating of the Japanization project in the special issue of the *Journal of Management Studies* (1995, hereafter *JMS 32/6*. See especially the introduction by Morris and Wilkinson) represents a bold attempt to locate the school within the wider contemporary debate concerning global restructuring. However, the outcome serves to reinforce existing weaknesses in the paradigm (concerning the 'specialness' of Japan and the portability of essentialist Japanese management practices), while revealing other drawbacks which were largely implicit in the 1988 and 1992 'Japanization' texts (The latter was couched specifically in terms of evidence offered by the International Motor Vehicle Program [IMVP] on auto sector competitiveness.) Gone, however, in the *JMS* special issue, is an explicit genuflection to the work of the IMVP group (1992: 5–9, 15) in establishing the empirical basis for the notion of Japanese managerial specificity (see the 'lean production school' below). As a consequence of this, greater emphasis is placed upon the theme of employee domination, which is seen to be inscribed in the very idea of Japanese management practices. On one level, this can be viewed as a positive emphasis because in the 1988 and 1992 'Japanization' texts, the problem of employee domination tended to be subsumed within a framework which emphasized the creative tension involved in the management of 'high dependency' relationships (1992: 82–7). The outcome of this for the management of human resources was that the question of employee domination was defined in terms of consensus-acquiescence. In this context, organizational and technical features of the new workplace, such as 'just-in-time', place employees in a potentially very powerful position despite the fact that they never (or rarely) seek to realize this power. The answer as to why this might be is that employees effectively acquiesce in a regime which, though management-inspired, allows for some element of employee benefit in welfare and involvement programmes. Outside Japan itself of course this would occur either through the direct implementation of these management processes or via proxies – 'functional equivalents'. One important problem with this thesis was that it had little direct empirical grounding and none in terms of workplace research based upon employee responses.

The major advance of the 1995 *JMS* special issue is that this absence of field research into employee responses is addressed by several of the contributors so that the 'dark side' of this management is stressed – 'the iron fist in the velvet glove', to quote the conclusion's epithet on Japanese management. Yet one consequence of the emphasis upon subordination is that the double-sided nature of management regimes is occluded. In some respects we are back where we started in still requiring a theoretical account of subordination-resistance. In the *JMS* project, the Japanese management system is repressive by its very nature and the only way out is through personal protest (or via an indirect kind of collectivism coded in culturally 'accepted' norms of disobedience. See Abdullah and Kennoy on Japanese management in Malaysia). Consensus-quiescence is in effect replaced by control-insubordination: the management process is now notable to the extent that it is repressive – the worst possible fate for labour under Taylorism (the end state for Taylorism?). Thus, in the *JMS* update, despite the cautionary note for labour, the inevitablist assumption about development – or, following the lean production school, One Best Way – is still explicit. In effect, the question of labour subordination and commitment is never fully resolved in the school, largely because of problems with the framework used to account for 'why it works'. This framework is torn between elaborating management codes of control based upon employee commitment and employee resistance derived from a regime of coercive subordination. Thus,

- the problem of labour control-insubordination/struggle is explicable either (mostly) in terms of the material *quid pro quo*, as in the 1988–92 texts or (mostly) coercion, as in *JMS* (32/6),

- it is difficult to make sense of the character of any labour regime unless it is remembered that this will be limited by the nature of social struggles in the wider political economy, the workplace and the labour process, and finally,

- if the sobriquet 'Japanization/Japanese management' really is intended to conjure up something distinctive then both the analysis of so-called Japanese practices and their various structural consequences must be capable of bearing rather closer scrutiny than is presently the case.

I now want to turn to another theme which only recently has become significant for the Japanization school – its relation to the current debate over globalization.

JAPANIZATION AND GLOBALIZATION

Indeed, in some respects the overarching significance of the Japanization paradigm must be judged in relation to conceptions of globalization. This is in part because the Japanization oeuvre, in its *JMS* incarnation, serves a specifically ideological role in legitimating a teleological reading of new developments in the international division of labour which is the hallmark of globalization theories (see Scott, 1996; Burnham, 1991; Panich, 1994; Hirst and Thompson, 1996). For exponents of the Japanization school (*JMS*, 1995) the debate is a debate over the 'how and why' of things Japanese, including, at its most radical, a discussion of the exploitative character of Japanese management practices (Delbridge, 1995; Abdullah and Keenoy, 1995). However, despite the criticism of management gurus implied by the latter (construed as advocates of the lean production school) the 'radicals' share a number of their assumptions. Primarily, the Japanization school holds that the current phase of restructuring depends upon the outcome of the fate of management systems which in their essentials are seen to be Japanese.

The extent to which these management processes are exploitative is seen to shed light on the wider problem of the relation between new forms of management (namely, Japanese) and the shift from fordism (Hirst and Zeitlin, 1991). The conclusion would seem to be that Japanese forms of management *are* new but that, contrary to the optimism of the exponents of either flexible specialization, 'the third Italy' or lean production, the outcome is worse for labour and for employees' democratic participation in the firm.[1] 'Japanization', 'lean production', call it what they will, is merely fordism perfected – *plus ça change…*[2] This is unfortunate because this view entirely overlooks the results of counter-factual evidence including the work of critics of the idea of globalization, such as Panich (1994), MacEwan (1994), Holloway (1995) and Hirst and Thompson (1996) who root discussion of globalization and the new international division of labour in the social opposition, conflicts and struggles within which it takes place. The dynamic of social class, and the place of labour antinomies specifically, is vitiated where ready assumptions about employee acceptance or individualized employee rejection of 'Japanese management' forms a significant agenda. This is a significant problem because the most systematic piece of research in the last decade into the question of the relation between new management practices, trade unions and employee attitudes, the *Social Class and Economic Life Initiative* (SCELI),[3] fails to support the assumptions of the Japanization paradigm. This is a telling absence indeed for a school which is concerned with the impact of managerial control strategies upon labour. But then, one of the contentions here is that the Japanization school mirrors some of the claims of management, particularly regarding the coherence and 'excellence' of the techniques themselves. In short, this derives from a less than adequate linkage of the investigative intention behind their empirical agenda (Morris and Wilkinson, 1995: 719–728) to the diagnosis of 'fordist decline'. Moreover, despite the fact that the intention is to assess the degree of 'transfer' in the context of societal-specific norms of development, a globalizing motive is derived from very limited casework. All the different aspects of Japanese management have something which is in essence definable as 'Japanese' and eminently portable: '…The new paradigm of production and work organization *does* travel everywhere with the Japanese' (p.728). It is this essentialism, among other peculiarities as we shall see, which links the Japanization and lean production schools – 'radical' critiques aside.

Furthermore, the *JMS* agenda represents an attempt to locate the project within broader accounts of the fragmentation of the fordist paradigm. On the one side, according to Morris and Wilkinson, are the mostly German research groups (the 'Continental European school' (ibid., p.719) concerned with the consequences of new production models and the impact of their consequent technological innovations for organizational development. On the other side is the Japanization school, with its emphasis upon a socio-technical account of the consequences of the 'departure from the "Taylorist" or "Fordist" production paradigm'. While the Continental European school is seen to be hampered by a tendency towards technological determinism, the Japanization school is privileged in so far as its paradigm is sensitive to empirical assessment of the impact of culture and history on organizational development. Finally, so the argument goes, the Continental European school is likely to be marginalized because of the growing hegemony of the 'Japanese model'. Yet for a broader assessment we also require an evaluation of the views of French and Spanish researchers (Boyer and Freyssenet in France and Castillo in Spain), and the Swedish 'Uddevalla group' is never mentioned (Ellegard *et al.*, 1992; Ellegard, 1993). In addition, apart from Humphrey's contribution, evaluation of the work of the GERPISA international research network is also absent (GERPISA is the Permanent Group for the Study of the Automobile Industry and its employees). This is an important oversight because the heterogeneous nature of GERPISA ensures that critical evaluation of the fundamental assumptions behind the idea of 'transfer' can be aired. It could be argued, *pace* the objectives of GERPISA itself, that in this environment the themes of complexity, innovation and fragmentation are perhaps the only clear guide to understanding the impact of so-called Japanese forms of organization. Revealingly, Berggren's (1993; 1995) fascinating argument about a third way between Japan and Sweden does not even warrant a mention. Berggren's pessimistic view (in particular, his 1995 evaluation) of the impact of globalization upon Japan's social settlement and its ensemble of various management-labour cultures, is in stark contrast to the role conceived for things Japanese by Morris and Wilkinson. For them, Japanization is seen as the bearer of modernization cum globalization.

Moreover, when we turn to the specifics of Japanese inward investment into the UK, the inability to properly lay down the ground rules for the assessment of change based on a more nuanced understanding of class, labour and conflict reduces the explanatory validity of the school still further.[4] For example, when trade unions are considered, the focus is put entirely upon an institutionalist interpretation of what should be considered as highly contested social relations in electronics and automotives (Morris *et al.*, 1992). Moreover, trade union and management activities in Japan and elsewhere are described, with respect to their institutional forms, as all-powerful regimes of domination.[5] The paradigm, in other words, defaults to an over-socialized view of the role of labour at the heart of capitalist production. It is as a result of a different emphasis upon this over-socialized view of 'Japanese' management practices that conflict, though important, is given a different twist from its incorporated status in the 1988 and 1992 'Japanization' texts. Indeed, the casework in *JMS* insists that we interrogate the management practices in a manner that reveals employee subordination.

This suggests that one of the major problems for researchers of the implications of Japanese inward investment is to begin the long process of conceptual clarification in order to allow for the contradictory character of new employment relations as borne by foreign inward investors (Elger and Smith, 1996). Consequently, my purpose is two-fold. In the first place I want to indicate the basis of an alternative agenda for making sense of the dynamics of new (and some not so new) labour processes and work organizations to allow for a reinterpretation of those employment relations designated 'Japanese'. Secondly, it is important to locate the ground rules for the debate about changes in work within a class analysis of contemporary forms of employment. In other words, in going 'beyond Japan' we need to escape the conceptual limitations of the Japanization paradigm which imposes constraints upon even some of its most demanding critics (Elger and Smith, 1994). However, to go beyond what has proved to be a theoretically restrictive view of Japanese management and employment practices to a more balanced account of the social relations of production requires that we also indicate how we might go beyond both the couplets 'consensus-quiescence' and 'control-insubordination'. This is crucial if we are to locate labour regimes in the context of the insecure nature of management strategies. To do so will lead us to an evaluation of the importance of those organizations and groups which although usually (but not always) numerically small are firmly rooted in the Japanese workplace – specifically, what are termed the 'minority', or 'second', trade unions (*shosuha kumiai*). This evaluation is necessary because in many respects the view of the Japanese workplace as being driven by quiescence does have a superficial plausibility, but only if we use the western yardstick as an index of the character of conflict (Kawanishi, 1992). By pointing towards the work and role of the 'minority' trade unions we can begin to appreciate some sense of the more complex character of 'Japanese management' practices and the social conflicts which are central to them. While I discuss the character of the *shosuha kumiai* in detail elsewhere (Stewart, forthcoming) suffice for present to note that enterprise unionism, contrary to popular misconception, does not in principle imply the existence of only one union in the company. Indeed, despite the fact that often there is only one union in a company this cannot be guaranteed under Japanese labour law. If two or more individuals are determined, as sometimes happens, to form a union then the company is legally obliged to recognize and negotiate with them (Zenroran, 1994–95). The 'minorities' thrive in many sectors and industries and, while they are considerably more significant in the public sector and in firms on the periphery, their political and ideological significance often compensates for their overall numerical weakness (Kawanishi, 1992). However, even in the auto sector where the numbers of individuals participating are often quite limited, they can score notable successes as occurred for example during the 1994 elections for union stewards at Toyota. Contrary to all expectations, the 'minority' representative gained just over seven per cent of the vote, out of a total workforce exceeding 80,000 (Stewart, forthcoming). Clearly, there are other dynamics than either consensus-quiescence or control and individualized insubordination at work here.

THE JAPANIZATION PARADIGM AND SOCIAL CHANGE: EXPLANATION, IDEOLOGY, DETOUR?

Having considered the main tenets of the Japanization school in the context of the questions of labour subordination and globalization, a final note needs to be added regarding two prominent assumptions. Below, I address some of the issues already considered – labour control, subordination-insubordination and management expertise – but from the standpoint of underlying problems of methodology. In short, the Japanization project more generally relies upon a functionalist understanding of the role played by employees and trade unions in the enterprise, both in the US and elsewhere (Kenney and Florida, 1991: 381–2; Oliver and Wilkinson, 1988; 1992; Morris *et al.* 1992). This functionalism in turn is tied to a teleological notion of change which is highly important for those arguments we have just considered with respect to globalization.

Despite some distinctive points of divergence (for an especially clear and cogent assessment of these see Elger and Smith, 1994[6]) 'Japanization' authors in the UK and USA share common points of analytical and substantive convergence. What is of significance for the argument here is the fact that they address issues of change within a framework which in all its essentials is driven by a search for an understanding of consensus-making institutions both in the wider economy but especially within the workplace. However, the difficulty is that since social change cannot easily be understood at the level of formal institutional consensus-quiescence making processes, an appreciation of the themes of change needs to move beyond a view of conflict as either residual and backward looking (Kenney and Florida 1991, 1993) or as problematical to the delicate organizational and social (not to mention economic) balance of JIT (Just In Time) production regimes. The latter of course, as pointed out above, are seen as axiomatic to Japanese production paradigms (Oliver and Wilkinson 1988, 1992). If this was the perception in the 1988 and 1992 versions of the 'Japanization' school perhaps balance was restored with the shift which occurred in the focus upon employee subordination in *JMS* 32/6. Yet the functionalism at the root of the paradigm did not allow for a re-evaluation of what is a homeostatic view of organizational development. Despite an agenda that addresses the down side of Japanese management processes, the issues of economic development, organizational rationality and broad social changes nevertheless require the implementation and adaptation of those technical and organizational variables which they label Japanese. The sub-text is that this form of development is worthy and sufficiently important to emulate. While the second edition of *The Japanisation of British Industry* (1992) and *JMS* 32/6 are somewhat more amenable to the salience of what Smith and Meiksins (1995) refer to as 'societal contingencies' as against what they define as 'dominance effects' (for our purposes, Japanese management processes) this is mitigated by the teleology implicit in the perception of the ascendancy of the Japanese line of march. That is to say, on the one hand, social characteristics sui generis in the country of origin are seen to be important for the model, while on the other hand where these are absent in the host country, 'functional equivalents' allow the Japanese management paradigm to operate.

It is important that this failing be addressed, for while much of great value has already been written about the overall problems of the Japanization school, insufficient emphasis has been placed upon this important ontological confusion. While there is insufficient space to rehearse all of the objections to the paradigm,[7] it is nevertheless worth mentioning the most trenchant and so far mostly unanswered assessment by Ackroyd *et al.* (1988).[8] For the latter, briefly, if Japanization as a concept refers to firm specific and labour process developments then it often misconstrues and confuses actual empirical processes. If, by contrast, it is suggestive of shifts 'towards Japan' at the macro level then it is a misnomer for sure. But for a very cautious salvage operation based on careful critique Elger and Smith (1994) have performed a sterling feat in bringing together the main confluence of work in relation to the problematics of Japanization. However, although they make reference to one of the most critical features of the Ackroyd *et al.* thesis regarding the problems with the concept 'Japanization', namely, the ideological import of the notion of 'Japanese' management, the full implications of this may to some extent be diluted in their insistence that at a minimum, it serves as a fairly open-ended agenda for investigation.[9]

However, and contrary to the projects of the Japanization school, Elger and Smith argue for the rigorous critique of Japanese production relations including everything dignified by that title. It is of course true as pointed out above that for the critical wing of this paradigm in the UK, most notably Delbridge (1995) and Sewell and Wilkinson (1992), the negative character of what they term Japanization is identified and confronted. However, the components of this critique – *inter alia*, work intensification, exclusion and domination – paradoxically consolidate rather than challenge the core teleology of the Japanization project. This is because Japanese production arrangements are seen to be pre-eminent because they are more rational (for management) and therefore must be/will be followed. There is no alternative! The implications of this are (and have been) somewhat debilitating since the lesson for management must be that the pursuit of something labelled Japanese can be a successful route in the emulation of Japan's 'success'. For labour, by contrast, what used to be termed the 'new realist' agenda, though perhaps now the 'new industrial relations', is the only path to survival. Both of these conclusions have been recited recently by Morris *et al.* (1992) in their assessment of the pattern and characteristics of Japanese FDI in south Wales, including its impact upon industrial relations. But even where the Japanization paradigm is most sophisticated, as with Sewell and Wilkinson (1992), the implications of control and surveillance strategies have a parallel resonance – labour as controlled, labour as subordinate and without choice.[10]

But perhaps this assessment is overly critical in that it inhibits even elementary work on things Japanese, forgetting that the paradigm for all its conceptual inadequacies at the very least promotes fundamental research. This is the starting point for Elger and Smith's *Global Japanisation* (1994) though it is not obvious that the concept 'Japanization' does allow for the investigative agenda they claim. Clearly, the casework in *Global Japanisation* is substantial in range and depth. However, it may also be reasonable to pursue the question of restructuring in the context of a more politically sensitive agenda, as some of the sharpest published empirical accounts, particularly in the UK, attempt to do. We can refer to the work of, *inter alia*, Grant (1994; 1996), Danford (1997) and Stephenson (1995). Ackers and Wilkinson (1995) also provide good casework on the usefulness of the concept from a largely institutionalist perspective. This research suggests that the notion of Japanization has limited use even as a rough and ready way of organizing initial incursions into the field.

When all is said and done, possibly the key problem with the concept of Japanization is that it conceals much more than it reveals. Thus, in going 'beyond Japan', the principal aim here is to present different organizational, economic and social readings of developments in different countries where the impact of new production arrangements cannot be constrained within the organizing ethos of the Japanization paradigm. A number of these accounts will allow us to lay the basis for an understanding of the extent to which new management practices are embedded in relations of, to quote Holloway (1995) 'subordination-insubordination'. At the very least this will allow us to question the taken-for-granted assumptions of the Japanization school about the coherence of a 'Japanese' model or practices, singularly or collectively, in which the point of origin is so marked as to act in a determinate manner upon those introduced to them – whatever the social and national context.

To some extent, this obsession with the powerful determining power of Japanese characteristics is all of a piece with the reification of Japan among many Western academics. Indeed, it could be said that there has been a mutual reinforcing – by both Western and Japanese scholars – of the reification of Japanese exceptionalism which has met with a peculiar response in Japan itself. Lie, recalling Harumi Befu (1990) sees this ready fixation with a packaged view of Japanese life by Japanese researchers as a kind of 'mass consumption commodity' (Lie, 1996: 9), an appropriation of the discourse of Japanese pre-eminence derived from a objectified understanding of Japanese social relations. The latter, according to Lie, is little more than the contrivance of some Japanologists. For Lie this has led to 'Theories of Japanese people and culture [which] constitute a sociology of the street' (Lie, 1996: 9), which is another way of indicting (occidental) social science (in particular) for the creation of an unwarranted contemporary myth. What is certain is that the Japanization school plays an important role in the naturalization of Japan as the exemplar for globalization strategies in the current phase of social and economic restructuring. The danger is that the assorted management techniques labelled Japanese serve to focus the attention of different industrial actors on one-dimensional responses and solutions to the various and complex crises underlying the current phase of restructuring.

To recapitulate, the central problems with the Japanization school are that:

- it eschews a broader understanding of social conflict because of its emphasis upon the impact of individualizing processes in the workplace – the paradigm cannot consider extant forms of collective opposition because workplace culture is seen to be entirely management centred;

- relatedly and particularly in *JMS* 32/6, it over-emphasizes subordination and control (the over-socialized view) at the expense of collective forms of dissent;

- too much credence is given to the institutionalist model of collectivism (notably in Morris *et al.* 1992); and finally,

- the reification of Japanese management techniques allows us to see these as variables which are (more or less) easily transferable.

FROM JAPANIZATION TO LEAN PRODUCTION?
CONTRASTS AND CONTINUITIES

With the development of the lean production paradigm at the end of 1980s, all of these discomforting problems can (so the evangelists hope) be left behind because for the first time the key reference points in the theme of Japanization can be stripped to its bare (technical) essentials. According to its advocates, lean production might well have been invented in Japan, but the conundrum ends there. By concentrating on the decultured and desocialized aspects of things Japanese, management can now, with cautious optimism, apply the lessons of the Japanese way just as they supposedly applied the verities of Taylorism in a previous era. With the lean production school there is precious little need to worry unduly about difficult issues of cultural transfer. This is not to say that social, cultural and organizational matters do not figure in the account, merely that they are seen to be secondary to the overriding technical imperatives of lean production. In a notable exception to the usual technological determinism underlying the assumptions of lean production school, Oliver *et al.* (1993) give some credence to the role of leadership in the implementation of lean strategies. However, even in this instance, social relations are perceived to be significant only in so far as they conform to the imperatives of 'lean' management behaviour. Technology and its proper implementation is the key to the 'one best way' of achieving manufacturing success.

This commitment by many researchers and practitioners to the view that Japanese pre-eminence can be reduced to production relations *qua* technological fixes perceives emulation as the way out of the competitivity crisis facing non-Japanese manufacturers (Oliver *et al.* 1994; Jones, 1992; Oliver, 1991). It is this emphasis upon the notion that Japan's success derives more realistically from a unique set of technical attributes, which given the proper conditions can be adopted by any company anywhere, that marks the attempt to resolve the tension between culture and technique in the Japanization school. Certainly elements of a technocratic narrative were significant in the 'Japanization' texts (and in the *JMS* 32/6 work) but the obsession with the peculiarities of Japanese culture saved these from an impulse to excessive technological determinism. Lean production represents this unashamedly technocratic account of Japanese pre-eminence but it also acts as a cipher both for the technological precepts of the Japanese management paradigm and the key to occidental catch-up.

The new panacea for economic despair in the West, according to the IMVP[11] authors of the *Machine that Changed the World* (1990), Womack, Jones and Roos, and more recently Andersen Consulting (Oliver *et al.* 1994) on world-wide manufacturing, must be lean production which will supposedly allow for an unbiased assessment of sector competitiveness. The claims of the lean production school are many and they have both social and technical implications, but for present purposes we can focus on those relating specifically to social agency in the context of labour unions. The key assumption of the IMVP group which concerns us here involves strategic issues for labour in so far as trade unions in the West are implored to face up to the demands of wider global transformation. In effect, trade unionism will be seen to be relevant to company success in so far as it eschews Anglo-Saxon forms of organizing. In this respect, lean production can allow the establishment of a new form of industrial citizenship. (Womack *et al.*, 1990: 103, and D. Jones, 1992)

This can be realized when management concentrates on the issues that it can immediately transform – labour in the guise of social agency is not in itself a significant variable in considering change to production regimes. On the contrary, it is just one among others – labour can then be stripped of its social and cultural characteristics which allows conflict and disagreement to be banished because they are seen as abnormal. Needless to say, this allows management to effect change in its own image and on its own terms, specifically by following the Toyota production philosophy – the One Best Way to achieve world class manufacturing (Womack *et al.*).[12]

Indeed, so hegemonic has the lean production paradigm become that there are very few who now contest, not only its claims to superiority, but also its efficacy as a useful social scientific perspective with some insight into the process of managerial change. (For notable exceptions see, *inter alia*, Masami, 1993; Nomura, 1993; Watanabe, 1993). Even within the labour movement in the UK and North America, those who are dubious as to its general claims regarding workplace humanization nevertheless take for granted the status given to it by its leading proponents as an adequate account of change (Huxley *et al.* 1991; Robertson, 1992a; 1992b). More generally, critics concentrate upon the social consequences of lean production including the impact upon workplace industrial relations. Some of this may derive from an accommodation to its status as a description of the 'best in the world', or as a prescriptive account of change. Many critics fail to challenge it on either count. Although the limitation on space does not permit elaboration of the arguments of all the critics of lean production, for present purposes I consider those offering perhaps the most cogent critique because they address lean production mostly on its own terms.

For some researchers, lean production is restricted as an account of new management techniques (most notably, Berggren, 1988 and 1993, Lyddon, 1996 and Milkman, 1991). Lyddon's typically thorough and incisive debunking of the claims of the lean production school provides a solid historical and sociological complement to the radical economic critique of the Williams-Haslam team in the UK (*Against Lean Production*, 1992a; *Ford Versus Fordism*, 1992; *Factories or Warehouses*, 1992b; *The Myth of the Line*, 1993; *Management Practice or Structural Factors*, 1995). Their argument, derived from a radical accounting and economic tradition, is that lean production provides an implausible understanding of the nature of new production and management practices. On this basis, they challenge the school's claims to originality as proffered by Womack *et al.* (1990) For the Williams group, it was the Ford's 'lean production' model, as opposed to

Toyota's, that was truly revolutionary. The first and major innovation established by Ford, initially at Highland Park between 1909 and 1916, was the ability to strip labour out of the labour process (Williams, *et al.*, 1992: 522). The significant advance was not in the extension of the principles of mass production; rather it was established through the creation of what Williams, Haslam and Williams describe as a 'proto-Japanese' (1992: 519) factory. It was with this factory regime that Ford really established the foundations of new production arrangements, the lessons of which were lost over the next forty or so years, only to be rediscovered by Toyota in the 1950s (1992: 546).

The second misunderstanding in the lean production thesis relates to the problem of conversion efficiency (linked to the level of firm integration). According to Williams *et al.*, while conversion efficiencies were maintained at Highland Park (1992: 520) the company began to ship kits to its other plants throughout the US from 1912 onwards, with over a score of 'branch assembly plants in all the "principal cities"' (1992: p.520). Nevertheless, Ford still built more of the Model-T in-house than contemporary auto producers, and in their weighting for this Williams, Haslam and Williams calculate that enormous advances were established by Ford operations. Finally, according to the authors, the third achievement of Ford was to wage a successful war against high inventories, and this is compared rather favourably with their 1988 findings of Toyota's experiences (1992: 523).

Life beyond Management?

In '*Management Practice or Structural Factors*' (1995) Williams *et al.* meet directly the challenge from Womack *et al.* to the effect that the strength of the *Machine That Changed the World* lies with its concern over things which management *can* change as opposed to those things which it cannot – that is, supposedly secondary issues associated with social agency, such as labour unions. While going some way to explaining what is the Achilles heel of the lean production approach their argument nevertheless points up a curious kind of strength. By ignoring labour, it is possible to contrive idealized assumptions about performance at plant level. The benefit of their approach is that where we might nevertheless adjudge social agency to be problematic, this difficulty is resolved where we correlate a set of congruent organizational variables as the basis of success – team working and *kaizen*, for example. If these are instituted where organizational problems arise, it is assumed that organizational synergy will develop (Williams *et al.*1993: 2–6). Of course, because the lean production approach is paradigmatic its leading protagonists envisage that success will only accrue where organizations adopt the full philosophy. In the event that problems might arise in the wake of full adoption of the production principles, dysfunctional operations are reducible to inadequate transference (Oliver *et al.* 1994). Strangely, it is not the 'real world' which is to be used to allow for adjustments to the model, rather it is the model – in effect, a reification of Toyota's Takaoka plant – which becomes the arbiter of organizational efficacy. This reification of the technical system finds a mirror image in the reification of the social organization of production. Yet by alleviating social and technical phenomena of the historical and cultural burden of what it is that allows for empirical differences, it is impossible to determine how actual variations can occur (Williams *et al.* 1993: 5–6). This performs the same end as does the methodological device of 'functional equivalence' for the Japanization school – social and organizational differences are sublimated to erode social barriers – to the implementation of the model.

The reality is that it is only by coming to terms with the significance of the political economy, including the character of state–civil society relationships in each environment, that both the origins of differences with respect to each society's automotive industry and its future trajectory can be ascertained. It is unsurprising therefore if the uncertainties of the real world continue to disrupt the calculated unreality of the lean production model. By positing that social agency is a non-variable in the equation it is spirited away. This is why the lean production paradigm cannot explain variations between plants and companies in any real world. As touched upon above, one response proffered by the protagonists of lean production to their critics (see *inter alia*, Fucini and Fucini 1990, the CAW 1993) is that where dissonance exists this can either be attributed to inept management in the implementation process, or to Fordist and hence anachronistic forms of industrial relations (Stewart and Garrahan 1995). In this case, what about the lacuna at the heart of the debate on Japanese management – conflictual, recalcitrant, and oppositional labour? To begin to address this absence, we need to go beyond consensus in a double sense. First, with respect to the hegemonic account of the Japanization school which defaults to a view of Japanese workplaces as constituted upon the normality of consensus – whether or not concensus is based upon an assumption of quiescence or subordination. Second and relatedly, to go beyond consensus requires the establishment of an agenda that recognizes the normality of the relatively independent power of labour in the workplace, including the ultimate unrealizability of management imperatives as delineated by any extant model.

CONCLUSION: BEYOND CONSENSUS – THE NORMALITY OF STRUGGLE AND OPPOSITION

Clearly therefore, it is axiomatic to the argument presented here that social struggle must be seen to be central to our understanding of production relations – just as they are in the west. In this concluding section, my aim is merely to open a different agenda for the analysis of workplace labour relations. The key problem with accounts which focus upon the consensual character of Japanese employment relationships (whether or not consensus is achieved by quiescence or subordination) is precisely that they distort the character of labour in the social relations of production. This is certainly not specific to the Japanization and lean production schools alone but is symptomatic of a more widely shared assumption about the nature of Japanese society. Citing Lie once again (1996: 9, 10–11) we can argue that the over-emphasis upon the normality of consensus (abnormality of conflict) has its origins in a taken-for-granted belief about the homogeneous character of Japanese culture and social relations which has been fed (in similar fashion to the idea of Japanese exceptionalism as pointed out above) by western and Japanese scholars alike. It is central to what Lie defines as 'Nihonjinron – theories about the nature of Japanese people' (Lie, 1996: 8) and its emphasis upon the cultural and societal distinctiveness of Japan's homogeneity. We can see how this underlies and distorts an understanding of the character of labour in the social relations of production. It is certainly convenient to see conflict and opposition as in some sense atypical of the standard norm for labour activity. This is often pursued by focusing, for example, upon the 'glory years' which supposedly ended in the 1950s, or by the description of the annual shunto ('spring offensive'), as the residual shibboleth of a once-proud trade union movement. This serves different researchers and commentators in different ways. For some on the left it suggests that opposition is indeed dead, and for management consultants (not to mention some leading Japanologists) that labour is so inextricably tied to management that all opposition other than the ritual shunto is inconceivable. For example, Tabata (1989) is enlisted by Morris and Wilkinson, to demonstrate the irrefutable power of management at Nissan, despite the former's data and analysis to the contrary. Nissan certainly took the iniative from the 'majority' union in the mid to late 1980s during a period of the economic transition, but Tabata's concern was to highlight the significant power exerted by the 'majority' union until the 1980s. Tabata is important because his account of the relative autonomy of a form of trade unionism offers the possibility of a significantly different reading of the life of the enterprise unions after the 'fall' in the 1950s. While his view of enterprise unionism at Nissan is not intended to be generalizable, he nevertheless offers compelling evidence of (a key) workplace as a contested domain in which even 'majority' enterprise unions have to, and on occasions can, battle around issues that are of fundamental importance to workers. Yet the model of Japanese unions as consensual-quiescent does not allow for these nuances to come through (see Stewart, forthcoming).

Going 'beyond consensus' is perhaps the best way to leave behind the condescension of the lean production paradigm. By going beyond consensus, this collection of articles will point towards an agenda for future research which recognizes the importance of both conflict and struggle within Japanese employment relationships (Totsuka, 1996; Nohara, 1993; Fujuta, 1988; Kawanishi, 1992; Yamamoto, 1990; 1992). This suggests the need to set aside the formalistic notion which argues that conflict has been either institutionalized (in the shunto) or marginalized (see especially Yamamoto's research on the Ohgi Kai, at 'T-Electric', 1990). Indeed, it is instructive that in the recent attempt to bolster the explanatory power of the

Japanese management paradigm, Morris and Wilkinson make reference to Yamamoto's account in order to highlight the all-encompassing nature of domination, despite Yamamoto's caution that the level of institutional surveillance is deemed necessary precisely due to the degree of opposition in the company. It could be countered that of course the object of the paradigm is to elaborate the institutional characteristics of Japanese management, yet this defence can only be accepted if the contours of opposition and contradiction are also highlighted.

The problem is that opposition does not rest easily in an account premised upon a one-dimensional notion of control. In the Japanization paradigm, institutions such as the *Ohgi Kai* are taken as marks of domination, when they are just as important analytically in drawing our attention to the persistence of insubordination. After all, as Gramsci pointed out, the double-edged nature of workplace hegemony is that it is founded upon conflict as well as consensus. Management strategies for subordination cannot only lead to quiescence for they are necessarily mediated in a context of employee power. If management strategies, in other words, do not operate in a vacuum but rather are constituted in a social dialectic of consent-dissent, then conflicts and social struggles must be seen to be inherently part of Japanese employment relations. This view is intended to convey the hope that it is not too late for researchers of 'Japanese management', in their various incarnations, to reassess their role as knowing or unknowing purveyors of the latest management discourse. Academics need to be clear about the 'politics' and 'ideology' of their sponsors, including the impact of these influences upon the soul (if that is not an outdated notion) of their research. Many people's lives are changed unrecognizably by the latest management whim, proselytized by academic consultants who knowing better should be wary of promised wonders. However, leaving aside the mantel of the organic intellectual will require a rather more extended critique of management practice than is possible within the constraints of the Japanization and lean production schools.

Indeed the exceptions illustrate that by focusing upon the concerns of labour it is possible to assess new management practices, whether or not inspired by Japan. Humphrey, below, addresses this in the context of Latin America where he considers the impact of social and cultural themes of organisation on new labour and management strategies. While the contribution from Ogasawara and Ueda draws attention to the complex variations both within and between Japanese auto producers, Durand's notion of a 'French way', in his analysis of French auto assemblers, suggests that society and company 'culture' considerations are important in the determination of new management processes. A similar point could be made in respect of Germany where Bochum and Dörrenbächer reflect upon the impact of international restructuring in the auto industry. Solutions will depend upon the way in which the sector shapes up to a double crisis – the current sector restructuring is itself provoking a crisis but this is being mediated by the national response to the 'crisis' of unification.

The contributions by Rawlinson and Wells (on the auto components sector) and Haslam *et al.* (on Japanese economic performance) stand as vital empirical critiques of the organizational and economic assumptions behind both the Japanization and lean production schools. Relatedly, Ellegard identifies the crucial importance of actually existing alternatives to the logic of lean production. Volvo may have allowed the faint hearts to triumph over the 'Uddevalla way', but her argument illustrates how limited is the lean production conception of work humanization. On this question of work humanization, the evidence presented by Babson from Ford and Ford-Mazda in the US reemphasizes the fundamental importance of labour intervention in mapping alternative pathways for the social and cultural organization of the firm. Finally, research by Lewchuk and Robertson from Canada reveals not only the downside of new production arrangements but also the profound role that labour unions can play in meeting management's challenge. Their research tells us that both change and the meanings attributed to it by management are open to other interpretations. An important challenge for researchers will be to offer alternative interpretations by challenging the taken-for-granted and the commonplace in management rhetoric.

ACKNOWLEDGEMENTS

Thanks to Miguel Martinez Lucio, as usual, and Ed Heery for critical and helpful comments on various versions of this article. In addition, I would like to express my thanks to the Japan Society for the Promotion of Science for their support in the collection of material in the preparation of the article.

NOTES

1. And by extension, the wider polity.
2. This draws on the Foucauldian current within the Japanization school which for reasons of space cannot be elaborated here. See especially Sewell and Wilkinson (1992).
3. Despite criticism about the sampling used by the SCELI team and its long overdue publication, it nevertheless represents a significant assessment across sectors and localities of the changing nature of work and employment in the 1980s. The reference here is to *Trade Unions in Recession*, (1996) Gallie *et al.*
4. This conclusion may appear odd, especially when one considers the conceptual scope for issues of conflict suggested by the Japanization paradigm. Nonetheless, the argument being made here is that conflict is seen to arise from the *technical* tension which exists in a JIT-no buffer system between planned production and the consequent enhancement of employee potential for disruption (Oliver and Wilkinson 1988, 1992). Indeed, the potential for conflict is never realized because social (surveillance) and organizational (teamwork) measures, which are fundamentally part of the system, intervene to prevent it occuring except in individualistic terms – so much for the need to develop an analysis derived from the way in which new production relations impact upon the struggle over the social surplus. Employees should be stronger in this system but the reason why this strength is rarely if ever realised is seen to result from the coercive nature of Japanese management techniques of surveillance in the form of practices such as TQM/JIT. However, the question has to be raised as to whether conflict can be entirely accounted for where subordination is over-emphasized.
5. One example of this is in the reference made to the *Ohgi Kai* at Toshiba in Japan in order to emphasize the omnipotence of managment – which is certainly powerful – as opposed to the persistence of insubordination. See Yamamoto, 1990.

6. On the historically and sociologically, limited nature of the concept of Japanization, see Ackers and Wilkinson, 1995 and Wood, 1991.

7. The most sustained assessment of the concept of Japanization is still probably the original one in the special issue of the Industrial Relations Journal (19:1) which published key proceedings from the Cardiff Employment Research Unit conference in 1987. See especially, in addition to Ackroyd *et al.*, the articles by Briggs, Dickens and Savage and Graham.

8. Extraordinarily, Ackroyd *et al.*'s assessment of the problems with the school are entirely ignored in JMS 32/6, as is Wood's (1991) careful and important critique.

9. 'We use the term with a question mark, to underline the disputed character of the social organization of production in Japanese manufacturing and the problematical influence of wider social, economic and political conditions on management efforts to adopt or adapt such innovations.' (p.8).

10. Delbridge's project focuses upon the contours of employee opposition, identified by way of a plant-based 'sociology of Japanization'.

11. The International Motor Vehicle Program was coordinated by the Massachusetts Institute of Technology

12. For a salutary critique on the empirical consequences of transfer, albeit in a non-automotive sector, see Milkman (1991) and on the logic of transfer more generally, Berggren (1988, 1993).

REFERENCES

Abdullah, S.R.S. and Keenoy, T. (1995) 'Japanese Management Practices in the Malaysian Electronics Industry' in *Journal of Management Studies* Vol.32, No.6 (Nov.), pp.747–66.

Ackers, P. and Wilkinson, A. (1995) 'When Two Cultures Meet: New Industrial Relations at Japanco' in *The International Journal of Human Resource Management* Vol.6, No.4 (Dec.) pp.849–71.

Ackroyd, S, Burrell, G. Hughes, H and Whitaker, A. (1988) 'The Japanisation of British Industry?' in *Industrial Relations Journal* Vol. 19 No.1 (Sept.) pp.11–23.

Berggren, C. (1988) '"New Production Concepts" in Final Assembly – the Swedish Experience' in Dankbaar B. *et al.*

Berggren, C. (1993) 'Lean Production: The End of History?' in *Work Employment and Society*, Vol.7, No.2 (June), pp.163–88.

Berggren, C (1995) 'Japan as Number Two: Competitive Problems and the Future of Alliance Capitalism after the Burst of the Bubble Economy' in *Work, Employment and Society* Vol.9, No.1 (Mar.), pp. 53–95.

Boyer, R. and M. Freyssenet (1996) 'Des Models Industriels Aux Strategies D'Internationalisation' in *L'Industrie Automobile Mondiale: Entre Homogénéisation et Hiérarchisation.* GERPISA, Paris (June).

Burnham, P. (1991) 'Neo-Gramscian Hegemony and the International Order', *Capital and Class,* Vol.45 (Aut.) pp.73–93.

Canadian Auto Workers (1993) CAW Statement on the Reorganisation of Work.

Castillo, Juan José (1994) 'Which Way Forward for the Sociology of Work', The Charles Babbage Research Seminar, Working Paper 101, Department of Sociology, Universidad Complutense Madrid.

Delbridge, R. (1995) 'Surviving JIT: Control and Resistance in a Japanese Transplant' in *Journal of Management Studies,* Vol.32, No.6 (Nov.), pp.803–17.

Elger, T. and C. Smith (1994) *Global Japanization: The Transformation of the Labour Process.* London: Routledge.

Ellegård, E. (1993) *The Creation of a New Production System at the Volvo Automobile Assembly Plant in Uddevalla, Sweden.* GERPISA, Paris.

Ellegård K., T. Engstrom and L. Nilsson (1992) 'Reforming Industrial Work – Principles and Realities', in *The Planning of Volvo's Assembly Plant in Uddevalla.* Stockholm: Arbetsmiljofonden.

da Costa, I. and A. Garanto (1993) 'Entreprises japonaises et syndicalisme en Europe' in *Le Mouvement Social* (Jan.–Mars), pp.95–128.

Danford, A. (1997) 'Japanization and the 'New Industrial Relations': an Ethnography of Class Struggle in the 1990s' in *Capital and Class* 6/1 February.

Fucini J, Fucini S (1990) *Working for the Japanese*, The Free Press.

Fujita, E (1988) 'Labour Process and Labour Management: the case of Toyota', in The Society of Social Sciences of Aichi Kyoiku University, No.28.

Gallie, D., R. Penn and M. Rose, (1996) *Trade Unionism in Recession*. Oxford University Press.

GERPISA (1993) 'Trajectories of Automobile Firms', Proceedings of the Group for the Study of the Auto Industry and its Employees, University d'Evry-Val d'Essone, Paris.

Gramsci, A. (1971) 'On the Intellectuals' in Q. Hoare and G. Nowell Smith (eds.), *Selections from the Prison Notebooks*.

Grant, D. (1994) 'New Style Agreements at Japanese Transplants in the UK: The Implications for Trade Union Decline' in Employee Relations, Vol.16, No.2, pp.65–83.

Grant, D. (1996) 'Japanisation and The New Industrial Relations', in Beardwell, I J (ed) *Contemporary Industrial Relations : A Critical Analysis*, Oxford University Press.

Hirst, P., G. Thompson (1996) *Globalisation in Question,* Oxford: Polity Press.

Hirst, P., J. Zeitlin (1991) 'Flexible Specialisation versus Post-Fordism: Theory, Evidence and Policy Implications', in *Economy and Society,* Vol.20, No.1, pp.1–56.

Holloway, J. (1995) 'Capital Moves', in *Capital and Class,* Vol.57 (Autumn) pp.137–44

Humphrey, J. (1995) 'The Adoption of Japanese Management Techniques in Brazilian Industry' in *Journal of Management Studies* Vol.32, No.6 (Nov.), pp.767–87.

Huxley, C., J. Rinehart and D. Robertson (1991) 'Team Concept: A Case Study of Japanese Production Concepts in a Unionised Canadian Auto Plant'. Paper presented to the Labour Process Conference, Manchester (April).

JAW Confederation of Japan Automobile Workers' Unions (1992) 'Towards coexistence with the world, consumers and employees' (Feb.).

Jones, D (1992) 'Lean Production (an update)'. Paper presented to the 'Lean Production and European Trade Union Co-operation' conference, TGWU Centre, 6–11 December 1992, Eastbourne, England.

Kenney, M. and R. Florida (1991) 'Transplanted Organisations: The Transfer of Japanese Industrial Organization to the US' in *American Sociological Review,* Vol.56 (June) pp.381–98.

Lie, J. (1996) 'Sociology of Contemporary Japan' in *Current Sociology*, Vol.44, No.1 (Spring), pp.1–95.

Lyddon, D. (1966) 'The Myth of Mass Production and the Mass Production of Myth', in *Historical Studies in Industrial Relations,* No.1, March, pp.77–105.

Masami, N (1993) 'Farewell to 'Toyotism'? Recent Trends of a Japanese Automobile Company'. GERPISA, Paris, (Feb.).

Milkman, R (1991) *Japan's Californian Factories – labour relations and economic globalisation,* Los Angeles: Institute of Industrial Relations, University of California.

MacEwan, A. (1994) 'Globalisation and Stagnation' in *Socialist Register* London: Merlin.

Morris, J., M. Munday, and B. Wilkinson (1992) *Japanese Investment in Wales: Social and Economic Consequences,* London: [publisher?]

Morris, J. and B. Wilkinson (1995) 'The Transfer of Japanese Management to Alien Institutional Environments' in *Journal of Managment Studies,* Vol.32, No.6 (Nov.) pp.719–30.

Nohara, (1993) 'The Average Worker of a Large Japanese Company', University of Hiroshima, Japan.

Nomura, M. (1993) 'The End Of Toyotism': Recent Trends in a Japanese Automobile Company'. Paper presented to the 'Lean Workplace Conference' Wayne State University, 3 October.

Oliver, N. (1991) 'The Dynamics of Just-In-Time' *New Technology, Work and Employment* Vol.6, No.1, pp.19–27.

Oliver, N., R. Delbridge, D. Jones, and J. Lowe (1993) 'World Class Manufacturing: Further Evidence in the Lean Production Debate'. Paper presented to the British Academy of Management Conference, Milton Keynes, September.

Oliver, N., D. Jones, R. Delbridge, and J. Lowe (1994) 'Worldwide Manufacturing Competitiveness Study'. The Second Lean Enterprise Report, Andersen Consulting.

Panich, L. (1994) 'Globalisation and the State' in *Socialist Register*, London: Merlin.

Robertson, D. (1992a) 'Canadian trade union experiences of the new management techniques and the development of counter strategies'. Paper presented to the TIE/Vauxhall Shop Stewards' Committee Conference on New Management Techniques. Liverpool, Jan./Feb.

Robertson, D. (1992b) 'The Canadian experience'. Paper presented to the 'Lean Production and European Trade Union Co-operation' seminar, TGWU Centre, 6–11 Dec., Eastbourne, England.

Scott, A. (Ed.) (1997) *The Limits of Globalisation: Cases and Arguments*, London: Routledge.

Sewell, G. and Wilkinson, B. (1992) '"Someone to Watch Over Me": Surveillance, Discipline and the Just-In-Time Labour Process', *Sociology,* Vol.26, No.2 (May) pp.271–89.

Smith, C. and P. Meiksins (1995) 'System, Society and Dominance Effects in Cross-National Organisational Analysis' in *Work, Employment and Society*, Vol.9, No.2 (June) pp.241–67.

Stephenson, C. (1995) 'The Different Experience of Trade Unionism in Two Japanese Transplants', in P. Acker, C. Smith, and P. Smith, *The New Workplace and Trade Unionism*. London: Routledge.

Stewart, P. (1997) 'The Silent Minorities: The Politics and Ideology of the *shosuha kumiai*' (*Asia Pacific Business Review*, forthcoming).

Stewart, P. and P. Garrahan (1995) 'Employee Responses to New Managment Techniques in the Auto Industry', *Work, Employment and Society*, Vol.9, No.3 (Sept.).

Stewart, P. and P. Garrahan (1997) 'Globalisation, the Company, and the Workplace' in A. Scott.

Stewart, P. and M. Martinez Lucio, (1996) 'New Models, Hybrids or Societal Effects? The Development of the Employment Relationship in General Motors Europe' in *L'Industrie Automobile Mondiale: Entre Homogénéisation et Hiérarchisation*. GERPISA, Paris, June.

Stewart, P. (forthcoming) 'The Silent Minorities: The Politics and Ideology of the *shosuha kumiai*'.

Tabata, H. (1989) 'Changes in Plant-Level Trade Union Organisations: A Case Study of the Automobile Industry' Institute of Social Science, University of Tokyo Occasional Papers.

Totsuka, H. (1996) 'Transformation of Japanese Industrial Relations: A Case Study of the Automobile Industry' in *Bulletin of the Centre for Transnational Labour Studies* No.1 (March) pp.9–23.

Turnbull, P. (1986) 'The "Japanization" of Production and Industrial Relations at Lucas Electrical'. *Industrial Relations Journal*, Vol.17, No.3, pp.193–206.

Watanabe, B. (1993) 'The Japanese Auto Industry: Is Lean Production on the Way Out?', Paper presented to the 'Lean Workplace Conference' Wayne State University, 3 October.

Williams, K. A. Adcroft and R. Willis (1995) 'Management Practice or Structural Factors: The Case of America versus Japan in the Car Industry', in *Economic and Industrial Democracy*, Vol.16, No.95, pp.9–37.

Williams K, C. Haslam and S. Johal (1987) 'The End of Mass Production', in *Economy and Society*, Vol.16, No.3, pp.404–38.

Williams K., C. Haslam, A. Adcroft, and S. Johal (1992a) 'Against Lean Production' in *Economy and Society* (Aug.) pp.321–54.

Williams, K. C. Haslam, A. Adcroft, and S. Johal , (1992b) 'Factories or Warehouses' [pub???]

Williams K, C. Haslam, A. Adcroft and S. Johal (1993) 'The Myth of the Line: Ford's Production of the Model T at Highland Park, 1909–16', in *Business History*, Vol.35, No.3 (July) pp.66–87.

Williams, K., C. Haslam, and J. Williams (1992) 'Ford v 'Fordism': the Beginning of Mass Production?' in *Work, Employment and Society*, Vol.6, No.4 (Dec.) pp.517–55.

Womack J.P., D.T. Jones and D. Roos (1990) *The Machine That Changed The World*, New York: Rawson.

Wood, S. (1991) 'Japanisation and/or Tayotaism' in *Work, Employment and Society*, Vol.5, No.4 (Dec), pp.567–600.

Yamamoto, K. (1990) 'The "Japanese Style Industrial Relations" and an "Informal" Employee Organisation: A Case Study of the Ohgi-Kai at T-Electric'. Institute of Social Science, University of Tokyo Occasional Papers.

Yamamoto, K. (1992) 'Labour Relations in Big Japanese Corporations: The Formal Framework and the Informal In-House Organisations'. Institute of Social Science, University of Tokyo Occasional Papers.

A Fallen Idol?
Japanese Management in the 1990s

COLIN HASLAM and KAREL WILLIAMS
with SUKHDEV JOHAL and JOHN WILLIAMS

Part of the extraordinary elevation of the status of management in Western social science in the 1970s and 1980s rested on perceptions of the sources of what was seen as Japanese manufacturing superiority. Text after text, popular and academic, traced an apparently permanent Japanese competitive advantage to new productive techniques devised and implemented by innovative Japanese managers. In the eighties there was a spate of books by knowledgeable authors like those by Schonberg, *Japanese Manufacturing Techniques: Nine Hidden Lessons in Simplicity* (1982) and *World Class Manufacturing* (1987), which draw attention to these developments and advocated their emulation in the West; throughout the decade and spilling well into the 1990s there were innumerable articles in such influential magazines as Fortune which took as axiomatic both the superiority of Japanese manufacturing and its basis in new and improved management practices; and the culmination was perhaps the publication in 1990 of *The Machine That Changed the World,* preaching the gospel of lean production and offering the promise of two-for-one improvement for all who followed these Japanese-initiated doctrines. The stress was largely on what could be achieved through the agency of management using such techniques as just-in-time, quality circles, and Kaizen. It is only a relatively mild overstatement to say that the message of much of this literature is that new management techniques have transcendent virtues which can be applied everywhere so that everyone can win if they make the right kind of management effort.

It is no part of the present purpose to question the existence and effect of such skills, nor to deny that Japanese manufacturing in the 1970s and 1980s developed productive methods which were, in some crucial respects, different from those currently practised in the West. The object is rather to shift the balance. The argument is that the evidence – both *before* and *after* the serious downturn in the Japanese economy around 1991 – suggests that much more weight needs to be given to the particular structural factors within which Japanese industry operated. Attention is thus drawn to the extent to which Japanese manufacturers operated in a domestic environment where the social settlement was favourable to them (especially in terms of

Colin Haslam and Sukhdev Johal, Royal Holloway University of London School of Management; Karel Williams, University of Manchester; John Williams, University of Aberystwyth wages, hours worked and managerial control over the labour process), and then their products were sold in export markets where quite different social settlements set prices at levels which generated a great deal of cash for Japanese producers. It is argued that the erosion, if not the disappearance, of these favourable conditions from the mid-1980s onwards has contributed substantially to the recent difficulties of Japanese producers. Further confirmation of the significance of structural factors is contained in the evidence that Japanese manufacturing affiliates abroad (the so-called transplants) have not been able to reproduce the levels of productive efficiency attained by the parent firms in Japan: the suggestion is that when firms – of whatever origin – are working under similar structural conditions the outcome is broadly similar. The object of the essay is thus to shift the balance by placing more weight on such structural factors and less on management success or failure. As so much weight has been given to management agency in accounting for Japanese advantage in 1970s and 1980s, the general force of the argument, it is suggested, is strengthened by using the evidence of Japanese manufacturing performance both domestically and through overseas affiliates.

REVERSAL OF FORTUNE: JAPANESE PARENTS IN THE 1980S AND THE 90s

When the world moves on, it often leaves social scientists trailing in its wake as they reiterate the discursive verities of the old order rather than engage the empirical realities of the new period. Thus, many organization theory and business policy texts continued to teach Chandlerism right through the 1970s and early 1980s and economists continued to test the superiority of 'M' form even as American 'M' forms were being soundly drubbed by Japanese competitors who were often organised on different lines. It is therefore not surprising to observe that some of the social science literature of the mid 1990s does not register any reversal of fortune and continues to present Japan as an exemplar of success and object of emulation; thus, the 1994 Lorriman and Kenjo book on Japanese management, training and education introduces its themes in cliched language that could have come from any 1980s best seller:

> Japan's continuing success is both inevitable and inexorable unless her competitors can learn the simple lessons explained in this book ... what is so extraordinary is that the West has made such little real effort to understand the reasons for Japan's success (Lorriman and Kenjo, 1994).

But it is equally encouraging to find that some academic social science recognises the 1990s are different and does register a reversal of fortune which has turned the Japanese parents from most feared competitors to peers with problems that sound familiar to most Western manufacturing firms. The most important, forceful and well informed of these reports is provided by Berggren whose summary is well worth quoting because it introduces a new and different Japan:

> Suddenly, it is obvious that Japan is not invincible ,and that the extrapolation of trends, which supported much of the 'Japan as number one' argument has collapsed. Within Japan, long standing issues about creativity – or the lack of it – in the educational system and corporate structures, are resurging. Other aspects of 'normalisation' are that growth rates will no longer be exceptional, and that the trade surplus will gradually diminish. At last, the Japanese economic players have started to realize that the surplus is as burden for them because it is driving the yen up, and thus making an increasing number of industries uncompetitive (Mimeo)

However, even this timely work is descriptively focused on the problems manifest since the end of the Hesei boom whose underlying results are presented ambiguously as part of a process of 'normalization'. The underlying structural mechanisms and their implications for the Japanese trajectory are not addressed; specifically, Berggren does not consider the question of whether and under what conditions, 'normalization' represents a stable outcome. Nor is the crucial question as to whether and what extent, an up-turn would solve the problems of Japanese manufacturing. Whilst it registers different results it does not decisively break with the mainstream tradition of writing about Japan which always neglected structural mechanisms and drivers because it focused on manufacturing systems and simply asserted superior results. This is what we find in many classic texts from the Womack, Roos and Jones presentation of Japan as lean production which we have critiqued elsewhere (Williams, *et al.* 1992) to the original work of Oliver and Wilkinson (1988) on emulation aka 'the Japanization of British industry'. The latter text represented Japan as the best way 'manufacturing system paradigm' and then went on lyrically to assert its promise: 'Japanese style manufacturing systems have captured the imagination of British industry because of the promise of leaps in productivity through efficiency of asset – including human asset – utilization' (Oliver and Wilkinson, 1988, p.160). The fact that Japanese manufacturing capital utilization had always been inferior and the suspicion that labour productivity was output driven was never registered in this story about the promise of a system; just as these empirics do not figure prominently in the new literature of disillusion.

Against this background, a structural analysis is generally useful because it broadens the field of the visible and intelligible by analysing mechanisms and drivers to show that the 1990s are not simply a break with the 1980s as it appears to be if we concentrate exclusively on results. The social accounting framework plus the empirical data below allow us to show how the Hesei boom in Japan covered accumulating problems about cash generation in the 1980s before the onset of recession dramatized the end of a trajectory in the 1990s: the implication is that the current outcome is not stable and that a cyclical upturn in the later 1990s would ease the symptoms but not cure the disease. All this is relevant to parents, Manufacturing Direct Investment (MDI) and affiliates because it illuminates the mechanisms and motives which have shaped and will determine the future flow of Japanese MDI. In terms of mechanism, MDI like any other kind of (re)investment requires the parent firm or sector to realize a cash surplus for capital over and above internal conversion costs after purchases and labour have been paid for. In terms of motives, the capital surplus can be applied strategically via MDI to cost recovery through investment in market access and/or cost reduction through low wage production. The Japanese manufacturing sector of the 1990s now has a permanently reduced cash surplus and an urgent need for cost reduction through (more) low wage offshore production; the implication is that cost recovery through 'transplant' investment in high income Europe and America was like much else in the 1980s, including soaring property prices and a stock market boom, just a phase the Japanese were going through.

In the 1970s and 1980s when the Japanese were feared competitors, they benefited structurally from a combination of low Asian wage costs and high Western prices which generated large cash surpluses as they increased their share of Western high income markets. As we demonstrated in our analysis of Japan v. America in *Cars* (Williams *et al.*, 1994), the Japanese physical advantage over the Americans in terms of sectoral build hours was usually modest, but their financial advantage was overwhelming for two reasons: first, in every year up to and including 1985, the wages paid by Japanese assemblers were in dollar terms half or less of those paid in Detroit; and second, the prices obtained in the American market reflected the cost recovery requirements of high wage producers which made low wage Japanese exports highly cash generative. As we pointed out in a more recent paper on the late capitalist crisis of cost recovery' (Williams *et al.*, 1995), the next generation of Asian new entrants has pulled exactly the same trick; in cars, the Koreans have reduced build hours so that they are physically competitive and, thanks to low wages, hugely cash generative. In both the auto and electricals sector, the Koreans all through the 1980s were realizing 70 cents in the $ as a cash surplus over labour costs which nicely inverts the 30/70 split between capital and labour which is usual in Western manufacturing.

The Japanese in their glory days of the 1970s were never as cash generative as the Koreans in the 1980s: labour's share of value added in Japanese manufacturing has been around 50 per cent since the late 1960s and depreciation's share of the residual available for capital has always been unusually high. This preliminary observation is hard to reconcile with the social scientific stereotype of the Japanese as masters of cost reduction through factory techniques which take labour out and masters of cost recovery through marketing which takes the product up market; if the stereotype were true, surely the Japanese should be effortlessly and always hyper cash generative and profitable. It is therefore worth proving the point by presenting some more systematic evidence on Japanese manufacturing as a whole over the past decade; the trends in sectors like automobiles and electronics are different in detail but consonant with the overall picture and will be considered later in this section.

If the Japanese were masters of cost reduction and cost recovery, we would expect the real value added per employee to increase steadily as labour comes out and value goes in. The reality is completely different. Table 1 shows that real value added per employee shows no sustained upward trend; in 1992 it is no more than 6.9 per cent higher than in 1983. A closer examination shows also that labour productivity is not being actively managed; with total numbers employed in Japanese manufacturing more or less flat, the trend in real output determines productivity which varies cyclically and passively. In years such as 1986 and 1992, when real sales drop, productivity falls sharply; conversely in the Hesei boom of the late 1980s a temporary increase in labour productivity of nearly 25 per cent more or less exactly matches the increase in output over the same period. This cyclically driven pattern overlaps with what we observe in British manufacturing; the British, like the Japanese, have a productivity miracle with each upswing although, unlike the Japanese so far, the British sack workers on the downturn so as to contain labour's share and maintain cash generation.

TABLE 1

PRODUCTIVITY AND CASH GENERATION IN JAPANESE MANUFACTURING

Year	Nos Employed	Real sales index	Nominal VA per employed index	Real VA per employee index	Labour share of VA	Labour +dep share of VA
1983	2,724	100.0	100.0	100.0	55.3	70.7
1984	2,738	105.6	110.1	101.7	52.7	67.7
1985	2,757	105.7	108.7	104.3	56.1	72.2
1986	2,719	97.3	102.2	97.5	60.1	78.0
1987	2,654	99.7	109.5	104.3	56.8	74.3
1988	2,659	108.9	124.0	117.4	53.2	69.2
1989	2,700	116.1	132.7	108.0	52.8	68.8
1990	2,771	123.4	137.7	123.7	53.8	70.3
1991	2,836	122.1	133.4	116.1	56.9	75.1
1992	2,858	116.0	124.9	106.9	60.4	80.4

Source: Japan Development Bank 1993

Notes: Calculations are averages based on a sample of 44 Japanese manufacturing firms which account for 22 per cent of total manufacturing output.

Japanese manufacturing as a whole has never had to sack on the downturn for two reasons; first, there was no serious downturn for nearly twenty years between the first oil crisis in 1973 and the end of the Hesei boom in 1991; second, the Japanese manufacturing sector has (like subsequent Asian new entrants) run with a labour share of value added (LSVA) which is rather lower than the norm in Western manufacturing sectors. In Western manufacturing, the long run average LSVA is typically around 70 per cent which leaves very little head room; when manufacturing output turns down and LSVA turns up, management must sack workers if cash generation is to be maintained. As Table 1 shows, in Japanese manufacturing since 1983 the LSVA ranges cyclically between 53 and 60 per cent. Unfortunately, this lower LSVA does not translate into a large profit surplus because the depreciation charge on the value added fund is proportionately much larger in Japanese manufacturing. In Western manufacturing the depreciation charge averages around 12 per cent of value added; as Table 1 shows, in Japanese manufacturing the depreciation charge ranges from 15 to 20 per cent of value added and that higher capital charge wipes out many of the benefits of a relatively lower labour share. Far from being distinguished by their ability to use labour ever more efficiently, Japanese manufacturers are distinguished by their profligate use of capital equipment. Japanese extravagance reflects the habits of an earlier period when Japanese manufacturing was steadily cash generative: many major companies have managed without elaborate systems of capital rationing and project appraisal; obsolescence has been used as a marketing tactic at the cost of massive expenditure on model renewal in cars and electronics; while Japanese techniques like cellular manufacturing obtain continuous labour utilization at the cost of capital underutilization. In this context, when labour's share drifted upwards whenever output turned down, Japanese manufacturing was not a miracle but an accident waiting to happen.

If the Japanese were physically unimpressive because they could neither start taking labour out nor stop putting capital in, the one variable which they did actively manage through the 1980s was the financial variable of next year's wage settlement. Internally generated cash equals sales turnover minus purchases plus wages; free cash equals sales turnover minus purchases plus wages plus depreciation. Given these fundamental relations, the management of the nominal wage bill in relation to nominal sales turnover is crucial to the maintenance of cash generation in any manufacturing sector whose residual is precarious. Table 2 shows how, when manufacturing employment was more or less flat, Japanese manufacturing rose to this challenge and held nominal wage increases in line with the increase in nominal sales. As Table 2 shows, the rising indexes of nominal wages and nominal sales track each other very closely; for more than a decade in every year, except 1986 when output fell, the two indexes are within 3 percentage points of each other. This pattern is all the more remarkable because the increase in nominal sales was modest and thus nominal wages increased very slowly; nominal wages increased by just over one third in the decade 1983–92 and most of that increase came after 1987 as the Hesei boom gathered pace. This containment of nominal wage increases was a major achievement in a period of general inflation and gently rising prices; as Table 2 shows, a 37 per cent rise in nominal wages translates into a much more modest 20 per cent rise in real wages up to 1991. What we see here is not mastery of productive technique or brilliant

TABLE 2

NOMINAL AND REAL WAGE INCREASES IN JAPANESE MANUFACTURING,
1983–92

Year	RPI	Nominal sale	Nominal sales index	Nominal wages per employee	Nominal wages per employee index	Real wages per employee index
1983	100.0	114,675	100.0	4.85	100.0	100.00
1984	102.2	123,734	107.9	5.09	104.9	102.69
1985	104.2	126,257	110.1	5.35	110.3	105.86
1986	104.8	116,968	102.0	5.39	111.1	106.04
1987	104.9	119,950	104.6	5.46	112.6	107.32
1988	105.6	131,876	115.0	5.79	119.4	113.05
1989	108.0	143,802	125.4	6.16	127.0	117.60
1990	111.3	157,563	137.4	6.50	134.0	120.41
1991	114.9	160,888	140.3	6.66	137.3	119.51
1992	116.8	155,384	135.5	6.62	136.5	116.86

Source: Japanese Development Bank 1993

Note: Calculation based on a sample of 44 Japanese manufacturing firms which together account for 22 per cent of the value of manufacturing output.

marketing but a set of labour market institutions which generates very modest nominal and real wage increases even in the frenetic boom which rounded off twenty years of full employment.

In Britain in the 1960s and 1970s, an earlier generation of social democratic politicians sought this kind of wage restraint through incomes policy and promised prosperity and jobs for all if we deferred gratification in the next pay round. The Japanese in the 1990s show how deferred gratification is a necessary but not sufficient condition for this kind of success. Although they were able to manage the internal aggregates in a way that maintained cash generation, the Japanese could not manage their exchange rate against the dollar which was rising in a way that undermined their international competitivity. Ironically, the Japanese were at this point victims of their earlier low wage export success which had resulted in very high export sales ratios: the export/sales ratio was 50 per cent in cars, 55 per cent in consumer electronics and 70 per cent in electronic components (IBJ, 1994a). This exposed them to appreciation of the yen against the dollar which could simultaneously make their exports unprofitable and turn them into a high wage exporter, regardless of the restraint exercised by wage negotiators back home.

Table 3 converts Japanese hourly labour costs per employee in major car assemblers into dollars at the prevailing exchange rate and does the same for other major industrial countries so as to establish Japan's place in the wages league table. The cars sector fairly represents broader trends; furthermore because (as we have demonstrated elsewhere) build hours are converging internationally, the hourly rate in dollars is a reasonable proxy for unit labour costs at least in trans Pacific trade. Japan in the early 1980s was a low wage industrial country whose labour costs were in dollar terms roughly equal to those of Italy or the UK. By 1990, Japanese assemblers were in dollar terms paying wages which were roughly equal to those paid by Detroit. By 1994 the Japanese had become the second highest labour cost industrial country behind Germany: in dollar terms, manufacturing costs per employee hour were now significantly higher than in the USA. The general lesson is that, if internally rising money wages do not in due course reduce successful new entrants to ordinariness, an externally appreciating currency will do much the same job.

TABLE 3

EMPLOYER LABOUR COST PER EMPLOYEE HOUR FOR MAJOR NATIONAL MOTOR INDUSTRIES 1980–94 (IN US $)

Country	1980	1985	1990	1991	1994
Japan	7.40	11.15	18.03	20.52	28.60
USA	12.67	22.65	20.22	21.24	24.87
France	10.03	10.20	15.57	16.42	18.54
Germany	13.70	13.72	26.03	26.95	35.88
Italy	9.05	10.40	16.94	19.13	17.23
UK	7.63	8.70	15.48	16.15	16.80
Spain	6.95	6.76	16.31	17.91	16.86
Sweden	15.70	12.33	26.40	27.52	24.70

Source: VDA, fax communication 1992; Financial Times.

When Japanese manufacturing was being represented as a brilliant success in the late 1980s, it was structurally exposed and vulnerable on two fronts: because the Japanese were unable to manage their physical inputs of labour and capital, continued cash generation depended on first, the maintenance of high output levels and second, a slowing of currency appreciation. Neither condition has been satisfied since 1992 when the Japanese economy turned down for the first time since the first oil crisis. By 1994, in electrical, and electronic engineering, motor vehicles and general machinery, volume sales on the home market were 20 per cent down on the cyclical peak year of 1991 (IBJ Monthly Report, August 1994a). The effects of this volume loss were compounded by rapid appreciation of the yen against the dollar; after a period of 'endaka', the yen was by early 1995 trading steadily at 100 to the dollar or lower. The Industrial Bank of Japan (1994b) observes that every appreciation of one yen against the dollar reduced manufacturing earnings by 5 billion yen.

The results were devastating and Table 4 establishes this point by summarizing the operating performance of 44 large Japanese corporations which are involved in the manufacture of cars and car components, household electrical goods and electronic equipment. All of these sectors are heavily oriented towards export and in all of them nominal and real sales have been falling since 1991. In each of the three sectors we have calculated the average real value added per employee in million yen, cash flow as a percent of sales and the labour plus depreciation share of value added.

TABLE 4

Value added per employee, cash flow to sales and break-even point of operations in Japanese automobiles, household electrical and computers/electrical equipment 1983–93.

	1983	1988	1993
Automobile Industry			
Cash flow as a % of Sales	8.6	7.9	4.7
Lab + Dep as % of value added[1]	73.1	74.1	95.0
Real VA/Employee (mill yen)	10.02	11.2	10.0
Household Electrical Ind.			
Cash flow as % of Sales	9.1	8.3	5.1
Lab + Dep as % of value added[1]	53.0	65.5	80.1
Real VA/Employee in mill yen	8.19	9.03	8.31
Computers and Electrical Equipment			
Cash flow as % of Sales	10.0	9.8	6.0
Lab + Dep as % of value added operations[1]	68.8	73.2	95.6
Real VA/Employee (mill yen)	10.75	9.74	7.95

Notes: 1. Labour costs plus depreciation as a per cent of the value added fund in each year also serves as a crude proxy for the break even point.
2. The 44 Japanese companies surveyed account for 22% of total Japanese manufacturing output.
3. The real value added per employee figure is for 1992 in household electricals and electrical equipment.

Sources: Handbook of Industrial Financial Data, Japan Development Bank, 1993; Quarterly Survey, Industrial Bank of Japan, No.100, 1994, IV.

The first observation must be that our pessimism about Japanese manufacturing as a whole is vindicated if we consider the record of these three sectors since 1983. Japanese inability to cost reduce by taking physical labour out or cost recover by moving the product up market emerges very clearly from the sectoral record on real value added per employee. Over the whole period 1983 to 1993, there is no sustained increase in any of the sectors; and in electronics, where cost recovery is difficult because of declining prices, real value added per employee declines sharply. The recent downturn has exposed the reluctance or inability of major manufacturers to shed labour by sacking workers. With employment maintained since the downturn began in 1991, the main adjustment has been a reduction in hours worked per week in manufacturing through the elimination of overtime and a reduction in the nominal working week from 41 to 38 hours (JETRO 1994b).

In these three sectors, as in Japanese manufacturing as a whole, accumulating problems were covered by output increases and high capacity utilization in the later stages of the Hesei boom. We do not see the classic upturn effect of a decline in labour's share as output increases. Instead, the share of labour plus depreciation in value added rose sharply in two of the three sectors between 1983 and 1988; in electronics, the combined share rises by more than 10 per cent. The downturn after 1991 simply dramatizes the underlying deterioration in structural fundamentals. In all three sectors, cash flow as per cent of sales is more or less halved and the labour plus depreciation share rises alarmingly in cars and electricals to squeeze residual operating profit. In both these sectors, a capacity utilization of around 95 per cent has now to be sustained before a positive contribution to net income is made after labour costs and depreciation have been covered. When these sectors operate in saturated and cyclical markets, this is a major problem because full capacity utilization cannot be sustained. Cyclical recovery would go some way to restoring cash generation but it could never restore the lost competitiveness of the pre 1985 period because structural conditions have changed irrevocably in a way that makes the Japanese not strong but vulnerable to every market downturn and exchange rate movement.

The implications are twofold: first, Japanese manufacturing in the 1990s can no longer be an object of emulation for the rest of the advanced countries; second, the internal agency and calculation explanation of Japan's earlier success should be discarded. Japanese manufacturing cannot be an object of emulation because, in terms of performance and results, it is becoming increasingly difficult to distinguish major Japanese manufacturers from embarrassed Western competitors who share similar structural problems. This is most clear in the case of German manufacturing which produces a different range of products, with a much stronger emphasis on premium mechanical engineering, but encounters the same problems about high labour plus dep shares and precarious cost recovery so that German manufacturing only generates a cash surplus if high levels of capacity utilization are maintained. The end of the reunification boom in Germany in 1991 had much the same effect as the end of the Hesei boom in Japan; it exposed underlying problems which had been covered by high rates of utilization. Germany and Japan now share a common status as high break even producers with precarious cost recovery. The status is unenviable because it involves short run risks with every market downturn or exchange rate shift and long term adjustments with attempts to reduce the breakeven point at the expense of domestic employment and maybe the domestic social settlement.

As for the secret of earlier Japanese success, we can paraphrase the old Jewish question and ask the Japanese parents: if your manufacturing system is so clever, why aren't you cash generative. The record of the Japanese parents in the 1980s, as much as after 1991, shows that the internal techniques and management systems of Japanese manufacturers do not infallibly deliver super-profits and cash flow regardless of structural circumstance: these techniques may be a necessary condition for the maintenance of a financially robust business but they are not in themselves sufficient to establish competitiveness. The whisky of advantage which might accrue from differences in management agency is drowned in the water of structural conditions. If this conclusion is a discursive lesson for social science, it is a practical lesson for the Japanese parents who must rethink all the fundamentals including their manufacturing direct investment strategies.

SHADES OF MEDIOCRITY: JAPANESE MANUFACTURING AFFILIATES IN THE UK AND EU

As a prelude it is necessary to get the scale of Japanese direct investment abroad into some general perspective. One major aspect is the relative insignificance of the contribution made by the foreign affiliates to the manufacturing output of the host economies. But since this is one of the characteristics to be demonstrated in the present section it can, for the moment, be left to a simple assertion. In addition, Japanese direct investment overseas has been of less significance to its domestic economy than similar foreign investment has been for other major industrial countries. This can be briefly indicated from two general measures; of FDI as a proportion of gross fixed capital formation (see Table 5), and of overseas production as a proportion of total (home and overseas) production. Even in the boom years of the late 1980s Japanese FDI, compared to the size of its domestic economy, was relatively small.

TABLE 5

RATIO OF FOREIGN DIRECT INVESTMENT TO DOMESTIC FIXED CAPITAL
FORMATION (IN NOMINAL TERMS)
BY MAIN INVESTING COUNTRY (AVERAGE)

	1980–85	1986–90	1991–93
UK	11.93	18.30	13.27
Germany	2.80	5.49	4.90
France	2.38	6.54	6.81
US	1.67	3.11	5.43
Japan	1.39	3.72	1.83

Source: JETRO White Paper on Foreign Direct Investment 1995, Summary, March 1995, p.6, Tables 1–5, Tokyo.

It may be unreasonable to compare Japan to the UK where the proportion is inflated by the low level of domestic investment, and where through the 1980s the government encouraged the illusion that a switch from a manufacturing to a rentier economy was possible and desirable. But even when compared to the US, which was running huge, growing payments deficit in the 1980s, Japanese FDI was unexceptional; and the importance of FDI to the economy at large was markedly less than that for

France and Germany. The point emerges even more starkly during the recession of the early 1990s and underlines the points made above about the effects of the ending of the boom on the Japanese parent companies. In these years the proportion of FDI to domestic gross fixed capital formation was the lowest of the major industrialized countries, and the proportionate fall in Japan had been greater than elsewhere. Another measure, more specific to manufacturing, reinforces the general impression: in 1992 the production overseas by Japanese firms represented just 6.6 per cent of total (domestic and overseas production) whereas the proportion of the US was 27.1 per cent. In Germany,generally not keen on moving production capacity out of the country, the proportion had been 20 per cent in 1989. (MITI, 22nd Survey of Overseas Activities of Japanese Corporations).

Any discussion of the significance for, especially, British industry of the presence of Japanese manufacturing affiliates needs to be set against this perspective. It also needs to take note of the direction of Japanese investment, especially manufacturing investment. Until the early 1980s most of this (54 per cent in 1980) went to Asia and latin America as Japanese firms looked mostly for opportunities to reduce costs. In the mid and late eighties there was a shift to Europe and, especially, the US (between them 77 per cent in 1990) when the concentration for Japanese firms was on cost recovery in affluent markets and using transplants to de-fuse political opposition to imports from Japan. The 1990s have seen a gradual shift back to investment in Asia (which took one-third of Japanese MDI in 1993) as cost reduction becomes increasingly important for Japanese parent firms.

If these preliminary points which are necessary to understand what can and should be expected from the operations of Japanese manufacturing affiliates (JMA) are often ignored, it is also the case that the extensive literature on Japan's UK 'transplant' includes very little systematic discussion of JMA firm and sector characteristics and performance. Insofar as the possibility of underperformance is recognized, the issue is usually sociologized and posed in terms of whether the technical potential of Japanese manufacturing systems will be obstructed by social obstacles such as British culture or institutions: locally, transplants and Japanization were an intellectual medium in which the right's 'British worker problem' (Nichols,1986) could be propagated just as the left's 'nasty to work for' refrain could again be rehearsed (Altmann, 1995). Thus, Trevor writing in 1987 on the broader internationalization of Japanese business presumed the issue was really about how the social obstacle was conceived;

> Dunning, for example, concludes that Japanese plants in Britain should be able to achieve 90 to 95 per cent of performance levels in Japan and one may agree with this view that the obstacles to achievement have more to do with 'inappropriate' institutions and unhelpful 'work attitudes' rather than some sort of 'cultural gap' or 'innate ability' (Trevor, p.24).

While this debate continued, none doubted the a priori assumption about the internal origins of JMA high performance in manufacturing systems and management practice.

The consensus was broad and durable because it had discursive, empirical and political conditions which led to the neglect of counter evidence about mediocre JMA performance and its connection to external causes. First, effective criticism required applied forms of knowledge which have been displaced by theory and the technical in mainstream academic life. Financial statement analysis is an irrelevance for economists distracted by algebra as for radical accountants overdosed on social theory. Second, the publicly available sources for such work, in the form of company reports and official statistics, provide out of date evidence on a relatively small transplant sector which was until very recently developing rapidly. Our earlier paper (Williams *et al.* 1992), based on the statistical evidence of the late 1980s, showed that the Japanese transplant sector was then small in size, mediocre in productivity, lacking in profit and probably heavily import dependent. This evidence was irrefutable, but its significance was less clear if the transplant sector was in its start up phase and could subsequently grow rapidly, develop local linkages and improve its performance. Third, for political reasons, key pieces of public interest evidence which were freely available in the US were unavailable in the UK whose government, under Mrs Thatcher, was determined to represent the arrival of the Japanese as a brilliant success and a vindication of its policies of encouraging inward investment through an open door and lower social charges. Thus, in the USA researchers can track transplant import content from the Bureau of Commerce series, but in Britain the government and the Japanese auto assemblers have instituted a meaningless count of the value of purchases made in the UK regardless of whether the purchased components originate outside the UK.

While all these difficulties remain, it is now increasingly possible to redress the absence through empirical work whose results can no longer be dismissed. To begin with, the basic questions about Japanese manufacturing affiliates in the UK are relatively straightforward and uncontroversial: the first set of issues concerns the size of the sector and its backward linkages through purchases to the British economy and to the Japanese parent and affiliates elsewhere; the second set of issues concerns the performance of the JMAs in terms of profitability and value added productivity. These questions are not all answerable because the evidence from UK official statistics remains out of date and fragmentary; but we are able to draw on the supplement of semi official Japanese surveys of EU transplant manufacturing which clarifies issues like local content. Finally, the time has come when the rapidly changing infant sector alibi can no longer serve as a plausible excuse for curtailing debate; the pace of growth and structural transformation has slowed and, as we have argued, Japanese parents are increasingly ill placed to commit further resources to supporting European JMAs. The time has come to survey the sector which has been created and to evaluate what has been achieved.

The first awkward fact is that the UK's JMA sector remains small in size and is no longer growing fast. Table 6 summarizes the most up to date publicly available and comprehensive evidence taken from the 1991 Census of Production. The table shows that in 1991, after a period of rapid growth from a very small base, the UK's JMA sector employed just 57,000 workers or 1.3 per cent of the manufacturing workforce. This made it roughly comparable in size to the French affiliate sector which is the largest of the EU 'transplant sectors' and 1/6th the size of the US affiliate sector which remains after all these years the only statistically significant foreign presence in UK manufacturing. The gap between the publication and collection of Census data is such that the evidence in Table 6 is of course four years out of date. But the rate of expansion has slowed in the past four years because the flow of inward investment has diminished and many established Japanese affiliates have been badly hurt by a recession during which parents deferred expansion plans and subsidiaries sacked workers. In a 1994 JETRO survey of Japanese manufacturing affiliates operating in Europe, more than 80 per cent of respondents admitted they had been 'hurt in one way or another' by the recent recession; when asked to be more specific about their responses, 38.7 per cent had 'dismissed employees', 36.6 per cent had 'scaled back their manufacturing plans' and 31.8 per cent were 'obliged to give up their intended capital investments'.

TABLE 6

FOREIGN AFFILIATE SHARES OF TOTAL UK MANUFACTURING EMPLOYMENT
AND VALUE ADDED, 1991

Ownership	Total employment	Percent of total employment	Percent of Value Added
Total	4,506.4	100.0	100
UK	3,731.6	82.8	78.3
Total overseas enterprises	774.8	20.2	21.7
France	56.0	1.2	1.5
Germany	37.0	0.8	0.8
Japan	56.6	1.3	1.6
Netherlands	33.7	0.7	0.7
US	374.0	8.3	11.2
Others	217.5	8.5	11.9

Source: Business Monitor, PA1002 Table 18, CSO, 1991.

The Japanese affiliate sector in the UK was less damaged by recession than its counterparts on the mainland because two of the three transplant car assemblers, Toyota and Honda, were still expanding: Toyota was in the start up phase and Honda tried a restart after its rival BMW bought its partner Rover early in 1994. But medium term prospects for transplant car assembly are poor because, in the UK and EU car markets, Nissan, Honda and Toyota are niche players with very weak positions; their reliable but boring mid market product is losing share of the EU market where in 1994 Japanese sales fell as the overall market rose so that the share of all Japanese marques fell from 12.3 to 10.9 per cent. Of the British based Japanese car assemblers, Nissan is losing share because the Primera has failed in the EU market place where in 1993 it sold just roughly 90,000 units and production was down 16.6 per cent in 1994 (Nissan Corporate Communication). Toyota and Honda maintain their positions and shift their smaller British outputs by discounting the product in a way which, as Honda dealers complain, undermines residuals and alienates traditional customers. Nissan Sunderland tries to maintain plant loading, as Toyota Derby and Honda Swindon will do, by running two models down the lines of a standard sized final assembly plant. This kind of low volume assembly operation cannot fund local model renewal or development and generates no volume contracts for the local component supply industry. In the case of the 300,000 a year capacity Sunderland plant, two models do not even produce a decent loading; in 1994 the plant operated at around two thirds capacity when it produced 205,000 cars and several hundred voluntary redundancies. (Financial Times, 31 January 1995). Perhaps it is not surprising that Toyota was then reported to be hesitating about whether to press ahead with the second phase of its Derby plant which would take capacity to 200,000 a year. The predicament of the transplant car assemblers was meanwhile sympathetically observed by their counterparts in electronics who faced very similar problems. After the Japanese parents lost any opportunity to push over indigenous European majors, like Philips and Thompson, their European affiliates were trapped as a fragmented collection of niche players whose world famous brands, like Sony, Panasonic and Hitachi did not command much of a price premium in a market place where everybody else had good product.

The backward linkages from a small, fragmented Japanese affiliate sector are unlikely to promote a broader economic transformation of the national economy; the sector is more likely to consolidate linkages with Japanese parents and their affiliates in low wage Asia which produce parallel imports in brown boxes for British distribution and components in polystyrene trays for British assembly. Optimists, such as Dillow (1991), used to argue that the arrival of the Japanese would redress the British trade deficit: the prediction of 1992 was that by 1995, Japanese investment would create 400,000 jobs, add 2 per cent to British output and improve the UK trade balance by some £4 billion. If Dillow was accidentally correct about the trend of the UK trade balance, he was entirely wrong about the contribution of the Japanese. The UK trade balance has improved mainly thanks to the forced devaluation against the DM and weak consumer demand which has encouraged a general diversion of car output from a depressed home market into mainland European export markets. As Table 7 shows, the UK's trade deficit with Japan has not fallen since the establishment of transplant operations. Recession normally damps the demand for imported manufactures and kits of components but in the three recession years of 1991–93 imports from Japan were maintained at a steady

TABLE 7

BALANCE OF TRADE DEFICIT UK WITH JAPAN 1987–93

Year	Exports in $ mill Japan to	UKImports in $ mill Japan from UK	Balance of Trade in mill $
1987	5,464	1,495	3,969
1988	5,531	1,743	3,788
1989	7,108	2,260	4,848
1990	6,726	2,596	4,130
1991	6,754	2,258	4,496
1992	7,444	2,227	5,217
1993	8,536	2,740	5,796

Source: PA 1023 UK Trade Statistics

annual rate of around $7.5 billion per annum and as a direct result, the bilateral UK deficit on manufactures with Japan averaged 5.1 billion US$ from 1991–93 which was nearly 25 per cent higher than the average deficit of 4.2 billion US$ in the three boom years of 1987–89.

A more focused analysis of component sourcing and local purchases from the host economy only confirms our pessimism. In general, any transplant sector with a high propensity to import is economically undesirable because it diverts value adding and employment from the host economy to the parent company. The accumulating evidence shows that Japan's American and European transplants do have these undesirable characteristics and we see no reason why British transplants should do much better. In our 1992 paper, we demonstrated from Bureau of Commerce data that Japanese transplants in the USA had a high propensity to import. We inferred that the position might be similar in the UK because the Japanese transplants in the UK had a suspiciously low value added/sales ratio but, in the absence of relevant official statistics, could not prove the point. Our suspicions have since been confirmed by the results of UK case study, especially the work of Munday (1995:15), a former enthusiast for the Japanese way, who now concedes that in his electronics affiliates 'local (British) content … was negligible' and in one case consisted of 'mostly packaging, PCBs, metal parts, harnesses and fuses'. More systematic confirmation comes in the form of a recent MITI survey which covers all of Japan's EU affiliates, including those in Britain as well as those in Asia and America. The unimpeachable results are summarised in Table 8 which shows that the Japanese transplants in the EU, like those in Asia and USA, import around 40 per cent of their procurement requirement from parent companies in Japan. The EU transplant operations are however different from those in Asia or America, because their level of local procurement from within the region is unusually low. In the EU case, the local procurement is low because a significant part of their component requirements comes from the Asian affiliates of the Japanese parents: 29.0 per cent of the value of Japan's EU transplant purchases is locally sourced against something like half the value

TABLE 8

BREAKDOWN OF PROCUREMENT SOURCE FOR JAPANESE MANUFACTURING
AFFILIATES (BY REGION AS OF FINANCIAL YEAR 1992)

Location of Japanese Manufacturing Affiliates by Region	Local Procurement %	Imported From Third Country Other Than Japan %	Imported from Japan %	Total Import Content of Japanese Affiliates
Asia	48.5	8.9	37.9	46.80
US	51.7	6.2	42.1	48.30
EU	29.0	21.8	44.4	66.20
World	46.5	12.6	40.9	53.50

Notes: Imported from third countries indicates mainly imports from low wage Asia.

Source: Overseas Business Activities of Japanese Corporations, Japanese Ministry of International Trade and Industry, 1992.

of purchases in the American and Asian cases. As a result, the import content of purchases is materially higher in the EU case where two thirds of purchases are imported from outside the EU. It is hard to see this changing because European electronic parts are an expensive substitute for low wage Asian output and the capacity of the auto transplants to source within the EU is limited by the fragmented, low volume nature of their operations. Low local procurement is a structural fact of life for the UK's Japanese transplants; the necessary consequence is that these transplants generate more tied imports and less (direct and indirect) employment.

If the Japanese affiliate sector in the UK remains economically negligible and heavily dependent on imported components, its profit and productivity performance has changed but by no means miraculously for the better. During the recent recession, profitability almost certainly deteriorated from the break even position which was the norm in the late 1980s. Again in the absence of relevant and up to date British evidence we can again cite a recent Japanese survey of EU transplants. According to a 1994 JETRO survey, 51.2 per cent of Japanese transplant affiliates in the EU were by 1992 making operating losses. Insofar as the position in the UK is unlikely to be any better, transplant operations are just one more financial problem for beleaguered Japanese parents who must cover operating losses by UK affiliates even though they are chronically short of cash for the basics of Japanese product and process renewal. This is the background to the current round of redundancies, investment cut backs and postponements of expansion in the UK's Japanese electrical and motor affiliates as damage limitation becomes the name of the game.

The one cause for optimism is an improvement of value added productivity in the UK's Japanese transplants which is documented in Table 9. In a couple of years between 1989 and 1991, the UK's Japanese transplants substantially closed the gap with the US affiliates whose productivity performance has long been one third better than that of indigenous British manufacturing. The performance improvement is not however without parallel and the observed improvement should not be automatically attributed to superior techniques of production which are unique to the Japanese. As Table 9 shows, the French transplant sector managed much the same kind of productivity improvement over the period 1989–91. And that should make us cautious about attribution; in relatively small affiliate sectors employing around 50,000, as in the Japanese or French cases, acquisition or expansion which takes the affiliates into new sectors is likely to be the main influence on productivity. The Japanese affiliates have in recent years expanded car assembly and component manufacture which have traditionally been high productivity sectors and this reduces the drag from electricals and electronics which are traditionally low productivity sectors. A sectoral shift towards inherently high productivity activities vindicates the structural interpretation rather than the alternative which emphasises magic manufacturing systems. Sectors, like the large and long established American sector, which outperform indigenous firms are likely to have some combination of structural advantages; in the American case, the advantage is concentration in high productivity sectors where firms like Ford or Kellogg have traditionally held market leading positions.

Sectoral evidence from the Census of Production provides the most obvious way of controlling for some of these differences because it allows us to compare the performance of the Japanese affiliates within each sector with the performance of indigenous firms and those owned by non Japanese parents. In the motor sector, the Census will not release gross output and gross value added figures on the grounds that individual firms could be identified ; but in the electrical and electronics sector, the Census has released these figures as well as employment, in response to our request, and the results are published below for the first time in Tables 10 and 11. JMAs are well established in UK Electrical and Electronic Engineering: nevertheless, they account for only 18.5 per cent of total foreign affiliate employment in this sector, a share which is only half as large as that of American owned affiliates. In terms of value added productivity, the Japanese affiliates perform no better than other foreign affiliates operating in electricals and electronics; our interpretation would be that the value added per employee of £21–23,000 is surprisingly more or less identical regardless of ownership even though the affiliates often compete in different product markets. As Table 10 shows, there are however significant differences in the value added to sales ratio between JMAs and other affiliates: the Japanese affiliates have a value added to sales ratio which is some 30 per cent below that of US and EC foreign affiliates. Japanese and European affiliates operating in UK electronics have very similar gross output figures of £1863 million for JMAs and £1833 million for ECMAs but Japanese affiliates generate 28 per cent less value added from this gross output. Strictly, this demonstrates only that Japanese operations are less vertically integrated and more dependent on external purchases which could be sourced from UK suppliers or Far Eastern associates. In the light of the MITI evidence on procurement, it is however reasonable to assume that all or

TABLE 9

VALUE ADDED PER HEAD AND RELATIVE VALUE ADDED PER HEAD OF UK
BASED FOREIGN AFFILIATES (MANUFACTURING DIVISIONS 2–4)

	Value Added per Head £ mill Nominal			Relative Value Added per Head USA = 100		
	1983	1989	1991	1983	1989	1991
UK	12947	20149	22048	72.3	59.0	70.1
EU (12)	14331	26148	25250	80.0	76.6	80.3
France	12073	30524	28716	67.4	89.4	91.3
Germany	16035	27750	24891	89.6	81.3	79.1
USA	17906	34153	31464	100.0	100.0	100.0
Japan	13880	23523	30547	77.5	68.9	97.1

Source: PA 1002 Census of production Table 18, 1983, 1989, 1991

TABLE 10

EMPLOYMENT IN ELECTRICAL AND ELECTRONIC ENGINEERING FOREIGN
AFFILIATES OPERATING IN THE UK IN 1992

Class 34	Total Employment	Admin and Technical	Operatives	% share of all Foreign Affiliates in UK
USA	38804	18036	20768	38.27
Japan	18803	5429	13374	18.54
EC	26911	10081	16830	26.54
Total	84518	33546	50972	100.00

Source: CSO Information Request.

TABLE 11

VALUE ADDED PER EMPLOYEE AND VALUE ADDED TO SALES RATIO IN
ELECTRICAL AND ELECTRONIC ENGINEERING OF FOREIGN AFFILIATES
OPERATING IN THE UK IN 1992

Class 34	Total Employees	Gross Output £ mill	Value added £ mill	VA to Sales ratio %	VA per Employee in £
USA	38804	2771	896	32.33	23,093
Japan	18803	1863	415	22.28	22,074
EC 11	26911	1833	575	31.37	21,375
Total	84518	6468	1886	29.16	22,320

Source: CSO Information Request.

most of the extra purchases come from Far Eastern associates. And on that
assumption we would conclude that, if the Japanese electronics affiliates had
the same purchase pattern as their American or European owned counterparts,
the Japanese would create 50 per cent more electronics jobs in the UK.

Overall, the pattern of Japanese transplant performance confirms the structural prediction that affiliates which operate in a host economy under the same structural conditions as local firms will perform much as indigenous firms do. Large supply side differences in hours worked and wages paid of the order of 2:1, as now exist between Northern Europe and Korea (Williams, *et al.* 1995), will produce large differences in performance ; so will differences in market access or product position on the demand side. But the Japanese affiliates in Europe cannot find advantage in this way against indigenous firms because they sell mundane products assembled under the terms of North European national social settlements which put a floor under wages and a cap on hours. They may gain a marginal advantage from locating in Britain where the Social Chapter does not run and hourly wages are relatively low by mainland North European standards; but the Japanese transplants cannot escape the saturated and cyclical markets for autos and electronics in which they and indigenous firms must sell their output. Contrary to what the Tory right believes, we suspect that the influence of demand side leverage through lower wages is much weaker than the influence of supply side equalization through market difficulties. It is significant, for example, that the few Japanese affiliates established in Spain do just as badly as in the UK for exactly the same market related reasons despite the leverage of UK style wages: Spain may be, like Britain, by North European standards, a low wage site for auto assembly but Nissan Motor Iberica, which assembles four wheel drives, has just turned in a fourth successive operating loss because the company cannot sell product and the Spanish plant is underutilised just like the British one (Financial Times, 31 January 1995). If they cannot find cost reduction leverage in the factory or cost recovery advantage in the market place, it is hardly surprising that so many Japanese affiliates turn in performance which is average in every way except for reliance on imported components which reflects their fragmentation and limits their employment creation.

Common Ground?

This article has been written to argue the case for a structural interpretation of the current underperformance of Japanese parents and their UK manufacturing affiliates. We recognise that this interpretation will not be acceptable to many social scientists and business school academics who start from the opposite a priori which emphasises management agency rather than structural forces. The JMAs and Japanization were congenial objects because they can be used to confirm assumptions about the importance and power of corporate organization and management techniques. Although this a priori has not been explicitly rejected, it is notable that the empirical work on the 'transplants' and Japan has recently grown much more cautious. The point can be proved by considering the shifts in position of erstwhile enthusiasts such as Oliver and Wilkinson between their 1988 and 1992 books on Japanization and Mundy (1995); equally relevant is the reinterpretation and qualification of the Japan equals high performance proposition between the first and second Andersen

Consultants bench marking reports. It therefore seems reasonable to ask whether there is any emerging common ground between ourselves and researchers who started from very different assumptions: what, if anything have we all learnt as we begin to recognise realities which were long denied?

Can we agree in retrospect that Japan, the transplants and Japanization in the UK was not a debate but a panic whose essentially rhetorical devices mimicked those of earlier panics about the threat of Germany before 1914 and the threat of America after 1945 as reflected in the Anglo American Council on Productivity (AACP) summary reports. As in previous panics, the problem was set up in terms of a simple A or B, good versus bad comparison. In this world of the good versus bad typology success is explained by the presence of magic techniques which guarantee high performance and failure explained by the absence of these techniques. From this point of view, technical education in Germany before 1914 had much the same significance as the presence of management accounting and materials handling in America after 1945 for the AACP; or team working and low stocks for the first Andersen bench marking report. The only novelty in the third panic was the cult of the transplant which, as Elgar and Smith observe (1994) introduced a semiotics about healthy organs from good donors; that had already in a way been adumbrated in the cult of the American affiliate in the business school literature of the 1970s. As national decline progressed, the theme of competition and loss which was central to the first panic inevitably gave way to the theme of emulation and renaissance which animated the agenda of the second and third panics.

Can we also agree that the rhetoric was powerful because it was never subjected to a classical intellectual critique which analyzed its discursive devices and evaluated its empirical support. In all three panics, the competitive superiority of the successful country was assumed without any serious moves either to broaden the debate to take in other cases beyond A and B or to decompose and evaluate the high performance which was endlessly asserted. When these two moves are made, the whole fragile rhetoric of panic inevitably falls apart because it immediately becomes clear that there is more than one way to skin a cat, performance is multi-dimensional and it is powerfully influenced by structural variables like wage costs which are invisible in the simpler forms of rhetoric. This is the point of disillusion and self refutation which the British panic has reached with the publication of the second Andersen Report (1994) on bench marking which makes significant concessions to all these positions. These concessions would have come more quickly and constructively if those who participated had been able to construct multi-dimensional performance profiles for companies and sectors from official statistics and company reports.

As for the Japanese 'transplants', can we now agree that their significance was mainly symbolic rather than real; a manufacturing sector employing not much more than 50,000 is of significance mainly as a role model for the Koreans who will undertake the next round of low wage investment in market access. Japanese transplants in cars and electronics are not the solution but another instalment of the problem of British decline. Thirty years ago, in cars and electronics, British industry consisted of too many small firms making too many products in short production runs; this fragmentation was and is a massive structural disadvantage in any business where new product development costs serious money. After a process of failed rationalization and protracted market failure, the indigenous producers collapsed or quit the field leaving the Japanese to recreate the same pattern of fragmentation through their transplants, although the parts now come from the Far East not the Midlands. With that significant qualification what do Nissan and Honda represent but the Hillman and Standard Triumph of the new millennium; just as Sony and Aiwa represent the Sobell and Ferranti of the digital age. Pietschrieder of BMW, which owns the sad remnant of British car manufacture, promises to 'bring back the marques' including Austin Healey and Riley. Japanese manufacturers have already fragmented the home an overseas markets they operate in without finding sustained financial success.

REFERENCES

Altmann, N. (1995) 'Japanese Work Policy: Opportunity, Challenge or Threat ?' In Sandberg, A. (Ed) *Enriching Production*. Aldershot: Avebury.

Anglo American Council on Productivity Report on Internal Combustion Engines (June 1950) and report on Management Accounting (Nov.1950).

Arthur Anderson Consultants (1994) 'Lean Enterprise Benchmarking Survey', London.

Berggen, C. 'Towards Normalisation' (Mimeo).

Dillow, C. (1991) 'Can the Japanese Eliminate the UK Trade Deficit?', Oct. Nomura Research Institute.

Elgar, T and Smith, C. (1994) *Global Japanisation?: The Transnational Transformation of the Labour Process*, London: Routledge.

Financial Times, 16 March 1994.

Industrial Bank of Japan (1994a) 'Monthly Report: Economic and Industrial Trends in Japan', Aug. No.275.

Industrial Bank of Japan (1994b) 'Quarterly Survey: Japanese Finance and Industry', Vol.99, No.III.

Industrial Bank of Japan (1994c) 'Quarterly Survey: Japanese Finance and Industry', Vol.100, No.IV.

Japanese Ministry of International Trade and Industry (1994) '4th Basic Survey on Japanese Business Activities Abroad'.MITI, Tokyo.

Japanese Ministry of International Trade and Industry (1992) 'Overseas Business Activities of Japanese Corporations', MITI, Tokyo.

Japanese Ministry of International Trade and Industry (1991) 'Survey on Globalisation of the Japanese Economy', MITI, Tokyo.

JETRO (1994a) 'White Paper on Foreign Direct Investment', Japan External Trade Organisation, March, Tokyo.

JETRO (1994b) *Nippon Business Facts and Figures*, Japan External Trade Organisation, Tokyo.

JTERO (1995) 'White Paper on Foreign Direct Investment', Japan External Trade Organisation, Mar. Tokyo.

Japan Development Bank (1994) *1993 Handbook of Industrial Financial Data*,

Management Research Institute, Tokyo.

Lorriman, J. and Kenjo, T. (1994) *Japan's Winning Margins: Mmanagement, Training and Education*. Oxford University Press.

Mundy, M. (1995) The Regional Consequences of the Japanese Second Wave: A Case Study,

Local Economy Vol.10 (May).

Nichols, T.(1986) *The British Worker Question*, Routledge and Kegan Paul.

Oliver, N and Wilkinson, B.(1988) *The Japanisation of British Industry*. Oxford: Blackwell.

Trevor, M.(1987) *The Internationalisation of Japanese Business: European and Japanese Perspective*. Boulder, Colorado: Westview Press.

Williams, K., Haslam, C. Williams, J. Adcroft, A. and Johal, S. (1992) Factories or Warehouses: Japanese Manufacturing Foreign Direct Investment in Britain and the United States, *University of East London Occasional Paper No. 6*

Williams, K., Haslam, C. Johal, S. and Williams, J. (1995) The Crisis of Cost Recovery and the Waste of the Industrialised Nations, *Journal of Global Competition and Change*, (Aug.)

Williams, K., Haslam, C., Johal, S. and Williams, J. (1994) *Cars: Analysis, History, Cases*. Oxford: Berghahn Books.

Womack, J., Roos, J. and Jones, D. (1990) *The Machine That Changed the World*. Rawson Associates.

The Changing Nature of Japanese Production Systems in the 1990s and Issues for Labour Studies

KOICHI OGASAWARA and HIROFUMI UEDA

PART I:
THE CHANGING NATURE OF JAPANESE PRODUCTION
SYSTEMS IN THE 1990s

At the beginning of the 1980s, Ford introduced quality control measures as part of its 'After Japan' strategy. A decade later, Toyota developed what they termed 'The medium-and long-range vision' to review its basic company strategy for production and man-management systems. These were also heralded as basic concepts for company development. This was a timely development, coming as it did around the period when the lean production thesis was coming to fruition. Yet a review of the management systems of the 1980s is required not only for Toyota and the auto industry, but for anyone wishing to determine the direction being taken by Japanese industry as a whole. This is clear from the fact that the Japanese Confederation of Management Organizations (NIKKEIREN) in May 1995, published what was in practice an agenda for the fundamental reform of the so-called 'Japanese management system' (NIKKEIREN, 1995). Thus, only a decade after the publication of the Ford strategic prognosis, Japanese industry has at last begun to seriously consider its own 'After Japan'.

The production system together with its related work organization has been at the centre of the changes in the 1990s. Significantly, management and labour are more or less in agreement that the problem with the industry lies more in its workings than in its overall philosophy and principles. An executive manager with responsibility for production technology at Japan's largest auto producer, for example, described his company's newly introduced production line as a 'human-machine friendly line', the object of which is to realize each worker's sense of achievement through the individually-defined content of production work. In other words, the work in the previous system was not a sophisticated complex of tasks allocated for each individual worker. However, the executive manager stressed that the basic idea of his company's (Company B) production system has remained unchanged (*Kojo-Kanri*, 1994: 18–21). On the other hand, the JAW (Confederation of Japan Automobile Workers' Unions) emphasizes that lean production is superior in its basic conception, while recognizing

Koichi Ogasawara, Faculty of Economics, Saitama University; Hirofumi Ueda, Institute for Economic Research, Osaka City University.

that there must be some improvement in the system such as 'reasonably culculated standard time' in order to check the excessive priority on production efficiency. This is because the system itself contains some problematical aspects which often impose heavy burdens on individual workers in the production process (JAW, 1992a; 1992b). These kinds of drawbacks to lean production have already been cited by Mike Parker in the American context, in his preface to the Japanese version of *Choosing Sides*. He repeats his view that the real nature of lean production is in its continuous stress on supervisors and workers (Parker and Slaughter, 1995: 55–6).

The most crucial aspect of Japanese production practice is surely in the structure of managerial control on the shop floor. The importance of supervisors within the context of the formation of skills, work organization, regulation and trouble-free industrial relations has been marked by many research publications.[1] This reflects what could be termed 'workplacism' in terms of research into Japanese management. Supervisory workers are at the same time the leaders of enterprise trade unions, and the Japanese system does not carry any legal and institutional mechanisms which allow for the regulation of one's parallel roles as a union leader and supervisor. Consequently, supervisors carry a heavy burden of responsibility in attempting to perform two fundamentally inconsistent roles in circumstances where there is pressure to ensure trouble-free production on a daily basis. Our first question in this article is whether the new production system might be able to relax this pressure on supervisors to take sides.

The 'basic idea' of Japanese production systems has been interpreted by both sides of the auto industry in terms of what we might term 'respect for people'. This was originally the idea of Taiichi Ohno, and it is now widely recognized as one of the fundamental principles of so-called Japanese management. 'Respect for people' implies the use of human potential, including their abilities wherever possible in the production process in order to secure job enrichment. The post-war industrial relations context has been profoundly concerned with the development of the idea. In the 1950s, many leading Japanese companies, including Toyota and Nissan, experienced major disputes around the question of rationalization of staff. In the second half of the 1950s and 1960s, against a background of relatively unstable product markets, there gradually emerged a framework for Japanese management practices which had as a fundamental condition a combination of reduced manpower and limited mechanization, together with the highest possible degree of production efficiency. The internal labour market is vitally important to the functioning of the overall system. It is characterized by discriminatory employment practices of relatively long-term employment, with flexible allocation of core employees and massively unstable peripheral employment acting as a buffer; sub-contracting and outsourcing as a system of vertical division of risks of low profitability; internal collaborative management-union relationships based on an understanding of the need for high productivity; and an individualized wage system linked to systematic appraisal. In short, these have become the institutional elements of the system. However, owing to the differences in the process for the termination of disputes and the overall industrial relations context, the implementation of 'human respectability' has worked differently from company to company. Toyota has stressed the productive abilities of workers, while Nissan has emphasized what they term 'humanized work standards'. In essence, this has reflected on the formation of different types of production system at each company. The change in the 1990s is common to Toyota, Nissan, and also Mazda in that it claims to be a system which is humane from a workers' point of view. Is it valid to anticipate that there will be some convergence between the production systems of the various companies, such that it will possible to speak of a new model? This is the second question we seek to examine here.

There has been relatively little Japanese research thus far conducted on this question of the possibility of the appearance of a new production system and so in consequence, the account provided here cannot be definitive. In the first part of this article we propose to describe in comparative terms the basic nature and features, including the determining factors, of the production systems of three major assembly plants in the auto industry in the 1990s. In conclusion, we suggest four issues for a future research agenda that can help us assess the nature of work with respect to individual workers and their supervisors.

CHANGES IN THE TOYOTA PRODUCTION SYSTEM

The Toyota production system not only is the production system which has been developed within the Toyota company but is also, in essence, the system which has been applied by many other Japanese manufacturers. Nevertheless, the actual composition of the production system varies between companies owing to factors as diverse as historical context, product line-up, company strategy, and local conditions. In addition, there have also been, as one can imagine, substantial differences between companies with respect to industrial relations and the organization of the division of labour. A recent major study comparing industrial relations at the two largest Japanese auto companies suggested that the 'flexible and efficient system of manpower usage' had different contents, at least by the mid 1980s, and that this was a reflection of the rather different social and historical contexts of the two companies (Totsuka and Hyodo, 1991). In relation to the socio-historical contexts, the study emphasized a number of key differences between the companies. In this respect a number of key factors were of relevance: the way in which major disputes in the 1950s were concluded, the effect which this had upon the unions' subsequent approach to industrial relations, and the way in which the recruitment of school leavers and personnel management practices which closely related to company location. Finally, the authors found that the production system at each company is based upon a particular industrial relations background.

They argued that the composition of each system can be seen as illustrating the specificity of each company's development against common trends.[2]

The change in the production system in the 1990s is still in progress, but we suggest a number of major characteristics and directions. For our comparison, two points are crucial. Firstly, change has become inevitable against the background of an absolute and long-term shortage of young male employees together with the necessity for the reform in working conditions. Secondly, as the potential for automation is extended, it is important for the assessment of change in production systems to analyse how and to what extent each plant has introduced automation technology. Especially we examine the different approaches of three companies to modular production.

THE NEW LINES IN THE 1990s

The fresh lines started in the 1990s[3] are the core lines for each car maker in the sense that the lines are designed as models for the twenty-first century. These are also expected to be strategically significant for the various companies' production activities, even though the actual operating capacity is only 60–70 per cent, owing to the current slump in the Japanese auto industry. The essential features of the lines are suggested in Table 1. The following description is of the assembly lines as typically followed at each plant.

The Kyushu Plant Company A

Plant outline: Company A's Kyushu plant (hereafter plant A) was founded in 1975 and it was the company's first plant outside the Kanto area near Tokyo. Originally an engine plant, it began to assemble vehicles around 1980. Plant A is now the company's largest production facility with an output of 50,000 vehicles per month. Recently, the company decided to close its major plant in the Kanto area (over 30 years old) in order to transfer production to plant A.

It was as a result of the projected labour shortage that Company A planned to build the new production line in plant A. The plant was conceptualized as 'the dream plant for the symbiosis of ecology, human kind, and auto vehicles'. It was designed as the plant of the twenty-first century which eliminates heavy/dangerous physical work, coexists with ecology, and has lines that enable it to assemble any type of vehicle with a sophisticated information network. The new production line (the second line) was set up in 1992 with maximum production capacity of 20,000 vehicles per month (eight types of four main models). However, at the end of 1994, the actual production was 12,000, four types (two main models), which is 60 per cent of the production capacity.

The Assembly Line: The new production line has just one process assembly track of 1,450 metres which can produce 20,000 vehicles per month. The

TABLE 1

FRESH ASSEMBLY LINES IN 1990s

Plants	Production Start-up Date(Plant Start-up Date)	Annual Outputs of Cars(Planned)	Type of Cars	Plant Employees	Tact Time (Planned in Minutes)	Tact Time (Real in Minutes)	Floor Area (m²)	Length of Assembly Line(m)	Plant Concept
A	Apr. 1992(1975)	240.000	Popular	670-680	1.0	1.8-1.9	84.000	1.450	Visionary Plant Pursuing Symbiosis among People, Automobile and Nature (Working Friendly Factory)
B	Dec. 1992	200.000	Popular	600	1.04-1.10	1.74	80.000	950	
C	Feb. 1992(1982)	156.000	Luxury	600	1.3	1.6	45.000	1.400	People Friendly Plant Tailored to Produce Upscale Vehicles

Note: Real tact time is the one when we visited the plants in the end of 1994.

Source: Authors' interviews from company A, B, and C.

FIGURE 1

ASSEMBLY PLANT OF COMPANY A

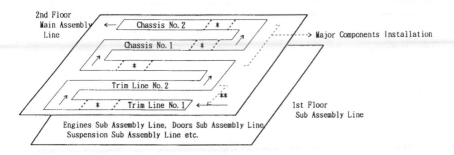

Notes: * The process of automation with robots.
** Intelligent, motor-driven dollies are collected.

Source: Authors' research into company A.

first production line kept three process lines which had a capacity of 10,000 vehicles per month. The ratio of the machine process is 20 per cent in terms of gross parts installing time, and the line comprises 60 robots, including an electronically controlled conveyance system. The plant is divided into the first floor which is a sub-assembly line of labour intensive process work and the second floor which comprises the main assembly line. The sub-assembly line is not a modular production system and the main assembly line is also different from a modular process.

The main assembly line comprises 256 work processes. At the start of the line the order sheet is placed on each vehicle to input into the line. The automated processes on the line are trim installation, unit-mounting, chassis No.1 (installation of tyres, glass), and chassis No.2 (installation of seats, battery, brakes). These processes are concentrated in the centre of the line. Company A has been active in promoting automation processes and the decision to automate was based on an assessment of a balance of factors such as the effect on staffing levels, investment efficiency and quality, the impact on heavy and dangerous work, machine size and level of pollution, and finally, whether or not it is crucial to safety and security.

The 'intelligent track' can be moved up and down at the worker's discretion and in relation to the size of the vehicle on the line. This has been designed in part for ergonomic reasons and also to allow for the flexible production of eight types of four basic models on one line.

The level of automation of the main assembly line on the second floor is almost at maximum and in order to promote further automation it would be necessary to introduce a modular system. In fact, although modular production was originally considered at the design stage, it was subsequently abandoned because it was felt that flexible production would have to be restricted to a limited variety of vehicles capable of being turned out on a modular basis. Indeed, given Plant A's position as a strategic production base for the company (where there is an expectation of a gradual concentration of production variations), it is crucial to retain full flexibility in terms of the kinds of vehicles manufactured there. This is the key difference between Plant A and, as we shall see Plant C, whereby production is designed around a limited model range on the basis of a fully modularized production system.

Kyushu Company B

Plant outline: Kyushu B Auto Company, founded in 1992, is formally independent of the company that originally developed the so called Toyota Production System. Kyushu B Auto Company (hereafter Plant B) is the first production base for the parent company outside the Tokai area, in the centre of the main island of Japan where the company has long concentrated its production base.[4]

Plant B, despite its legal independence, has no R&D, marketing and parts purchasing functions. It is an assembly plant producing vehicles using the parts, specifications and prices regulated by the parent company. The reason for the organizational independence of Plant B is very much related to the personnel management element. Because of the plant's relatively low age profile,[5] it has been possible for the plant to introduce innovations in both the personnel management and the payment systems.

FIGURE 2

ASSEMBLY PLANT OF COMPANY B

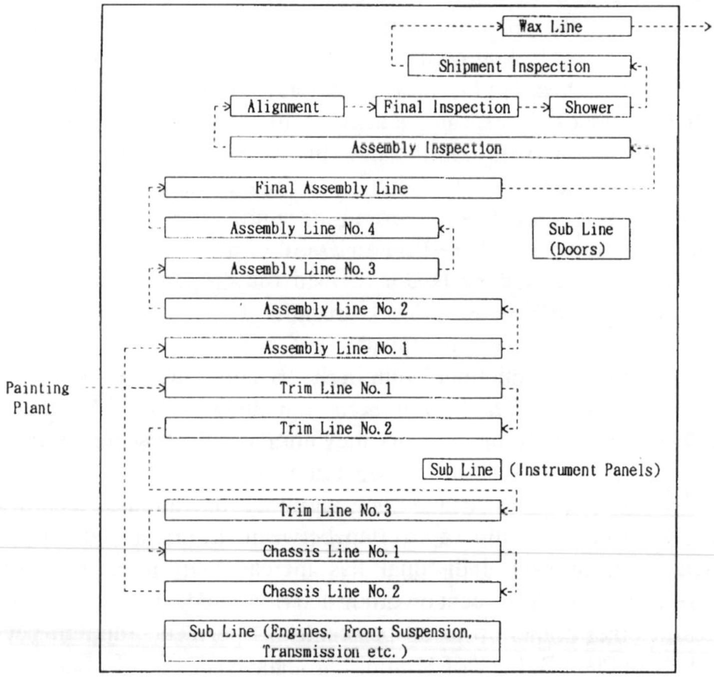

Source: Authors' research into company B.

T No.4 plant of the parent company – the latest innovation: At its T No. 4 plant, the parent company attempted an experiment which was later transposed to Plant B. In October 1991, T No.4 plant began production which was oriented around the basic concepts of the work environment, the formation of work organization, line layout, and personnel management. As regards improvements to work processes, the moving floor with hydraulic equipment, for example, has been introduced in order to eliminate heavy, difficult and dangerous work. As to improvements in work organization and process layout, work tasks have been consolidated in a functional unit on an individual and team basis so as to allow each operator the kind of sense of achievement which is hardly possible where work needs to be organized to take into account the imperatives of traditional assembly line principles, line productivity and effective line balancing. Moreover, this has ensured that people-management nostrums (specifically, the extension of the range of individual skills and training opportunities) have become institutionalized. Additionally, widening the automated area in the final assembly line has been pursued with a high level of investment in automation facilities, including electronic sensors, and the trial introduction of a modular system on assembly parts is in train. The line has been divided into 12 mini-lines, each of which is kept relatively independent of the other. In this respect, trucks with hydraulic lift equipment, as opposed to traditional conveyers, have been introduced in order to improve the ergonomics of the line.

Thus, it is clear that the company has attempted to significantly reform T No.4 plant. However, the economic costs incurred by automation in the body and the process assembly lines have come as to be judged 'excessive'. The modular system has also carried the problems of augmentation in the weight of parts, including an increase in the overall total number of work elements and there was a lot of pressure on the R&D division. The type of automation introduced in the assembly process area of plant B has to be seen as a response to these.

The assembly process at Plant B: The layout of the assembly line in Plant B is described in Figure 2. Plant B is defined as a 'Worker Friendly Factory' where the following three points are stressed.[6]

To begin with, the line is composed of 11 mini-lines, each of which is a relatively independent functional unit. In the first instance, the work elements are unified into a number of minimum functional units per worker, then consolidated into sub-groups. Finally they are placed in a series of relatively independent units per section. Each of the units at these three levels is expected to have a clear idea of one another's operations. According to company sources, the ratio of overlap between the ideal and substantive classified work of each individual has increased from 32 per cent on individual activities, 52 per cent on group activities, and 34 per cent on section activities in other plants up to 88 per cent , 90 per cent , and 55 per cent respectively in Plant B. Each of 11 mini-lines has its own quality check station on line, and a buffer of between three and ten vehicles. As indicated in Figure

2, some parts assembly is conducted off-line in sub-assembly modules.

The second point refers to the issue of the automated facilities on the assembly line. The parent company believes that its previous approaches to automation carried many negative features. Operators experienced stress, feelings of estrangement and a stagnation of work motivation (and decline in *kaizen* activities). Combined with these was the problem of scarcity in the number of workers with a sufficient level of technical skill. As to the problems caused by automation itself, this required considerable and expensive use of space. Because of the additional cost problems this created, it was necessary to avoid as much disruption as possible. In response to these problems, the parent company took the path of ensuring that the automation facilities would both co-exist with and be controlled by workers. Specifically, the structure of the automation facilities should be as simple and compact as possible with a high level of functional coherence. Last but not least, it has been emphasized that there should be sufficient room for *kaizen* activities. In fact, not only is the amount of investment in automation facilities at Plant B relatively low, but the automation ratio is less than that at T No.4 plant. There is no division in Plant B between the automated zone and the manual work zone, as can be seen in Plant C. The idea is to have a simplified, compact and low cost solution to automation in Plant B as can be seen, for example, by the way in which machinery operations are organized.

Thirdly, at Plant B an original measurement system known as the Toyota Verification of Assembly Line (TVAL) has been invented in order to analyse work load. TVAL is a system designed to reduce heavy and difficult tasks by assessing what these tasks consist of: specifically, the number of individual work positions; the weight of tools; the difficulty of parts installation; and the duration of physical work. Thus, the higher the score, the more 'difficult' the job.

Hofu No.2 Plant, Company C

Plant outline: Company C, Hofu No.2 Plant (hereafter Plant C) began operations in 1992, following the establishment of its transmission plant which was set up in 1982. The ground design of plant C was drawn up in the middle of the Japanese 'bubble economy', and production targets were set in relation to the luxury car market. Plant C is projected as, to quote the company, a 'Human-friendly luxury car plant'. However, due to the current depression in the market, line utilization is only around 60 per cent .

There are three main characteristics of the assembly process at Plant C. First of all, the length of the main line is 1400 metres, which is half the usual length of assembly lines in the company, and the part of the line which contains relatively heavy work has been modularized. The modular production system in this line is the most advanced in Japan. It comprises five modules of front-end, inside-panel, engine and suspension, doors, and dashboard. Secondly, the main line is also divided into the automated zone and manual zone, as illustrated in Figure 3. This is quite distinct from the

FIGURE 3

ASSEMBLY PLANT OF COMPANY C

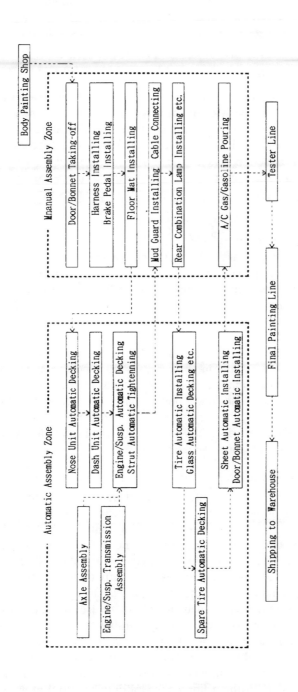

Source: Authors' research into company C.

routes taken by the other two companies in this article (Plants A and B). Thirdly, as regards the tracks themselves, a linear motor track system has been introduced in the automated zone and an electrically controlled track is in the manual zone.

THE PRODUCTION SYSTEMS IN THE NEW PLANTS

The three production systems begun in the 1990s contain a common theme in attempting to cope with the difficulties faced by Japanese car makers. Nevertheless, the actual organization of the assembly line and work systems themselves show certain differences stemming from the peculiarities in the idea of the production system, and both aspects co-exist at the present time. Therefore, we are concerned to examine the common points of reference and also the implications which company differences throw up for further research.

The Concept of the New Plants

The Japanese auto makers are facing contextual changes such as a change in the work-consciousness of the younger generation, the pressure on labour markets, and an intensification in international competition. The basic concepts of the new plants begun in the 1990s represent a positive reaction to these changing circumstances. The common targets here are a reduction in the burden of heavy work, improvement in the work environment and finally, co-existence with the natural environmental. Inside the plants, it is possible to see a gradual improvement with respect to safer and healthier conditions (for example, the environment tends to be rather more dustproof, machine vibration and noise levels have been reduced, there is air-conditioning and layout is better). As to efforts to reduce work load, the three plants, in their distinctive ways, are moving gradually towards the elimination of heavy and dangerous work.

The Modular Production System

The modular production system, in which Japanese car makers have been lagging behind the American and European producers, carries several merits from the point of view of production control, when introduced in the assembly process[7]). At the same time, the system inevitably requires an increase in the number of parts, vehicle weights and costs. The system also inevitably changes the R&D process. It is difficult to accommodate models designed for a non-modular process on a modular system.

Plants A and B have divided part of the process into a sub-assembly line, but the introduction of a modular system has been stymied. Plant A has avoided specification of a modular system in order to maintain flexibility in model variation on the line. Plant B has avoided modular production mainly on account of costs, but also because of a basic commitment by the company to the full use of human capabilities in pursuit of the principle of the 'co-existence of man and machine'.

As regards the case of Plant C, the timing was crucial for the introduction of the modular system. The theme of modularity was central both in the construction of the plant and in the development of the luxury cars due to be assembled there. However, this in itself is insufficient as a condition for success. The fundamental problems are that sales of luxury cars are low, and the input of non-modular cars are bound to reduce the merits of the system. While the modular system introduced at Plant C is surely progressive in technological terms, it is somewhat lacking when it comes to dealing with market fluctuations.

Approaches to the Automation

The approach to automation of the assembly process is varied. The attitude at Plant B is interesting. This outlook derives from the basic understanding of work as it is conceived at Company B (Toyota Production System). In the company's terms, the 'humanization of work' is not only concerned with eliminating heavy and dangerous work, but also with eliminating waste and non-value added physical activity. From this standpoint, the company was interested not only in developing a technologically rational approach, for it was crucial that automation did not disturb employee control of the automated machine facilities. As a result, the automation ratio of the assembly line at Plant B is lower than that at the other two plants.

The Functional Units at Plant B

The functional units introduced at plant B suggest the basis upon which to evaluate the new direction of the Japanese production system. One view is that the system moves further from Taylorism by the fact that the range and content of each employee's work is enclosed in a meaningful unit, firstly at the individual level, then at the level of the team and finally at section level. However, another key question is whether the new system constitutes a qualitative development away from the Toyota Production System or little more than a partial reform of it. Further detailed research on the change which has been occurring in the multi-skilling and *kaizen* activities needs to be conducted, although some recognized points for discussion will be suggested in the next section.

PART 2
ISSUES FOR DISCUSSION: 'BEYOND JAPAN?'

Our observations on the new plants are at an early stage in our research programme and therefore we can only go so far in our arguments. Nonetheless, what we can do in this conclusion is to suggest some implications for the discussion of the future direction of the Japanese Production System.

The Types of Production System

It is clear that the three plants have as a common theme the elimination of heavy and dangerous work. Behind this idea, there is the problem of recruitment of young males to traditional manufacturing organizations. Research carried out by the Japanese Automotive Workers Union (the JAW) in 1990 suggested that only a small minority of union members said 'yes' to the question 'Do you want your children to be employed in the auto industry?'. Work in the auto industry is seen to lack much attraction even among existing employees in the industry. The new plants chose not only to alter the production system, but also to move to green-field sites in the Kyushu area, far from their own local business environments and labour markets. This was seen to be the only way in which the auto makers could create new conditions for new production, including a dependable labour force. However, while they claim a new concept in the 'humanization of work', the various types of production system differ in terms of the form of automation at each company.

In the first type, we have an active modular production system. The Japanese producers have been prudent in moving towards a modular system. Even where one takes the case of Plant C, the expected merits of the system have not been fully realized.

In the second type, automating the main line by splitting off the labour-intensive assembly line, has not seen the introduction of a modular system. Plant A has prompted the automation of the main line, while the strategy to keep flexible production of model variety took precedence over the requirement for uniformity in modular production.

The third type pursues the co-existence between man and machine and automation occurs within this framework, although on the basis of a division between the sub-assembly and main lines. This approach seems to have been reasonably effective in terms of avoiding unreasonable cost pressures, as was the case at Plant B. The point is that this was possible on the basis of the company's existing production system.

The Third Type: Plant B

In the context of the notion of 'Beyond Japan' we focus attention on the third type in the sense that the plant is backed by the traditional Toyota Production System and has chosen a form of automation at the least possible cost. This approach has maintained a production system with a highly labour-intensive regime. To retain a high level of human involvement, the assembly line has been simplified by instituting functional units. The insertion of wire harnesses, or tubing, for example, is concentrated as a functional unit on an independent line. A line is called a 'group' which constitutes three teams on average and each team consists of 15–20 workers. Each worker can clearly understand their span of work and their position both within a group and the whole production process. In addition, every employee is required to develop their functions, initially within the team before then moving on to another group. The system targets detailed work progression and motivation control, clarifying individual task responsibility in a way which makes real time feedback possible.

In order to abolish night work, the plant has introduced related double shifts from early morning to late in the evening. A recent research report suggests that the net working hours are substantially the same as they were under the previous Toyota system, although with less overtime pay (Nakagawa 1994, 453–4). A future research agenda will examine whether this system can reduce the stress which employees experience both at work and, as a consequence of work, in their home life.

The New Burdens Placed on Supervisors

Where the functions of each group, team, and individual are made self-inclusive, the supervisory tasks have also become more detailed and expanded. As a consequence of this, the number of tasks and responsibilities of front line management has increased. The company, from the initial planning stage, expected 'the roles of group leaders (KUMICHO) to become more onerous' (*Kojo-Kanri* 1994: 19). The plant director pointed out that the group leaders on the new line 'can perform more detailed line control and man-management, in-depth' and also 'take responsibility for the quality control of each line'. Accordingly, 'for the group leaders, the line demands tight management with greater responsibility.' (*Kojo-Kanri* 1994: 44).

We need to carefully examine the changes that will take place with respect to what is happening to the supervisory role on the line. What is obvious, however, is the fact that the organization of the line presupposes the initiative of group leaders which also places a heavy burden on supervisors. As to the training of group members, each group leader is required to take the initiative on the effective use of the so-called 'training corner', an area for training and *kaizen* which is set out for each group. In March 1992, 56 per cent of the group leaders' tasks at Company B as a whole were already related to actual line work and constituted cover for absence, relief and recovery of delay, and so on (Saruta 1995: 271). Under Company B's production system, front line supervisors have inevitably performed the dual role of supervision and line work. What is crucial is whether the new system contains an in-built mechanism for the elimination of the heavy load currently being placed on supervisory workers. However, at this stage, despite a favourable research report on the workings of the new system(Shimizu 1995) we cannot perceive such a mechanism.

The Implications for Trade Unions

In this conclusion, we want to focus on the implications of the changes elaborated above for trade unions at the three companies. A recent detailed study of the union-management council system at Company A suggests that the collaborative enterprise union has succeeded through each level of the council's procedures to gain a certain degree of power to control management's activities at least up to the mid 1980s. The study also pointed out that this control has now collapsed as a result of an aggressive challenge from the management in order to open the road to flexible production (Kamii 1994). To assess whether flexibility is opposed to the functions of the union, it is significant to note that the International Metal Workers' Federation (IMF), B Company World Auto Council in 1992 concluded that: 'When companies use lean production, they often emphasize the company's objectives and values. Unions are concerned that this may overshadow their values and objectives.' (IMF 1992). This view is of practical importance because it expresses the preliminary, yet fundamental, standpoint of the union on the relationship between the so-called 'man-machine system of peaceful co-existence' and the union presence. It is important to remember that the union at Plant B operates under the umbrella of the federation of Company B unions. Having said this, recent research highlights the fact that the union at Plant B has no full-time official, and that union affairs are dealt by staff from the company's general affairs division (Saruta 1995: 487).

The study of the union at Company A also suggests that the union's power is structurally linked to the power of supervisory workers within the work organization. This exposes the fragility of union control in the workplace which is dependant upon the power of core workers, since if management can take the initiative with respect to supervisors then union control will be drastically curtailed. Finally, at Plant B, future research will need to carefully assess the reasons why the new production system imposes such heavy burdens on the supervisors.

NOTES

1. There has been a lack of research exclusively on the issue of supervision. A brief survey on the Japanese supervision issue will be published by Ogasawara and Sato (1996).
2. In the Japanese context where a federation of enterprise unions is organized within a group of companies headed by a large manufacturer, the difference in industrial relations also has crucial influence on industrial relations in the companies under the umbrella of the parent company. The difference in production systems in the Japanese auto industry has also been described by Klark and Fujimoto (1991).
3. The research relating to the following description of the new production lines was conducted at the end of 1994 by the Production System Research Project to which Hirofumi Ueda belongs. The description here is based upon discussions which have taken place within the project. An interim report of the research is available: *Production System Research Project* 1995.
4. Company B has sub-contracted a part of the assembly process to a group of companies outside the Tokai area.
5. The average age of employees at Plant B is 29, while at Company B as a whole the average age is 34.
6. Kawamura 1993.
7. Nikkei-Mechanical 1992 p.26.

REFERENCES

Clark, Kim and Fujimoto, Takahiro (1991) *Product Development Performance*, Harvard Business School Press (English).
IMF (1992) *Conclusions: IMF B World Auto Council*, May 27–28 (English).
JAW (1992a) *Japanese Automobile Industry In The Future: Toward Coexistence With The World, Consumers And Employees.*
JAW (1992b) *The Report Of The Second IMF-JC/IGMetal Meeting*, IMF-JC.
Kamii, Yoshihiko (1994) *The Influence of the Enterprise Union at the Shopfloor Level: A Case*

Study of the Automobile Industry in Japan, Tokyo University Press.

Kawamura, Teruya (1993) 'The Coming of the Worker-Friendly Factory', in *Toyota Technical Review* 1993; Vol.43, No.2.

Kojo-Kanri (1994) Vol.40, No.11.

Nakagawa, Junko (1994) 'Family life and living time', in *The Work and Living Research Group, Enterprise Society and Humanity*, Horitsu-Bunka-Sha.

Nikkei-Mechanical (1992) Issue of 7th September, 1992.

Nikkeiren (1995) Japanese Management In The New Era – New Japanese Management Study Project Report.

Ogasawara, Koichi and Hiroki Sato (1996) 'The First Line Management In Japanese CTV Plants and Transplants', in *Denki-Rengo Chosa-Jiho* (forthcoming).

Parker, Mike and Slaughter, Jane (1995) *Choosing Sides* (Japanese Version, Totsuka, Hideo translation and edition, Ryoku fu-Shuppan).

Production System Research Project (1995) Research Report (I), Working Paper no. 9502, Institute For Economic Research, Osaka City University.

Saruta, Masaki (1995) *Toyotism and Personnel Management*, Zeimu-Keiri-Kyokai.

Shimizu, Koichi (1995) 'The Humanization of Work in B Auto Company (I)', in *Okayama Economic Review*, Vol.27, No.1.

Totsuka, Hideo and Tsutomu, Hyodo (1991) *Transformation and Choice of Industrial Relations: The Japanese Auto Industry*, Nippon-Hyoron-Sha.

Working Conditions under Lean Production: A Worker-based Benchmarking Study

WAYNE LEWCHUK and DAVID ROBERTSON

INTRODUCTION: BENCHMARKING THE QUALITY OF WORKING LIFE

Benchmarking is being used extensively in management's drive to achieve 'world class' levels of performance. Those aspects of a corporation's current performance which companies and consultants identify as critical to achieving world class manufacturing practice are measured and compared with similar operations anywhere in the world.[1] Aspects such as throughput, productivity, WIP (work in process), set-up times, space utilization, direct/indirect employee ratios, rework, sales per employee, and robot counts are regularly measured.[2] The majority of benchmarking studies have little if anything to say about working conditions nor the tradeoffs between productivity improvements and the conditions of working life. They rarely if ever ask workers about their jobs.

This article is based on a study which focuses on working conditions as described by workers. It raises questions about the tradeoffs between work reorganization and the quality of working life under lean production.

To fully appreciate the implications of omitting working conditions from benchmarking studies, it is essential to realize that while benchmarking is the formal process of measuring and comparing operations, its proponents are quick to point out that it is not primarily a data-gathering exercise. Rather the aim is to learn how other companies have achieved their results and to instil in organizations a commitment to continuous improvement. In a recent publication, *The Economist Intelligence Unit* defined benchmarking as '…a process of continuous improvement in the search for competitive advantage. It measures a company's products, services and practices against those of its competitors or other acknowledged leaders in their fields.'

In an already competitive environment, benchmarking shifts the goal posts and redefines our understanding of an acceptable level of productivity or a normal rate of improvement. For example, a recent study entitled the *Worldwide Manufacturing Competitiveness Study: The Second Lean Enterprise Report* conducted by Andersen Consulting compared the performance of 71 automotive components plants in nine countries. The study concluded that there was a 2:1 difference in performance between world class plants and the rest. The implicit message is that if one is to survive one must adopt the practices of those companies that score high in

Wayne Lewchuk, McMaster University, David Robertson, CAW Work Organization Department.

benchmarking studies. These studies create an environment which encourages companies, and their workforces, to accept certain types of radical changes in work practices in order to reach world class performance.

Most benchmarking studies are incomplete and ignore one side of the production equation, the working conditions and the wellbeing of those involved in the operations. This creates two potential problems. First, such incomplete studies run the risk of falsely crediting practices such as JIT with improving productivity when in fact JIT may simply be acting as a proxy for some omitted variable such as work pace or workload. Second, because working conditions are all but ignored in the studies, improvements in productivity may come at the cost of poorer working conditions. Benchmarks in some aspects of a company's operations, which can only be achieved through practices that undermine safety or which lead to a deterioration in working conditions, are of questionable value. If a particular company, for example, had the highest throughput in the industry but also had the fastest line speed, the highest incidence of RSIs (repetitive strain injuries), the highest accident claims, and the most problems with the placement of injured workers, then its status as best-in-class around throughput would have to be offset against those other measures. If there are to be sustainable workplaces it is necessary to balance measures of performance with assessments of working conditions and to examine directly the tradeoffs involved. This is what the current study attempts to do.

BENCHMARKING, LEAN PRODUCTION AND THE QUALITY OF WORKING LIFE

Benchmarking studies are used extensively by academics and consultants promoting lean production as a means of improving productivity and the competitive position of North American and European manufacturers.[3] Based on extremely limited information on actual working conditions, the proponents of lean production have also speculated that it will improve the quality of work life. Lean production is said to offer workers a means of escaping the monotony and boredom associated with mass production systems based on Fordist principles. Jobs will become more challenging. Workers will be given more responsibility and more control over their work. They will be asked to learn professional skills and apply these in a team setting.[4] Womack et al.argued, '...by the end of the century we expect that lean-assembly plants will be populated almost entirely by highly skilled problem solvers whose task will be to think continually of ways to make the system run more smoothly and productively.'[5]

Popular discussions of lean production by authors such as Womack et al. (1990) or MacDuffie (1995) have little to say about the affect of lean production on physical effort norms, work pace, workloads or stress. Where effort is discussed it is usually in the context of workers contributing their knowledge to the process. The impression given is that workers will be working smarter, but not harder. The failure to even discuss physical effort intensification is in part a result of how the popular analysis of lean production has been structured. Following a long-standing tradition in economics, authors such as Womack *et al.*, and MacDuffie have equated physical effort and time.[6] The weakness of this approach is that it makes sense only if the level of effort per unit of time is constant. The promoters of lean production have simply assumed that the question of effort intensification is not a problem.

A growing number of empirical studies by critics of lean production paint a more negative picture of its affect on working conditions. The CAW, in a previous study using longitudinal data from a greenfield lean production automobile assembly plant, describes the growing dissatisfaction of workers with the lean system of production.[7] Authors such as Marsh have raised concerns about how far the Japanese system has in fact actually gone in giving Japanese workers more power to make decisions, compared with workers in North America.[8] Fucini and Fucini (1990), Garrahan and Stewart (1992) and Stewart and Garrahan (1995) have all stressed the negative aspects of lean production, including significant increases in physical effort.[9]

THE QUALITY OF WORKING LIFE IN THE AUTOMOBILE COMPONENTS SECTOR

Survey Methodology

This article is based on a survey of 1,670 workers employed in the independent automotive components sector in Canada.[10] Sixteen workplaces participated in the study which involved both site visits and the administration of two survey instruments. One survey focussed on workload and health issues and the other on training, skill, control and other workplace issues. The site visits included an in-depth tour of the operations and separate interviews with management and union leadership. Following the site visits, the surveys were distributed and subsequently returned to the CAW. The sample was comprised of 73 per cent direct workers, 18 per cent indirect, and 9 per cent tradespeople. Although 41 per cent of the sample was female, five workplaces employed only men in production tasks. The average age of the sample was 39 with 12 years of seniority. All the workers in the study were unionized and all were members of the Canadian Automobile Workers.

The 16 workplaces represented a cross-section of the automotive parts sector in Canada. Five plants moulded plastic components. All of these plants did some assembly and all but one had painting facilities. Three plants were engaged in casting metal parts, including two that manufactured wheel and brake components. There were six stamping/assembly plants in the study, including two that were involved mainly in stamping bumpers, two manufactured radiators and oil coolers, and two manufactured seat assemblies. One company moulded glass and one manufactured electronic circuit boards. Employment levels ranged from a low of 131 to a high of 830. Three of the plants had less than 200 employees, ten employed between 201 and 500 employees, and three had more than 500 employees. Six of the workplaces had head offices in Canada, seven had head offices in the United States, two in Europe, and one was a joint Japanese/American operation. Two of the plants began producing automotive components more than 50 years ago, seven began operations during the 1960s and 1970s, and seven had entered the industry since 1980.

Trends in Work Reorganization in the Components Sector

Driven by competitive pressures and the cost-down restructuring initiatives of the original equipment manufacturers (OEMs), automobile components companies are seeking ways to improve their operations on a variety of performance measures. The trend is towards vehicle assemblers out-sourcing the design and production of components to independent suppliers. Across the sector, companies are investing in machinery and equipment, tightening up managerial practices, and reorganizing work processes. Some placed more emphasis on new investment, others on work reorganization. Some continued to follow traditional Fordist forms of work organization, others were strongly influenced by the principles of lean production. Companies were shifting from push- to pull-production, introducing flow lines and process cells, and paying more attention to cycle times, set-up times, line balancing and production smoothing. Kanbans and visual controls are being introduced and problem-solving teams were in place at many companies.

Many companies are moving away from the batch production system where components are moved from one part of the plant to another for different operations and are moved in and out of work-in-process inventory. Instead, the manufacturing process is being simplified. The number of processing steps is being reduced and product flows are being streamlined so as to reduce overall cycle times, especially the move, store, and expedite functions. There are more process cells organized around particular machines, products, or sets of operations. Flow lines are used to facilitate the move from push- to pull-production. Most companies have cut WIP buffers and have reduced finished goods inventories. There is increased managerial control and co-ordination of production operations.

The following case study notes are typical of what we observed during our site visits.

> There have been many changes in the last year since the company's customers demanded they find ways to give back ten per cent of its costs. This was made possible through a combination of measures...
> The company introduced what management terms 'synchronous manufacturing' which largely dealt with work methods and involved time studies. As well the company introduced more process cells...the company is on a pull system. Although the plant does not have kanbans,

it does have a kanban board on the floor whereby the scheduling department will use this information to tell workers how much has to be produced. Management believes that the company is 100 times better now than what it was five years ago in terms of buffers.

The main goal is to reduce the elapsed time from the first part to the last part shipped out...the process cells have reduced buffers between the work stations and the open layout of the plant allows for a recognizable buffer.

In response to competitive pressures, management's emphasis has been on addressing both the way in which work is organized and the layout of the plant. While there has been investment in new equipment, this has largely been done to replace old and wornout machinery. In the last five years, management has streamlined work so that as much as possible can be done in one step. This is in contrast to the old methods whereby, for example, a piece would be worked on, sent to inventory and then pulled out to be worked on again. The company has also moved towards process cells organized around one machine where workers can build parts without having to move around and/or depend on material handlers to retrieve parts from storage. There are also some work cells comprised of assembly workers. Currently approximately 50 to 60 per cent of the workforce is organized into process cells and it is anticipated that this will increase in the future.

Even though the case notes from our site visits reveal a clear trend, some qualifications are required. First, the changes are not even across the sector. In fact, some plants were largely unaffected by these developments. Their operations, with the exception of some minor changes, were basically the same as they were ten years ago. Second, the changes are not independent of the production process. It is obviously easier to re-organize a plastics plant or small-part fabrication operation into process cells than it is to change a foundry in the same way. Third, the changes within a plant are often uneven. One part of the plant could be operating with new equipment, different processes, and changed job content while the rest of the plant is relatively unchanged.

Consistent with the philosophy of lean production, most companies are talking about making greater use of labour knowledge and some have created mechanisms for gathering information from workers. The most common arrangements are temporary joint worker/management task-oriented groups. More often than not, the objectives of these groups are set by management and, once achieved, they are dissolved. While these exercises are tempting to workers wishing to have their voice heard, in virtually every case workers were frustrated at the limited role they played and the uses managers made of their knowledge. The groups we observed bore little resemblance to the teams described in management-based surveys. We did not observe any increase in worker authority to make decisions, nor did we see permanent area-based self-directed teams.

The following descriptions of worker involvement from our case notes are examples of what we observed.

> The teams are voluntary and project oriented, for example, how to get scrap down. They are not by work area. The teams are still largely management, but there will be one or two workers per team. In the machine shop there is a team on how to get set-up times reduced. There is no formal rewards system but successful teams do get taken out for dinner.

> Task oriented teams are very much a part of the company's strategy. They are voluntary, although some people were selected. There are probably about 30 different teams in operation...They are task-oriented, not area-oriented...About 25 per cent of the workforce participate in teams. Of those who participate about 75 per cent take it seriously...Recently they set up Value Focus teams. These teams are corporate policy, all the company's plants will have them. The other teams are local initiatives.

> The company made much effort to expropriate labour knowledge. They had a clearly articulated philosophy of incremental change and an institutional structure to support it. Some 9,000 suggestions had been implemented thus far. The system was highly organized.

CONDITIONS OF WORK IN THE INDUSTRY:
CURRENT CONDITIONS AND TRENDS

Using data from the entire sample, this section will look at the conditions of working life in the components sector and how it is changing. The following section will provide a more detailed analysis including the impact of workforce and workplace characteristics on responses. It will focus on the tradeoffs between work reorganization and the quality of working life.

Control and Skill Levels

Workers in the components industry are employed in jobs which offer them little real control over working conditions and at tasks which can be learned in a short time. Reflecting the lack of real control, despite management claims of worker empowerment, the majority of workers were unable to change things they did not like about their jobs. Over one third were unable to even vary their work pace during the day. Almost half the workforce reported they could train someone to do their job in a few days or less. The trend appears to be towards even greater management control over workers, with over one-third reporting that management was collecting more information on their performance. Workers did not tend to describe their workplaces as democratic. More felt their workplace was becoming less democratic rather than more democratic. Most regarded even the concept of democratic control as foreign to life at work.

- 17 per cent reported that it would be easy to change the things they did not like about their jobs.
- 35 per cent reported they had little if any opportunity to vary the pace of their work during the day.
- 31 per cent had to find a replacement worker before they could go to the washroom.
- 48 per cent reported they could train someone to do their jobs in a few days or less.
- 19 per cent reported receiving some classroom-based training in the last three months.
- 35 per cent reported management was now collecting more information on their work performance.

Workload

There were strong indications that workload was both excessive and increasing in the industry.

- 61 per cent of those surveyed (61 per cent of women and 61 per cent of men) reported that their workload was either too fast, too heavy, had to be done by too few people, or in too little time.
- 52 per cent of those surveyed (59 per cent of women and 48 per cent of men) reported that in the last two years their workload had increased, becoming either heavier, faster, or having to be done in less time. (6 per cent reported their workload had been reduced.)

Health

There was also evidence that work was stressful and unhealthy and becoming more stressful and less healthy.

- 51 per cent of those surveyed (58 per cent of women and 47 per cent of men) reported high levels of workplace health risks. Health risks were considered to be high if workers reported at least two health risks from a list which included: working in pain at least half the days in the last month, working in an awkward position at least half the time, feeling tired after work most days, or being tense at work.
- 41 per cent of those surveyed (50 per cent of women and 34 per cent of men) reported their work had become less healthy in the last two years.
- 40 per cent of those surveyed (42 per cent of women and 39 per cent of men) reported working in pain or physical discomfort half the days in the last month.
- 37 per cent of those surveyed (40 per cent of women and 35 per cent of men) reported working in physically awkward positions at least half of each day.

- 44 per cent of those surveyed (50 per cent of women and 40 per cent of men) reported that compared with a couple of years ago, their current job was more tense.

- 45 per cent of those surveyed (56 per cent of women and 38 per cent of men) reported that compared with a couple of years ago, they were more tired lately after 8 hours of work.

Overall, the data presented above does not paint a positive picture of working conditions in this industry in the mid-1990s. Workers have limited control of shop floor conditions, they can train someone to do their job in a short period time, they are experiencing heavy and increasing workloads, and face high and increasing health risks. In short, there is little evidence of the improvement in working conditions which the proponents of lean production have associated with work reorganization.

WORKFORCE AND WORKPLACE CHARACTERISTICS AND THE QUALITY OF WORKING LIFE

In the previous section we found little evidence of improved working conditions in the industry as a whole. This last section will examine how specific workforce and workplace characteristics influenced the quality of working life. Our focus will be the tradeoffs between different forms of work organization and the quality of working life. The analysis will be presented at two levels of detail. In the first part we look only at how systems of work organization influenced responses to our survey questions. Companies were assigned to one of four different work organization systems: Traditional Fordist, Lean, Change or Exploitative. The second part will take account of the fact that workplaces differed not only in terms of the system of work organization employed, but also the characteristics of their workforce and the sector of the industry. This second section will employ multivariate regression analysis.

Systems of Work Organization

Unlike other studies which relied on management responses to standardized surveys to classify companies, we classified firms after detailed semi-structured interviews with labour and management and observation of the organization of work during plant tours. This reflected our view that responses to standardized questions such as 'do you employ teams', or 'do you practice just-in-time', are for the most part meaningless. We listened to labour and management describe their production systems and then observed these systems in operation. To classify a company as a lean company, we looked for evidence of established and operating kanban systems, JIT practices, redistribution of tasks between direct, indirect and low level supervisors, and systems for exploiting labour knowledge of the production process. Our criteria for being a lean company were strict, and in the end only two were designated as such. One was a joint Japanese/

American company, the other had won a major contract to supply a joint Japanese/American assembler. A number of other companies had implemented aspects of lean production but not to such a degree that we felt they should be classified as lean. Work organization here was described as 'changing to lean'. Other companies had invested in new capital equipment, but showed little evidence of the work reorganization practices associated with lean production. Work organization here was described as 'traditional'. A final group of companies relied on an older strategy of employing workers with limited bargaining power to demand higher effort norms while holding wage levels low. Work organization here was described as 'exploitative'.

None of our companies are perfectly described by just one of the four types of work organization. For example, most companies claimed to employ at least some aspects of the lean system of production in some parts of their operation. This overlap between types of work organization reduces our chances of finding any significant correlation between survey responses and work organization characteristics.

Some may also question whether any of the companies in our study are truly lean. Indeed a favoured response of proponents of lean production in dealing with their critics is to deny that what others observe is actually lean production. Management at the two companies identified as lean were clear in their own minds that they had adopted a lean production approach to work organization and production practices. However, it is also clear that these companies did not employ all of the HRM practices that have been described in the management literature by authors such as Womack *et al.* or Florida and Kenney.[11] As is the case with most North American and European companies, the lean companies in our sample did not employ a person-specific wage system, nor did they offer lifetime employment although both companies have made strong informal commitments to not laying off workers. Workers worked in groups and rotated jobs within these groups. While management saw these groups as teams, we would not describe them this way. The work groups did not have overall responsibility for coordinating shop floor activity nor were they used to encourage suggestions or continuous improvement, except in the case of a stand-alone kaizen team. Had we talked only to management, as many of the existing studies of lean production have, we would have been convinced that teams were in place at these companies and that workers were participating in decisions about day to day operations affecting them. It was only when we probed deeper that we found that the reality on the shop floor was seriously different and that the empowerment and participation that management described did not exist in the view of workers. We would argue that our two companies are representative of lean systems of production and work organization, and that closer examination of companies described as lean by other authors would likely reveal a system of work organization much like what we found.

The four work organization categories are described in detail below.

Lean companies: There were two companies far enough along the path to lean production to be called lean companies. One was the only joint Japanese/American venture in the sample. Both shipped a significant percentage of their output to a regional Japanese/American assembler. At each company, the JIT system was well developed, the responsibilities of direct production workers had been blurred as they were allocated inspection and material handling tasks, and a kanban system was in place. Both management and labour pointed to the Japanese influence in their current shop floor organization.

Companies changing to lean production: There were four companies in the process of reorganizing production. They had shifted towards Just-in-Time production, had invested in new capital equipment, and had made some attempt to access labour knowledge. However, these changes were either in their early stages or had only been implemented in a small part of the operation.

Traditional companies: Eight companies continued to operate a highly hierarchical control system of management based on Fordist principles. Workers tended to have a large degree of job ownership through the job posting/seniority system. Workers were rarely if ever consulted formally regarding how to run the plant. These eight companies had made experienced some investment in new capital equipment, but it tended to be organized along traditional lines with management retaining virtually complete control of coordination, planning and supervision tasks. The union locals in this group tended to be the strongest locals.

Exploitative companies: Productivity was increased at two companies by driving labour harder. These companies had high numbers of women and the highest number of visible minorities in the workforce. They had local unions who felt powerless in the face of competitive pressures, and paid the lowest wages in the study. These workers were in the worst position to resist managerial demands. Neither company had made significant investments in new technology nor had they undergone major organizational changes with the intention of implementing lean production.

The seven diagrams below give an overall impression of how systems of work organization influenced responses to our survey questions. The marked points on the vertical line in each graph represent the average response to a particular question from workers employed by companies using the indicated system of work organization. The horizontal line in each graph represents the average response to a particular question for the entire sample.

Figures 1 and 2 provide evidence that workload was excessive and increasing at lean companies compared with those employing a more

FIGURE 1
% REPORTING WORK LOAD EXCESSIVE

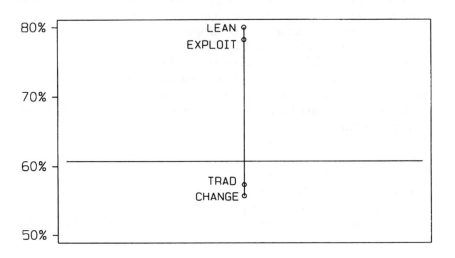

FIGURE 2
% REPORTING WORK LOAD INCREASING

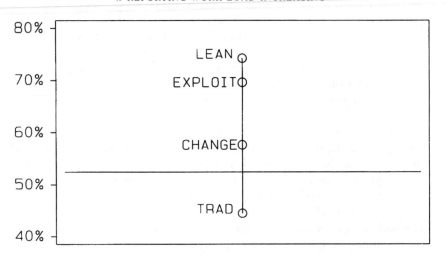

traditional Fordist system of work organization. Workload was considered excessive if work was described as either too fast, too heavy, having to be done in too little time, or with too few people. Workload was increasing if it was becoming faster, heavier, or had to be done in less time.

The pace of work was a particular concern for those employed under lean systems of production. Figures 3 and 4 indicate that those at lean plants were much more likely to report their work was too fast and that it was becoming faster compared with workers at traditional workplaces.

FIGURE 3

% REPORTING WORK PACE TOO FAST

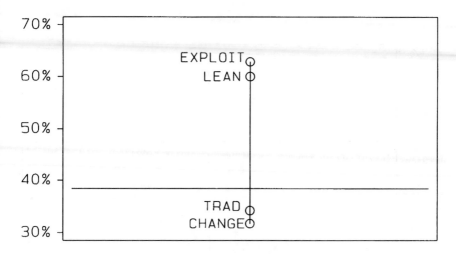

FIGURE 4

% REPORTING INCREASE IN WORK PACE

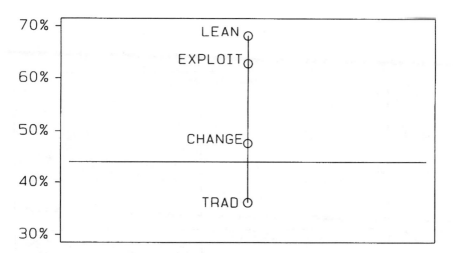

A key claim of those promoting lean production is that workers are empowered and that work becomes more rewarding. Our survey tells a very different story. Figure 5 suggests that rather than being more empowered, workers at our lean companies were the most likely to report they could not change the things they did not like about their jobs. Figure 6 suggests that workers at lean companies had lost some control over their own time and found it much more difficult to get time off for unscheduled absences such as a sick child, compared with workers at traditional companies.

FIGURE 5

% REPORTING DIFFICULT TO CHANGE JOB FEATURES

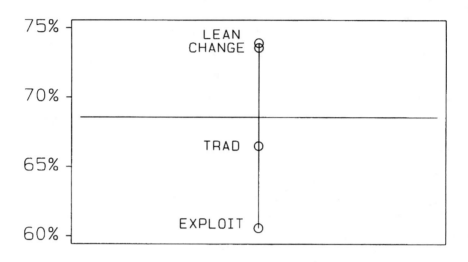

FIGURE 6

% REPORTING DIFFICULT TO GET TIME OFF

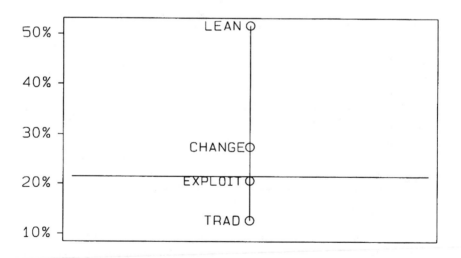

The high workloads, inability to improve working conditions and the loss of control over personal time all translated into a high level of job dissatisfaction at lean plants. Figure 7 indicates that workers at lean plants were the most likely to report distaste at going to work at least half the time.

FIGURE 7

% REPORTING DISTASTE GOING TO WORK AT LEAST ½ THE TIME

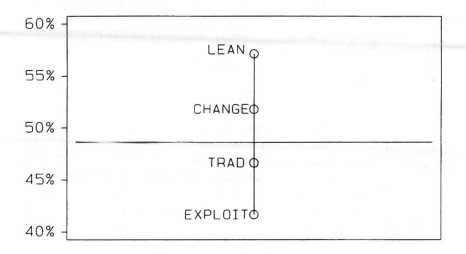

Impact of Workforce and Workplace Characteristics on the Quality of Working Life

The previous section simply divided our survey responses into four different categories representing different systems of work organization and reported average responses to our questions. While such an analysis is easy to grasp, it is limited in that there are a number of other variables we would like to control for as well as systems of work organization. Our companies employed work forces with different characteristics such as age and gender, and were occupied in different segments of the automobile parts industry. By using multiple regression techniques we can simultaneously correct for all of these differences and get a purer estimate of the impact of work organization.

We included in our regressions variables representing the four systems of work organization discussed above variables representing sex, age, and type of work (for example, direct versus indirect), and variables to correct for the sector of the industry in which companies operated (such as plastics versus stamping/assembly). We report below estimates of the impact of these variables on responses to our survey questions in percentage terms. The figures in the row next to the label FEMALE in each table indicates the estimated impact of being female on the responses to the indicated question. For example, in Table 1, women were 3.1 per cent more likely to report that their workload was too heavy.

To interpret these numbers it is sufficient to keep in mind two things. First, the average response from the entire sample is given in the final row of each table and gives a sense of the size of the relative impact of each workforce or workplace characteristic. Second, it is necessary to appreciate that the numbers in the tables indicate the difference between a worker with the specific characteristic in question (or working for a company with a specific workplace characteristic) from a standard worker. In all cases the standard worker is male, age 30, a direct worker, employed in a traditional Fordist style company in the metal stamping/assembly sector. The statistical methodology and the variables employed are described in detail in the Technical Appendix.

Workload

There were no significant differences between men and women in responses to our workload questions. Age was also not very important. The only significant result was that older workers were more likely to report their work was too heavy. Skilled trades workers were more likely to report there were too few people to do the work in their area, but significantly less likely to report that their work was too heavy or too fast. Indirect workers reported workloads similar to direct workers.

Our work organization variables were highly relevant. Workers at companies using lean production methods were 17 per cent more likely to report their workload was too heavy overall compared with workers in traditional plants. They were more likely to report their work had to be done by too few people, that the work pace was too fast, or that they had too little time to do the work. Those employed at companies in the process of shifting to lean reported lower workloads overall. They reported that their work was less likely to be too physically heavy and less likely to be too fast but were more likely to report it had to be done by too few people.

TABLE 1

WORKLOAD

(% change in responding yes to question)

	TOTAL LOAD TOO HEAVY	TOO FEW PEOPLE	PHYSICALLY TOO HEAVY	TOO FAST	TOO LITTLE TIME
FEMALE	3.1	-0.4	3.7	3.8	5.1
AGE -30	-0.8	0.8	5.8***	0.1	-2.9*
TRADES	-5.1	12.8**	-15.5***	-31.1***	-0.8
INDIRECT	-3.3	4.5	-6.5	-4.4	6.8
LEAN	16.9**	29.9***	10.5	17.5**	32.5***
CHANGE	-11.0**	10.3**	-8.7*	-11.8**	-2.3
EXPLOIT	6.4	4.3	-10.1	10.2	8.4
SAMPLE MEAN	60.7	36.0	26.9	38.2	31.7

* Statistically significant at the .10 level;** at the .05 level;*** at the .01 level.

Change in Workload

Workforce and workplace characteristics influenced changes in workload over the last couple of years differently than workload itself. Women were more likely to report increasing workloads. They were more likely to report increases in physical load and work pace. Age was not a discriminating variable. Compared with direct workers, skilled trades workers were less likely to report increases in workload, especially in the area of work pace. There were only minor differences between direct and indirect workers.

Workplace organization was highly relevant. Compared with traditional plants, those employed at lean plants were over 25 per cent more likely to report their workload was increasing. They reported increases in physical workload, increases in the pace of work, and being given less time to do their work. Workers employed at companies in transition and at exploitative companies reported similar changes in workload to those at traditional companies.

TABLE 2

CHANGE IN WORKLOAD

(% change in responding yes to question)

	WORKLOAD INCREASING	PHYSICAL LOAD INCREASING	WORK PACE INCREASING	LESS TIME TO DO WORK ASSIGNED
FEMALE	12.1**	8.3**	10.8**	2.6
AGE -30	0.6	0.6	-1.8	0.1
TRADES	-6.7**	-6.7	-21.2***	-2.0
INDIRECT	-3.7	-3.7	-1.1	7.3*
LEAN	25.9***	17.3***	30.0***	19.1***
CHANGE	3.6	8.8**	5.0	-0.6
EXPLOIT	12.3	12.4*	13.0	5.9
SAMPLE MEAN	52.2	23.4	43.6	52.8

* Statistically significant at the .10 level;** at the .05 level;*** at the .01 level.

Shop Floor Control and Worker Autonomy

Neither our workforce nor workplace characteristics showed a consistent pattern in terms of control and autonomy. Women were more likely to report having to work as fast as they could to keep up and less likely to have the freedom to go to the washroom. Older workers were more likely to have to work as fast as they could to keep up, but found it easier to get time off and felt the absenteeism policy had eased recently. They also reported it was easier to change things they did not like about their jobs. Not surprising, skilled trades workers enjoyed the most control and autonomy. In general, indirect workers also reported greater autonomy than direct workers.

There was little evidence to support the hypothesis that workers at companies employing lean production enjoyed greater autonomy. If anything they enjoyed less. They were over 38 per cent more likely to report that it was difficult to get time off and over 31 per cent more likely to report they had to find someone to do their job before they could go to the washroom. There was no evidence that those employed at lean plants had any greater freedom to vary their pace of work or change things they did not like about their jobs. This raises serious doubts that lean production will improve these aspects of the quality of working life.

TABLE 3

SHOP FLOOR CONTROL/AUTONOMY

(% change in responding yes to question)

	WORK AS FAST AS YOU CAN TO KEEP UP	DIFFICULT TO GET TIME OFF	ABSENTEEISM POLICY TIGHTER	FREE TO LEAVE JOB TO GO TO WASHROOM
FEMALE	9.2*	4.5	-3.6	-9.9**
AGE -30	4.8**	-4.1***	-9.8***	-2.9
TRADES	-33.3***	6.1	-13.7*	25.0***
INDIRECT	-16.5***	-6.1*	6.9	22.9***
LEAN	9.5	38.2***	-9.4	-31.3***
CHANGE	-7.5	4.8	20.7***	6.5
EXPLOIT	10.0	10.5	-22.8***	13.5**
SAMPLE MEAN	52.8	21.4	58.3	68.8

* Statistically significant at the .10 level;** at the .05 level;*** at the .01 level.

TABLE 3 (continued)

SHOP FLOOR CONTROL/AUTONOMY

(% change in responding yes to question)

	CANNOT VARY WORK PACE	DIFFICULT TO CHANGE ASPECTS OF JOB	MANAGEMENT COLLECTS MORE INFORMATION ON JOB PERFORMANCE
FEMALE	8.2	-4.9	-7.3
AGE -30	3.4	-5.3**	2.0
TRADES	-26.6***	-5.3	-7.0
INDIRECT	-11.7**	-2.3	-11.7**
LEAN	1.0	3.9	-13.1**
CHANGE	-12.2**	3.7	1.9
EXPLOIT	-8.9	-0.8	1.4
SAMPLE MEAN	35.3	68.6	35.5

* Statistically significant at the .10 level;** at the .05 level;*** at the .01 level.

Skill Levels and Future Prospects

Women were less likely than men to have received training in the last three months. However men and women reported it would take about the same time to train someone to do their job once we corrected for age, job type and work organization. Skilled trades workers were much less likely to report they could train someone to do their job in a few days or less. Our direct workers were the most likely to report concerns about their future prospects. They were more likely than either skilled trades or indirect workers to report they could not maintain their current work pace until age 60 but less likely to report they expected to have a better job at their firm when they reached age 60.

Compared with workers in traditional plants, workers at lean companies were less likely to report they could train someone to do their job in a few days. However, they were also less likely to report they had received classroom-based training in the last three months. Workers employed at lean workplaces were almost 15 per cent more likely to report they would be unable to keep the current work pace until age 60 compared with workers at traditional companies but were as likely to report they would have a better job at age 60.

TABLE 4

SKILL/FUTURE PROSPECTS

(% change in responding yes to question)

	TRAINING TIME A FEW DAYS OR LESS	RECEIVED TRAINING LAST 3 MONTHS	UNLIKELY TO KEEP PACE UNTIL 60	UNLIKELY TO HAVE BETTER JOB AGE 60
FEMALE	3.4	-14.1***	3.6	7.1
AGE -30	2.5	-1.1	-9.8***	12.9***
TRADES	-51.9***	-11.7*	-39.6***	27.8***
INDIRECT	-36.9***	8.3	-17.6***	11.4**
LEAN	-21.4***	-15.1**	14.7**	7.0
CHANGE	-17.3***	-7.5	-19.1***	15.4**
EXPLOIT	-15.5*	10.1	-22.3***	-26.8***
SAMPLE MEAN	48.4	19.0	48.8	70.5

* Statistically significant at the .10 level;** at the .05 level;*** at the .01 level.

Health and Stress at Work

Table 5 suggests that men and women reported similar health risks. The one significant difference was women were more likely to report being tired after work. There were few differences between young and old workers other than older workers reporting working in pain marginally more often. Direct workers consistently reported more serious health risks compared with those employed as skilled trades workers or indirect workers.

Workers at companies employing lean production reported similar health risks to those in traditional plants. They were neither better nor worse off. Those employed by companies in transition to lean reported working fewer days in pain and spending less of their day in awkward positions, but were more likely to report concern over job loss.

TABLE 5

HEALTH RISKS

(% change in responding yes to question)

	TENSE AT WORK	WORK IN PAIN AT LEAST HALF THE DAYS	WORK IN AWKWARD POSITION HALF THE TIME	TIRED MOST DAYS	CONCERNED OVER JOB LOSS
FEMALE	3.1	-0.4	5.9	18.6***	-0.7
AGE -30	-1.6	-1.7***	0.5	3.5*	-2.2
TRADES	-10.3**	-22.6***	-29.1***	-11.1	-16.0***
INDIRECT	4.3	-7.7	-12.2**	4.7	-21.8***
LEAN	4.4	-11.4	-2.6	5.9	-6.9
CHANGE	9.3**	-13.1**	-13.3**	-5.6	7.7**
EXPLOIT	6.2	-23.7***	-3.8	-4.5	-4.2
SAMPLE MEAN	49.6	40.2	37.8	53.6	73.8

* Statistically significant at the .10 level;** at the .05 level;*** at the .01 level.

Change in Health Risks over the Last Two Years

We found that workforce and workplace characteristics had significant impacts on changes in health risks over the last couple of years. Women were almost 16 per cent more likely to report being tired more often after work. Skilled trades workers reported being tired less often, while indirect workers were the most likely to report increases in tension and being tired more often after work.

Workers at companies employing lean production were over 20 per cent more likely to report increases in tension and almost 17 per cent more likely to report being tired after work more often compared with those employed in traditional plants. Workers at companies in transition to lean production were also more likely to report being more tense after work.

TABLE 6

CHANGE IN HEALTH AND STRESS OVER THE LAST TWO YEARS

(% change in responding yes to question)

	MORE TENSE	TIRED MORE OFTEN AFTER WORK		MORE TENSE	TIRED MORE OFTEN AFTER WORK
FEMALE	3.8	15.6***	CHANGE	10.5***	0.5
AGE -30	-0.6	4.5**	EXPLOIT	8.1	2.7
TRADES	-3.6	-10.5*	SAMPLE MEAN	43.6	45.1
INDIRECT	10.2***	8.4*			
LEAN	20.7***	16.7**			

* Statistically significant at the .10 level;** at the .05 level;*** at the .01 level.

CONCLUSIONS AND IMPLICATIONS

The results of our survey of working conditions in the Canadian automobile components sector paints an unattractive picture of working life. Workers are employed in jobs which offer them little real control over working conditions and at tasks which can be learned in a very short period of time. Most workers lack any real control over how they work, how fast they work, or when they work. Workloads are high and increasing, health risks are high and increasing, work is stressful and becoming more stressful.

One of our main objectives in this article was to examine the tradeoff between working conditions and new types of work organization, in particular lean production. We wanted to test the thesis put forward by supporters of lean production that under the new system of work organization, workers will be asked to work smarter, will have more control over working conditions, and will become problem solvers. The results of our study, based on a survey of 1670 workers at 16 different companies do not support this hypothesis. Compared with workers in traditional Fordist-style plants, those at lean companies reported their workload was heavier and faster. They reported workloads were increasing and becoming even faster. They did not report it was easier to change things they did not like about their job. They did report that it was becoming more difficult to get time off and were more likely to have to find a replacement worker before they could go to the washroom. They were more likely to report that they would be unable to maintain their current work pace until age 60. The only area where we found any support for the propositions put forward by supporters of lean production was in the area of time needed to train someone to do one's job. Those at lean plants reported it would take longer to train someone to do their job.

Our survey is based on a small sample of companies, geographically constrained to one area of North America and to one sector of the automobile industry. Nonetheless this is the first mass inquiry which asks workers how they are being affected by the spread of lean production. Our survey results suggest that working in traditional Fordist plants is far from paradise. They also suggest that working in lean plants is worse. At a minimum, our results should be viewed as a wake-up call to those who have painted a positive picture of work under lean production.

ACKNOWLEDGEMENTS

This project was organized by the Canadian Auto Workers. We would like to thank the 1,670 workers who participated in this study as well as the many union representatives and managers who assisted us. We would like to thank Jim Duerr, Cara Macdonald, Dale Brown, Delia Hutchinson, Ann-Marie Quinn, Sonia Lowe and Linda Cantin for their contribution to this project. Financial support was provided by the Ontario Government through its Sector Partnership Fund.

NOTES

1. For descriptions of benchmarking and its use as a management tool see, The Economist Intelligence Unit, *Global Benchmarking for Competitive Edge*, (London, 1993); J.G. Miller, *Benchmarking Global Manufacturing: Understanding International Suppliers, Customers & Competitors* (Homewood, 1992); Karen Bemowski, 'The Benchmarking Bandwagon', *Quality Progress* (January 1991), pp.19–24; Lawrence S. Pryor, 'Benchmarking: A Self-Improvement Strategy', *Journal of Business Strategy*, (November/December, 1989), pp.28–32; 'Beg Borrow – And Benchmarking', *Business Week* (30 November 1992), pp.74–5.

2. See 'The Lean Enterprise Benchmarking Project' (Andersen Consulting, 1993); 'Worldwide Manufacturing Competitiveness Study: The Second Lean Enterprise Report' (Andersen Consulting, 1994).

3. The MIT International Motor Vehicle Project, which looked at 70 plants across the globe, has made extensive use of this technique. See James P. Womack, Daniel Jones and Daniel Roos, *The Machine That Changed the World: The Story of Lean Production* (New York, 1990). See also John Paul MacDuffie, *Human Resources Bundles and Manufacturing Performance*, ILRR, (1995). For an alternative perspective on the adoption of lean production in an automobile plant see CAW-Canada Research Group on CAMI, *The CAMI Report: Lean Production in a Unionized Auto Plant* (Willowdale, 1993). The critical components of a lean production strategy continue to be debated. Womack *et.al.* offer the following definition of why lean production is lean. 'Lean production ...is 'lean' because it uses less of everything compared with mass production – half the human effort in the factory, half the manufacturing space, half the investment in tools, half the engineering hours to develop a new product in half the time.' Womack, Jones and Roos (1990), p.13. See also Kenney and Florida, *Beyond Mass Production: The Japanese System and its Transfer to the U.S (1993)*. Critiques of lean production include, Christian Berggren, *Alternatives to Lean Production: Work Organization in the Swedish Auto Industry* (Ithaca, 1992); Ulrich Jurgens *et.al.*, *Breaking from Taylorism: Changing Forms of Work in the Automobile Industry* (Cambridge, 1993); Karel Williams *et.al.*, 'Against Lean Production', *Economy and Society*, (1992, Vol.21), pp.321–54; Karel Williams *et.al.*, *Cars: Analysis, History, Cases*, (Providence, 1994); Philip Garrahan and Paul Stewart, *The Nissan Enigma: Flexibility at Work in a Local Economy* (London, 1992); Steve Babson (ed.) *Lean Work, Empowerment and Exploitation in the Global Auto Industry (Detroit, 1995)*.

4. Womack *et.al.*, pp.13–14.

5. Womack *et.al.*, p.102. See also, Paul S. Adler and Robert E. Cole, 'Designed for Learning: A Tale of Two Auto Plants', *Sloan Management Review*, (1993, Vol.34), pp.85–94; Paul S. Adler, 'The Learning Bureaucracy: New United Motor Manufacturing Inc.' *Research in Organizational Behavior* (1992, Vol.15), pp.111–94.

6. MacDuffie uses 'hours of effort' as his measure of productivity. See MacDuffie (note 3 above 1995), p.205.

7. See, CAW-Canada Research Group on CAMI, *The CAMI Report: Lean Production in a Unionized Auto Plant* (Willowdale, 1993).

8. Robert M. Marsh, 'The Difference Between Participation and Power in Japanese Factories', *Industrial and Labor Relations Review* (1992, Vol.45), pp.250–57.

9. Joseph J. Fucini and Suzy Fucini, *Working for the Japanese: Inside Mazda's American Auto Plant* (New York, 1990); Garrahan and Stewart, (1992); Paul Stewart and Philip Garrahan, 'Employee Responses to New Management Techniques in the Auto Industry', *Work, Employment and Society*, (September 1995, Vol.9) pp.517–36.

10. The in-house operations of the major vehicle producers are not included.

11. For a recent discussion of the Japanese system of production in North America see, Tetsuo Abo (ed.), *Hybrid Factory, the Japanese Production System in the United States* (New York, 1994).

STATISTICAL APPENDIX

All responses to our survey, other than age, were converted into binary variables (0 or 1). Logit regressions were run on each dependent variable and the 11 workforce and workplace characteristics. For each group of independent variables the omitted categories were: male, age 30, direct worker, employed at a traditional plant involved in stamping metal and assembly. The estimated coefficients were converted into the percentage impact of each variable by first calculating the estimated probability that the value of the dependent variable would equal one for the base worker with the omitted workforce and workplace characteristic. This base worker represented the largest cohort in the study. We then calculated the probability that the dependent variable would equal one if the worker differed from this base worker. This was simply done by changing one of our dummy variables to 1. In the case of age we calculated the impact of adding ten years to the base age of 30. By subtracting these two numbers we obtained an estimate of the impact of a specific workforce or workplace characteristic.

Variables Employed

The workforce characteristics we examined were sex, age, and job type. Age was measured as the individual's actual age minus 30. Workers were divided into three job types: indirect workers, direct workers and skilled workers. In our regressions we also included variables for the sector of the industry in which our companies operated. We had five companies producing plastic components, six involved in metal stamping/assembly, three foundries, a glass plant and an electronics plant. We do not report these results as they are not directly relevant to the questions we are asking. The full range of variables used in the regressions are reported below

Workforce and Workplace Characteristics

FEMALE   =   1
AGE   =   actual age of individual -30
TRADES   =   1 if a worker was a skilled trades worker
INDIRECT =   1 if worker was an indirect worker
LEAN   =   1 if workplace organized on lean principles
CHANGE   =   1 if workplace in transition to lean production
EXPLOIT =   1 if workplace organized on exploitative principles
PLASTIC =   1 if workplace produces plastic components
METAL   =   1 if workplace involved in melting metal
GLASS   =   1 if workplace produces glass
ELECTRIC =   1 if workplace produces electric components

A New Model Ford?

STEVE BABSON

You can stand inside Ford's body and stamping plant in Wayne, Michigan and imagine yourself halfway around the world in Hofu, Japan: huge Komatsu transfer presses pound out body panels, just as they do in Mazda's Hofu assembly plant; automated guided vehicles retrieve panels from the same Murata high-rise stacking equipment used at Hofu, and deliver them to the same array of 265 welding robots; even the Escort bodies emerging from the parallel welding lines have a Japanese counterpart, sharing many design elements with the Mazda 323, produced in Mazda's Hiroshima plant.

'Japanese Methods Flower at Ford', according to the front-page headline in *Automotive News* heralding the new Wayne plant opened in suburban Detroit in 1990. 'From the assembly line to the executive offices, Ford's product development and manufacturing are becoming increasingly Japan-like.' Media coverage welcomed this Japanization in confident terms, though there was less certainty about the Wayne plant's corporate lineage. According to *Automotive News*, 'the Wayne setup mimics Mazda's'; according to the *Detroit Free Press*, on the other hand, 'it might as well be one of Honda's plants.' No matter: with a made-in-Japan trademark, the new plant would automatically be 'world class' in the eyes of many investors, business writers, and management consultants.[1]

To more critical eyes, this Japan-idolatry begs the question. To what degree is the Ford Escort body plant really 'Japan-like'? Are Ford workers 'just like Japanese workers', as *Automotive News* insists, simply because they eat beside plant managers in a common cafeteria, as in Japan, or because they use the same technology? In either case, what is the actual organization of teamwork at Ford Wayne, and how do workers evaluate and respond to the system? Finally, to what degree is the Wayne plant a measure of things to come, and to what degree is it unique, perhaps even anomalous?

AFTER JAPAN

Even if Japanization is less coherent and less complete than many observers would allow, there is little doubt that the success of the Japanese auto industry, particularly its stunning conquest of the North American market, has made Japan a near fetish of auto management. Adopting some variant of the Japanese model has become the litmus of managerial competence in the Big Three, and outright purchase is deemed better still: accordingly, GM has taken a 37 per cent share of Isuzu and a three per cent position in

Steve Babson, Labor Studies Center, Detroit, Michigan.

Suzuki, and since 1979 Ford has owned 25 per cent of Mazda. Joint ventures have widened access to Japanese methods and provided a training ground for American champions of Japanese practice. GM's partnerships with Toyota (building Corollas and Geo Prizms at the NUMMI plant in Fremont, California) and with Suzuki (building Sidekicks and Geo Trackers at the CAMI plant in Ingersoll, Ontario) have graduated a cadre of proselytizing managers who carry the message of lean production to plants across North America and Europe. Ford has also pursued joint ventures with Japanese partners, including Nissan (building minivans in Lorrain, Ohio) and Mazda (building Mazda compacts and Ford Probes at Auto Alliance International [AAI] in Flat Rock, Michigan, south of Detroit). Ford's 1992 investment of $380 million to buy a half share of Mazda's Flat Rock plant capped a growing collaboration between the two companies, already marked by Mazda's lead role in designing Ford's Festiva, Probe, and Escort-Tracer models.[2]

At the Escort body and stamping plant, this heavy borrowing is particularly evident in the technology and layout of the production process. The very existence of the plant is a concession to Japanese practice, since the old Wayne Assembly operation had no in-house stamping capacity; as in the Big Three generally, Wayne previously sourced its body panels and other stampings from off-site suppliers, including Ford's own centralized press shops. With Mazda taking the lead in both the product and process engineering for the new model Escort, the Wayne operation underwent a $600 million facelift in 1989 patterned after Mazda's Flat Rock and Hofu plants, both with integral stamping capacity.[3]

The result is a unique hybrid: in the refurbished Wayne Assembly plant, some 2,500 members of the United Auto Workers Local 900 still paint, assemble, and trim the Escort under work rules that retain more than 60 job classifications; next door is the new 'Integrated Stamping and Assembly' plant (ISA), connected by a 700 ft. covered bridge, where 1,200 worker 'Technicians' under a separate bargaining agreement with Local 900 stamp and weld Escort bodies using Japanese technology and team-based production methods. Like Mazda Flat Rock, where UAW production workers are also designated by a single 'Team Member' classification, Wayne ISA has only one production worker classification ('Body Stamping Technician') with a corresponding single pay rate. Skilled workers at Wayne ISA (numbering 220) retain their specific craft classification, but as at Flat Rock, they are all paid the same top rate (rather than the minutely calibrated spread that previously defined the trades hierarchy) and they are all grouped under three 'umbrellas' – tool and die, electrical, and mechanical – that permit some flexibility in assigning 'incidental' work across craft lines. As at Mazda, production workers at Wayne ISA are encouraged to suggest improvements in the system; likewise, each worker is not only responsible for a defined set of direct labour tasks, but also for inspecting the product and repairing defects 'in station' rather than passing them along to down-stream repair bays. As at Mazda, workers at Wayne ISA are formally authorized to stop the line when serious problems cannot be resolved within the prescribed cycle time; prominent 'Andon' boards also provide a continual display of such conditions, including which robots are off line (red light) and which welding lines are down (yellow lights). Supervisors at both Mazda Flat Rock and Wayne ISA can redeploy workers as conditions warrant – to fill in for absentees, to perform special projects when the line is down, or shift workloads when there is an adverse model mix. In both plants, a considerable investment in worker training preceded the implementation of these new work practices.[4]

TALE OF TWO PLANTS

Wayne ISA looks very similar to the body and stamping department at Flat Rock, and certain important practices do overlap – most evident in the technical organization of a highly automated stamping and welding process paced by a moving assembly line. Yet, the two operations are fundamentally different in key aspects of their social organization. In Ford Wayne's body plant, worker-centred teams wield routine authority over specified areas of their work environment. At Flat Rock, on the other hand, supervisor-centred work units, rather than teams, are the constituent element of the work process.

The distinction between the two is evident in the comparison of decision boundaries in Table 1. At Mazda Flat Rock, despite the nominal designation of workers as 'Team Members', there are no functioning teams with specified decision-making authority. Instead, supervisors wield routine authority at the level of the unit, encompassing from two to four teams. Meetings are only convened by unit, not by teams, and the supervisor controls the proceedings. As 'Unit Leader', the supervisor can determine whether and how workers rotate through job assignments in the unit; who gets training; who is 'able and capable' to perform overtime work; and how workloads are rebalanced. Some supervisors delegate a portion of these responsibilities to the team leaders in their unit, but this augmented role for team leaders – who are hourly workers and UAW members paid a 50-cent premium – is not formally protected by the collective bargaining agreement with UAW Local 3000. Until 1991, the team leader more often served as an adjunct of the supervisor, who played the dominant role in selecting team leaders and defining their role. Concerned that team leaders were thereby becoming 'junior foremen', UAW members ratified a new collective bargaining agreement in 1991 that incorporated recall and election of these shop-floor leaders every six months (later stretched to 12). Consequently, team leaders now have to serve the interests of team members as well as supervision, but their role has remained murky in a production system where teams have no specified function. Indeed, many team boundaries were never defined until the 1991 contract required elections and, therefore, designation of who voted in which 'team'.

At Wayne ISA, in contrast, it is the work team rather than the

TABLE 1

DECISION BOUNDARIES AT FORD ESCORT AND MAZDA: (1991–94)

	Ford Wayne	Mazda Flat Rock
Team leader election by	Team	Team (51–4)
Meetings convened by	Team	Unit
Meetings chaired by	Team leader	Unit leader
Rotation boundary by	Team (12–13)	Unit (81–2)
Rotation scheduling by	Team (12–13)	Unit leader, except jointly defined ergo jobs (25%) 112–113
Temporary reassignments (<2 days) in dept/plant	Team ('pool' job)	Unit leader (182)
Training schedule by	Team (12)	Unit and Dept. (81–3)
Overtime equalization by	Area, by elected rep (25)	Unit leader (81, 241)
Transfers to openings by	Area (16–17)	Unit (46)
Vacation scheduling by	Team (12–13)	Unit (98)
Pay-for-know evaluation by	Team (15)	(none)
Job rebalancing by	Team (22)	Unit leader & senior team leader
Team decisions:	10 of 12	1 of 12

Note: * team = hourly workers
  * Area (Ford) and Unit (Mazda) = supervision
  * numbers in parentheses = contract page (where applicable)

supervisory unit that plays the front-line role in plant operations. Workers meet by team at least once a week for a half hour before the start of shift, with elected team leaders chairing the meetings. The supervisor or the union's district committee member might make brief announcements, arrange for coordination with other teams or plant resources, or, occasionally, mediate disputes, but the supervisor is otherwise absent and the team is expected to manage its own affairs. This includes scheduling of job rotation, training, vacations, and personal leaves. Teams decide how to improve the work process in terms of safety and quality, how to rebalance workloads, and how to implement engineering changes; as stipulated in the collective bargaining agreement with Local 900, supervisors intervene only when team members cannot agree on job changes across shifts. Team members also implement the 'pay-for-knowledge' system by collectively determining the progress of their co-workers through a five-step progression (entry to the team; knowing 25 per cent of team jobs; 50 per cent of jobs; 75 per cent; and 100 per cent) that can increase hourly pay by roughly four per cent. Even when issues are decided at the next highest level of plant organization – 'Areas', which include as many as six or seven teams – the collective bargaining agreement stipulates a kind of democratic procedure entirely absent at the Flat Rock plant. At Wayne ISA, instead of supervisors 'equalizing' overtime hours by Area according to their assessment of who is able and capable of performing the work, this responsibility is assumed by an elected hourly worker in each Area who is paid the same premium as elected team leaders (50 cents an hour) for the extra duty.

Table 2 defines another contrasting feature in the work organization of these two plants. 'Body Framing' is a common element in the production process for both locations, indicating the point in the assembly process where the body sides and floorpan are 'framed' in a large welding fixture and spot welded to form the actual unibody. The technical process is very

TABLE 2

TEAM JOBS

Body Framing (1994)

Ford Escort*	Mazda
Team Leader (1) Elected for 6-month term; co-ordinates rotation, chairs weekly meeting, schedules training, trouble shoots, spot relief, liason	Team Leader (1) Elected for 12-month term; absentee replacement, spot relief, trouble shoots, liason
Process Operator (1) Minor maintenance, dress/change weld tips, pry-checks, paperwork	Equipment Service Operator (1) Minor maintenance, dress/change weld tips, pry-checks, paperwork
Weld / Load / Monitor Stations (5)	Weld / Load / Monitor Stations (5)
Dimensional Control (1) Check incoming panels, paperwork	(done in previous unit)
Platform Inspection (2) Inspect welds, minor repair, drill out holes, etc.	(done in previous unit)
Repair (1) Fix jobs tagged by platform inspectors	(Team leader, or Metal Finishing)
Relief (1) Tag relief, stock lineside inventory	(none – mass relief)
Lineside Material Handling (1) Hi-Lo, from dock to lineside	(none – separate unit)
Pool Job (1) Fills for absentees, training, or loaned to other team	(none – team leader or unit fills)
Team size: 10–15	Team size: 5–10

* includes some respot

similar in the two plants, but the social organization is substantially different. At Mazda Flat Rock, the scope of team jobs for Body Framing is relatively limited: beyond the team leader and robot operator (or 'Equipment Service Operator' as the latter is called), the jobs consist of direct labour tasks related to the loading and monitoring of the machinery. Even with full rotation there is little variety in the work, and many supervisors implement only partial rotation, or just the minimum required by the UAW-negotiated ergonomics programme. The only 'off-line' job is servicing and operating the welding robots, and management at Flat Rock has consistently limited training for this semi-skilled task and thereby precluded rotation into a favoured job. In contrast, the team boundaries at Wayne ISA are drawn in a way that incorporates more varied tasks, including inspection, repair, relief, and lineside material handling, in addition to robot operator. Moreover, the contract stipulates that every team member has the opportunity for training and rotation through the full range of team jobs, though many team members may decide to 'swap' with fellow workers or forgo the top pay increment for knowing every job. This contrasting range of team jobs at Flat Rock and Wayne ISA can be overstated by focusing on a single team in the body welding process (there are, for example, inspection jobs in other units at Flat Rock), but there is no doubt that the overall scope of job rotation is wider and more protected at Wayne ISA.

While 'teamwork' exists at Flat Rock primarily as a rhetorical device to obscure the dominant role of supervision, at Wayne ISA teams are worker-centred groups that wield genuine authority. By some accounts, such teams warrant the designation 'self-directed' or 'autonomous', though both these descriptors (especially the latter) exaggerate the degree of choice in an environment where work is still paced by the moving assembly line and jobs are defined by cycle times of between one and three minutes. The difference between the Flat Rock and Wayne factories is best conveyed, not by categorical definitions, but by a spectrum that stretches from 'supervisor-centred' to 'worker-centred', with Flat Rock closer to the first and Wayne ISA closer to the second. As indicated in Table 3, middle points between these extremes are marked by the balance of control between workers and supervisors, measured along multiple continuums of decision-making. If the social organization of a particular workplace is organized around teams that elect their team leader, hold meetings without the supervisor, and decide their own rotation schedule, then it is likely that such teams would also be on the right-hand side of additional decision continuums that could be added to the benchmark. However team structures may also be internally contradictory: at Flat Rock, for example, team leaders are elected, but teams still have no contractually protected role in plant operations.[5]

As such, the Flat Rock plant occupies an awkward position straddling the Japanese model. As a supervisor-centred system focused on continuous improvement, it incorporates select features of Japanese lean production; but concessions to American practice, including election of team leaders

TABLE 3
WHOSE TEAM?

Supervisor Centered   or   Worker Centered

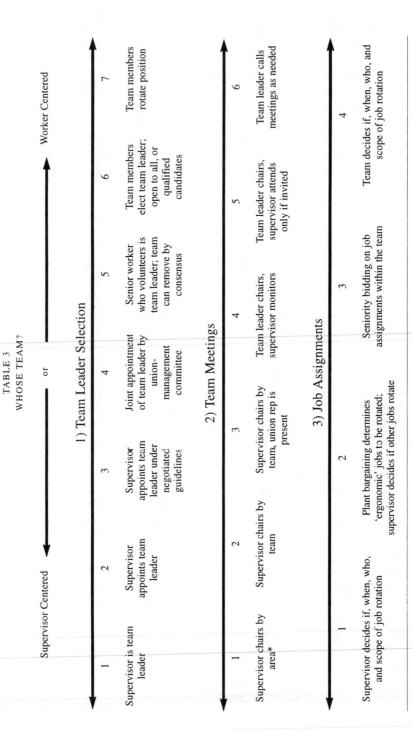

1) Team Leader Selection

1	2	3	4	5	6	7
Supervisor is team leader	Supervisor appoints team leader	Supervisor appoints team leader under negotiated guidelines	Joint appointment of team leader by union-management committee	Senior worker who volunteers is team leader; team can remove by consensus	Team members elect team leader; open to all, or qualified candidates	Team members rotate position

2) Team Meetings

1	2	3	4	5	6
Supervisor chairs by area*	Supervisor chairs by team	Supervisor chairs by team, union rep is present	Team leader chairs, supervisor monitors	Team leader chairs, supervisor attends only if invited	Team leader calls meetings as needed

3) Job Assignments

1	2	3	4
Supervisor decides if, when, who, and scope of job rotation	Plant bargaining determines 'ergonomic' jobs to be rotated; supervisor decides if other jobs rotate	Seniority bidding on job assignments within the team	Team decides if, when, who, and scope of job rotation

* 'area' indicates supervisor's unit, incorporating two or more teams

and plant-level contract bargaining with an independent union, are anomalous to the management-driven logic and conformist practice of Japanese automaking. This contradictory structure reflects the unique history of the Flat Rock plant. When Mazda announced its decision in 1984 to build a transplant in suburban Detroit, a thankful UAW, recently savaged by massive layoffs in the Big Three and grateful to any new employer willing to locate in the union's backyard, gave company managers a wide latitude in defining the plant's initial team structure and decision boundaries. The union chartered Local 3000 to represent the Flat Rock workforce, but the local did not hold its first leadership elections until 1989, two years after the plant began production. With this balloting, labour–management relations changed abruptly as a militant slate of opposition candidates, tapping widespread disappointment with the narrow range of worker participation, defeated the initial group of appointed officers. Adversarial bargaining followed for the next three years, marked by strike votes, informational picketing, in-plant demonstrations, and work-to-rule campaigns, with the single most important outcome being a new local contract that provided for election rather than the appointment of team leaders. By 1992, when Ford bought a half interest in the plant, economic recession and declining production at Flat Rock had substantially tempered worker militancy. Yet plant practices continued to mutate as Ford managers took control, and contract bargaining with the UAW began to borrow more heavily from language already codified in the UAW–Ford national agreement.

By comparison, the bargaining history at Wayne Escort was far more comprehensive, and, consequently, the results more internally consistent. Rather than late arrivals to a structure unilaterally imposed by management, Local 900's officers played a substantial role in defining the team structure at the new body and stamping operation. Before the new facility was constructed, union leaders and their management counterparts visited existing team-concept plants in North America, and Local 900 conducted a sustained round of meetings with plant workers to solicit their proposals for the new work arrangements. It became evident in these discussions that production workers were divided in their appraisal of team concept, particularly the proposed elimination of the numerous and narrowly defined job classifications in the old plant. Younger workers with little seniority felt they were stuck in dead-end jobs under the old system and looked forward to rotation; many older workers, on the other hand, favoured the existing classification system, since their seniority gave them first call to transfer into more favoured jobs – rotation therefore meant a partial return to the direct-labour jobs they wanted to escape. Local 900 addressed these concerns in the negotiations that followed. By 1988, a full year before the ISA plant began operations, the UAW and plant management had already initialed a 'conceptual agreement' that included election of team leaders and other basic features of the new system. In bargaining the more detailed contract that followed, union negotiators pushed for a system that retained certain features of the old seniority system, but with a new set of boundaries; instead of bidding for openings by job classification, seniority transfers applied to eight zones within the plant, three of them off-line areas reserved for senior workers: material handling, quality control, and 'environmental' – the latter including groundskeeping and feeding the ducks in the plant-side pond.

When this detailed contract proposal was put to a vote in 1989, its terms were well known to local members, and largely acceptable: 97 per cent of production workers and 83 per cent of skilled trades voted to ratify the tentative agreement.

WORKERS' VOICE

Given the choice, most auto workers would reject the supervisor-centred production system that Mazda installed at Flat Rock in favour of the worker-centred teams that the UAW and Ford negotiated at Wayne ISA. Of course, the choice is rarely posed in these either-or terms, but the available evidence strongly indicates that workers prefer the wider job rotation and team authority exemplified by the Wayne ISA plant.

That is certainly the sentiment expressed in surveys and interviews at Wayne ISA. 'One of the best changes I've seen in my area [is that] the team decides who's doing what job,' as one UAW member expressed it during focus-group discussions in 1995. 'The [supervisor] does not come up and tell me who's doing what job… The team decides.' There are fewer supervisors in any case, and most are cooperative – 'they leave you alone if you get the job done,' as one team leader observed. Occasionally, a new supervisor might try to 'hang around' the team meeting and dominate the proceedings, 'but everybody gets real ugly,' according to one team member, 'and throws the supervisor out.' Asked to compare their workplace with the way things were done before team concept, 70 per cent of those surveyed said they liked their current job better, 18 per cent said it was worse, and the balance reported no difference. Workers felt they still did not have enough control over what went on in the plant: on a scale from one (no control) to five (a great deal of control), survey respondents rated hourly workers as a group at 2.79, slightly lower than supervisors as a group at 3.24; asked what the balance of control *should* be, they reversed the order, with hourly workers at 4.06 and supervisors at 3.57. While Wayne's ISA's teams are not sufficiently worker-centred in the eyes of UAW members, the experiment increases their appetite for more control, rather than less. 'I have a lot more to say about what goes on, I'm more involved in everything that happens,' one worker observed 'and that makes me feel good about coming to work every day.' Overall, 73 per cent reported that they had benefited from team concept, while only seven per cent said they had been hurt by it.[6]

There is no comparable sentiment favouring the supervisor-centred groups at Mazda Flat Rock. When Local 3000 collected surveys from 2,400 members to prepare for contract negotiations in 1991, 14 per cent reported that their supervisor 'always considered their needs and interests,' while 28 per cent said this was rare and 14 per cent said it never happened. Seventy-three per cent reported that their jobs had been unilaterally changed by supervisors or engineers without their consultation, and 67 per cent of these respondents said the changes made their jobs harder. Only 16 per cent favoured the then current system of team leader selection dominated by the supervisor, while 30 per cent favoured seniority or rotation of the position and 48 per cent favoured election (which the new contract subsequently incorporated). Overall, 73 per cent agreed with the statement 'If the present intensity of work continues, I will likely be injured or worn out before I retire.'[7]

It is difficult to compare these sentiments with those expressed by Wayne ISA workers, since the surveys at the two plants were conducted at different times, with different questions, and for different purposes. A bargaining survey, particularly one conducted by newly elected and militant union leaders, as at Flat Rock, is more likely to provoke negative answers about management than a sample survey conducted, as at Wayne ISA, by outside investigators. However, the sharp contrast in tone between the relatively positive sentiments expressed by workers at Wayne ISA and the negative appraisals voiced at Flat Rock is consistent with the known bargaining history of these two plants: relatively stable and constructive at Wayne ISA, and tumultuous and confrontational at Mazda Flat Rock. It is hard to imagine that Flat Rock workers, given the choice in 1991, would not have volunteered for transfer to the Wayne body and stamping plant.

It is also likely, however, that most Big Three autoworkers would refuse to transfer to *either* Wayne or Flat Rock. This is not because autoworkers prefer the tightly scripted, fragmented, and deskilled work that has characterized American mass production since the 1920s. Survey data indicates that most blue-collar workers (auto included) want to participate in workplace decisions, with an overwhelming proportion (70–90 per cent) favouring 'some say' or 'a lot of say' over work methods, pace, and new technology, and a majority (50–60 per cent) favouring the same when it comes to job assignments. These positive assessments change dramatically, however, when abstract proposals for 'empowerment' are inserted into the real-life context of corporate downsizing, plant closures, and intensified competition in the global auto industry. In this turbulent environment, many workers conclude that radical changes in work organization will make them all the more vulnerable, particularly as new and untried systems replace customary and hard-won rights. The perception that team-based production systems are a step backward is further substantiated, in the eyes of older auto workers, by the fact that GM in the 1970s first used these new approaches in its non-union southern plants as part of a strategy for fending off the UAW. While that particular effort failed, non-union Japanese transplants are now widely regarded as the champions of a 'team concept' strategy designed to keep the UAW at bay.[8]

It is management, then, and not the union or its members, that usually initiates the movement towards new forms of work organization. And in many cases, the company's initial proposal is delivered in a way that further diminishes the appeal of 'empowerment': either workers agree to cooperate with the implementation of a team-based production system, or the company will close the plant. Under these circumstances, management's dictum – 'participate or die' – can produce compliance, but not much enthusiasm. In this sombre environment, fine distinctions between supervisor-centred and worker-centred teams are often lost.

THE BOTTOM LINE

American management has overlapping, evolving, and sometimes contradictory motivations for promoting some variant of the Japanese model of lean production.

Some corporations are drawn to lean production for reasons that have little to do, at least initially, with productivity and profits, and more to do with improving the company's image and access to capital markets. Unlike Japan and to some degree Europe, where stock ownership is closely held by keiretsus, banks, families, or governments, America's Big Three automakers have to compete in highly liquid capital markets against 'sunrise' companies that enjoy fast-growing sales and profits. In a business world where consultants, investment analysts, and the commercial media have loudly proclaimed the superiority of Japanese methods for the last two decades, adopting at least the symbolic trappings of the Toyota Production System becomes de regueur for managers who want Wall Street to look favourably on their company.

Beyond short-term appeasement of portfolio investors, lean production also promises tangible payoffs in terms of bottom-line performance. By widening each production worker's responsibilities to include inspection, minor repair, preventive maintenance, and housekeeping, factory managers can dramatically cut the number of 'non-value added' workers and supervisors who would otherwise support the production process in a traditional Fordist plant. Since these 'indirect' job classifications are often higher paid, there is a corresponding savings in payroll, particularly when staffing of production teams is kept to the bare minimum and team members have to cover for absenteeism. Since the workforce is 'cross trained' and capable of filling some or all of the jobs on the team, production workers can be flexibly deployed in response to a wide range of contingencies, including absenteeism, adverse model mix, and down time.

These advantages become especially important to management as auto buyers become more quality conscious, as competing automakers offer a wider line of models and options, and as global competition shortens the 'shelf life' of the product. Instead of prolonged production runs of a relatively simple product line – the conditions that characterized Fordist mass production until the 1970s – auto makers now put a premium on accelerated model launches and diverse model-option mixes on the same production line. In the late 1970s and early 1980s, GM and Ford tried to solicit worker participation in managing this complex process by installing off-line quality circles (also patterned after Japanese practice) that discussed production issues and made suggestions for improvement. Under terms negotiated by the UAW, GM's 'Quality of Work Life' and Ford's 'Employee Involvement' circles were voluntary and workers were paid for their participation. After an initial burst of enthusiasm, however, the programmes faded for lack of support from workers and managers: workers because, over a period of time, fewer of their suggestions were implemented, and managers because, in some cases, they resented worker meddling, and in other cases, they could see no measurable payoff that justified the expense of training and convening these groups. Increasingly, QWL and EI seemed like half-way measures – after each meeting, workers returned to the same fragmented jobs with the same top-down command structure and the same cumbersome decision process.[9]

Team concept, in contrast, promises a radical break with past practice. It is mandatory, and it requires substantial decentralization of decision making to 'empowered' supervisors and, sometimes, team members. Workers who rotate jobs learn a wider range of tasks and thereby acquire a better understanding of the interconnections between one job and the next. To the degree that this helps workers identify problems at their source, and to the degree that they have the authority to implement solutions, the result should be faster model launches, improved quality, and a widened capacity for complex model-option mixes.

Ideally, these results can serve both workers and managers. 'We expect Ford to reciprocate by keeping jobs on this shore and not sending them overseas,' as one UAW Bargaining Committee member at Wayne ISA put it. 'And what does the company get out of this? They get more productivity, they get solutions to persistent problems at a much lower level, a wider range of responsibilities for employees, better attendance, and a happier workforce.'[10]

Ford had reason to be happy as well with the initial performance of its new factory. 'The goal,' according to the plant's programme operations manager, 'is to compete with the transplants on the basis of quality, cost, productivity and [the use of] new methods.' By the industry's standard benchmarks, the plant fulfilled these goals. In 1992, the combined Wayne Assembly and Wayne ISA operation ranked eighth among 47 North American car plants rated for quality by J.D. Powers, trailing Toyota's transplants, but leading Honda, Nissan, Mitsubishi, and Mazda Flat Rock. According to the oft-cited productivity rankings published by Harbour and Associates, Wayne Assembly and ISA (including ISA's body plant but not stamping) also ranked near the top, fifth among 29 Big Three car plants in North America. Productivity comparisons with Japanese transplants were unavailable since the Japanese failed to submit the necessary data in 1992, but Harbour estimated that Toyota and Honda probably ranked ahead of Wayne, if only slightly. Such comparisons are notoriously crude, since it is virtually impossible to correct for the many differences in product complexity, design, and outsourcing that impact productivity. Even so, the available evidence indicated that the Wayne Escort operation was somewhere near the top of the heap.[11]

THE PATH(S) AHEAD

Wayne ISA represents what the AFL-CIO commends in a 'High Performance' workplace: unionized, worker-centred, high-wage, and capable of matching if not out-performing its non-union competition. Yet, despite its competitive showing, the Wayne plant may mark a detour rather than a path to the future.[12]

One such path may lie closer to Hermosillo, Mexico, where Ford builds Escorts and Mercury Tracers with much the same technology used at the Wayne Escort plant. In fact, Mazda's collaboration with Ford in developing the Escort took its initial form at Hermosillo, with Mazda not only designing the plant and managing its start-up in 1986 but also importing the engines, transmissions, and other parts from Hofu and Hiroshima. Many of the organizational features that distinguished Wayne ISA at its start-up were first implemented at Hermosillo: single production worker classification, team organization, cross training, job rotation, election of team leaders. An obvious difference, however, was wages. In 1992, when workers at Wayne ISA earned nearly $17 an hour, Ford Hermosillo paid only $2.40 an hour, and this gap widened all the more when it came to benefits and total compensation. Ford Hermosillo did not have to finance the expensive job and income security provisions that protected Wayne ISA workers, nor did it bear the same burden of pension and healthcare costs. As a result, total compensation at Hermosillo was only $4.50 an hour in 1992, dwarfed by the $40-an-hour price tag at Wayne ISA.[13]

Hermosillo's cost advantage is balanced in part by the expense of importing powertrains and parts, by the disruption of annual turnover rates that have run as high as 44 per cent, and by the labour turmoil that has periodically paralyzed production. Since 1986, there have been three major strikes at Hermosillo (focused primarily on wages), numerous wildcats, minor sabotage, and mass firings of local union militants. Yet even under these daunting conditions, the Hermosillo plant has consistently performed at high levels of productivity and quality. The same J.D. Powers quality survey that ranked Wayne ISA near the top of North American car plants in 1992 placed Hermosillo two rankings *higher*, at sixth overall and first among Ford's North American assembly plants. Productivity performance was also competitive, as indicated in Table 4. While Hermosillo lagged behind Wayne in 1992, it subsequently improved at a faster rate, nearly closing the gap by 1994.

Hermosillo's low wages must have looked all the more attractive to Ford management after the massive 1994 devaluation of the peso. The subsequent collapse of the Mexican auto market had no impact on

TABLE 4

LABOUR PRODUCTIVITY AT FORD WAYNE AND FORD HERMOSILLO

Workers per Vehicle of
Daily Straight-Time Output

	1992	1993	1994
Wayne	3.03	2.91	2.84
Hermosillo	3.50	3.10	2.99

Source: Harbour and Associates, *The Harbour Report 1995*, (Troy, Michigan: Harbour and Associates, 1995), pp.24 and 30; John McElroy, 'Ranking the Assembly Plants', *Automotive Industries*, January 1993, p.36.

Hermosillo since it exports its entire output, but the cheaper peso cut the cost of its payroll in half. The prospect of sourcing powertrains from Ford's Chihuahua engine factory, thereby eliminating shipping costs for imported components, promises further improvement in the plant's bottom line. For similar reasons, GM and Chrysler are also positioned to reap the benefits of their Mexican export strategy. As indicated in Table 5, each of the Big Three now produces their major compact and subcompact models in twin plants, one in Mexico and one in the United States. The Cuautitlan, Toluca, and Ramos Arizpe plants all trail Hermosillo in labour productivity, but the Chrysler and GM plants score respectable above-average ratings in quality. With each company also producing light trucks in Mexico, total Big Three capacity grew to nearly one million units by 1995, with Nissan and VW representing another 600,000 units, and Honda planning to add several hundred thousand more.

TABLE 5

MEXICAN–US SOURCING BY BIG THREE,
1996 COMPACT AND SUBCOMPACT MODELS

Company	Model	Mexican Plant	US Plant
Ford	Escort	Hermosillo	Wayne, Mi.
Ford	Contour/Mystique	Cuautitlan	Kansas City, Mo.
GM	Cavalier/Sunbird	Ramos Arizpe	Lordstown, Oh.
Chrylser	Neon	Toluca	Belvidere, Il.
Compact/Subcompact Capacity:		612,559	1,474,632

Source: Compiled from Arco Chemical, '1996 World wide Vehicle Production', *Automotive Industries*, October 1995, supplement.

The conditions that have made Mexico an attractive low-wage export platform could, in the foreseeable future, provoke a destabilizing social unrest that undermines investor confidence, much as the 1987 mass strikes and political upheaval in South Korea burst the bubble of that country's auto investment boom. In the meantime, however, the Mexican alternative marks a path that leads away from the 'High Performance' model exemplified by Wayne ISA. This is not because there would likely be a wholesale shift of production south of the border. Rather, the growth of a parallel production system will permit the Big Three to play one side off against the other, with Mexico serving as a laboratory for innovations that cannot be unilaterally imposed on the UAW, but which can become 'facts' that change the bargaining relationship. The Hermosillo plant is one such 'fact.' Its low wages, high productivity, and superior quality put considerable pressure on UAW members at Wayne to cut corners and 'self-manage' their own speed-up. In 1993, a new plant manager at Wayne wanted to eliminate scheduled team meetings to improve plant productivity; the union successfully resisted this proposed innovation, which would have substantially diminished the role of work teams in co-managing the plant. In Mexico, there are far fewer obstacles to such 'innovation.' Initially, Ford favoured a worker-centred team organization at its Hermosillo plant, permitting election of team leaders and a wider range of discretion in the teams' managing of personnel issues. However this began to change in 1987, following a two-month strike over wages which the union lost, and the subsequent election of a militant union leadership pledged to improve working conditions; in 1988, Ford fired the dissident leaders (45 in all) and the compliant national labour federation, the CTM, put the Hermosillo local in receivership. By the early 1990s, management had taken over the appointment of team leaders, redefined them as supervisors, and cut the training for new employees by 50 per cent.[14]

Hermosillo was therefore moving towards a supervisor-centred production system at the same time that Mazda Flat Rock moved in the opposite direction and Wayne ISA held to its worker-centred teams. These varied outcomes had little to do with the technology and layout of the production process – in this regard, the three plants were remarkably similar given their common Ford-Mazda lineage. More determining was the social terrain upon which workers and managers negotiated their respective interests: at Hermosillo, the union was defeated and management increased supervisory power; at Flat Rock, management had a free hand until the late emergence of union opposition; at Wayne, a long-established union helped shape the team structure from the start.

CONCLUSION

Contrary to most popular accounts of lean production, the Japanese model contains no constitutional imperative for worker empowerment. Instead, the system requires worker *commitment* to the systematic improvement of productivity and quality. Under Japanese lean production, worker participation is passive, largely consultative, and narrowly prescribed by supervisor-centred work groups.

In Japan, worker commitment to this tightly scripted process is reinforced by an inclusive and conformist mono-culture: company housing, company sponsored social activities, company unions (dominated by foremen), individual merit pay (determined by foremen), and lifetime jobs for the 25 per cent who work in assembly or major component plants. In the US and Canada, Japanese transplants and their native imitators attempt to reproduce this commitment with a different array of social controls: locating the plant in rural areas far from centres of minority population and UAW strength; screening the workforce for 'cooperative' attitudes; paying wages and benefits above local norms; and structuring teams to maximize peer pressure on wayward individuals.

High performance production systems characterized by worker-centred teams can sometimes match the performance of these transplants, and they are surely better places to work. They cannot survive, however, if they are solely dependent on enlightened management. There are supervisors and plant managers who prefer a worker-centred system because it can generate a different kind of commitment, one that is founded on a modest degree of self-actualization. Even if these enlightened managers were more numerous at the plant level, however, they would still answer to a system that is fundamentally autocratic in its top-down command structures, particularly when stockholders demand immediate returns. At Hermosillo, there is no seniority system, groundskeeping is contracted out, and if there are any ducks in the pond, no worker is paid to feed them.

As managers come and go, only an independent union can insure the continuity of a worker-centred system. And this is where the downward path towards Hermosillo steepens, for there is an accelerating trend towards de-unionization in American automaking, reflecting a national trend evident in virtually every sector of the economy. By 1990, 39 per cent of total auto industry employment was non-union; outside the Big Three, as independent suppliers closed older facilities and repelled UAW organizing drives at newer plants, the non-union sector grew from 41 to 76 per cent of employment. Public policy pushes in this direction, strengthening the hand of corporate leaders who invoke the spectre of global competition at every turn, while working to widen its play via NAFTA and GATT.[15]

In the new world auto industry, it is loudly broadcast, workers will not need or want a union. And feeding the ducks is a luxury no 'empowered' worker will have time for.

NOTES

1. Laura Clark, 'Japanese Methods Flower at Ford', *Automotive News*, 19 March 1990, p.1, 10; Janet Braunstein, 'Learning Team Concept', *Detroit Free Press*, 21 December 1989.
2. Greg Gardner, 'Ford Seals Flat Rock Deal, Gets Half Stake', *Detroit Free Press*, 2 July 1992; Clark, 'Japanese Methods Flower at Ford', p.10.
3. Clark, 'Japanese Methods Flower at Ford', p.10.
4. Information concerning the Wayne and Flat Rock plants is drawn from prolonged association with the unions at these two locations, UAW Local 900 at Wayne and UAW Local 3000 at Flat Rock. Planning meetings, formal interviews, surveys, plant visits (especially to Flat Rock), classroom exchanges, and documents provided by both locals are the principal sources I have relied on. Unless otherwise indicated, source references for this essay are Steve Babson, 'Lean or Mean: The MIT Model and Lean Production at Mazda', *Labor Studies Journal* Vol.18, No.2 (summer 1993) pp.3–24; Steve Babson, 'Whose Team? Lean Production at Mazda U.S.A.', in Steve Babson (ed.) *Lean Work: Empowerment and*

Exploitation in the Global Auto Industry (Detroit: Wayne State University Press, 1995), pp.235–46; Steve Babson, 'Mazda and Ford at Flat Rock: Transfer and Hybridization of the Japanese Model', paper presented at the Third International Colloquium, 'New Industrial Models', Groupe d'Etudes et de Recherches Permanent sur l'Industrie et les Salaries de l'Automobile, Paris, 15–17 June 1995; and Joseph Fucini and Suzy Fucini, *Working for the Japanese: Inside Mazda's American Auto Plant* (New York: The Free Press, 1990). For Ford Wayne, see Michelle Kaminski, 'Wayne Integrated Stamping and Assembly Plant', in Michelle Kaminski, Domenick Bertelli, Melisa Moye, and Joel Yudken, *Making Change Happen: Six Cases of Unions and Companies Transforming Their Workplaces* (Washington DC: Work and Technology Institute, 1995, in press).

5. For contrasting perspectives on 'self-directed' teams, see Richard Wellins, William Byham, and Jeanne Wilson, *Empowered Teams: Creating Self-Directed Work Groups That Improve Quality, Productivity, and Participation* (San Francisco: Jossey-Bass Publishers, 1991), a how-to manual published by a leading consulting firm in the field, Development Dimensions International; and Eileen Appelbaum and Rosemary Batt, *The New American Workplace: Transforming Work Systems in the United States* (Ithaca, NY: ILR Press, 1994), a critical and comprehensive review of workplace change that contrasts Lean Production with Team Production in ways that parallel the distinction drawn here between supervisor-centred and worker-centred teams.

6. Quotes are from Kaminski, 'Wayne Integrated Stamping and Assembly'; and interviews with Edward Smith and Darrin Green, 22 April 1993, audio tape and transcript in author's possesion. Survey data is from Kaminski, 'Wayne Integrated Stamping and Assembly.'

7. For details on the bargaining survey, see Babson, 'Lean or Mean', and Babson, 'Whose Team?'

8. For survey data on worker attitudes towards participation, see Thomas Kochan, Harry Katz, and Robert McKersie, *The Transformation of American Industrial Relations* (Ithaca, New York: ILR Press, 1994), p.212, and pp.148–62 for a review of the particular dynamics of work reorganization in the auto industry, including GM's 'southern strategy.'

9. On the marginal impact of QWL on plant performance, see Harry Katz, *Shifting Gears: Changing Labor Relations in the U.S. Automobile Industry* (Cambridge, MA: MIT Press, 1985), pp.122–31.

10. Dave Ramsey, speaking at 'Union Power in the Workplace of the Future', conference sponsored by Wayne State University, Labor Studies Center, held at UAW Local 157, Romulus, Michigan, 23 November 1991. Audio tape and transcript in author's possession.

11. Christoper Sawyer, 'Building the New Escort', *Automotive Industries*, January 1990, p.50; J.D. Power and Associates, '1992 New Car Initial Quality Study', unpublished data; John McElroy, 'Ranking the Assembly Plants', *Automotive Industries*, January 1993, p.36. On the difficulties in comparing productivity plant by plant, see Karel Williams *et al.*, 'Beyond Management: Problems of the Average Car Company', in Babson, *Lean Work*, pp.131–55.

12. For the AFL-CIO position on work restructuring, see AFL-CIO Committee on the Evolution of Work, *The New American Workplace: A Labor Perspective*, pamphlet (Washington DC: AFL-CIO, 1994).

13. For a detailed examination of Mexican lean production, including the Hermosillo plant, see Harley Shaiken, *Mexico in the Global Economy: High Technology and Work Organiztion in Export Industries* (La Jolla: Center for U.S.-Mexican Studies, University of California, San Diego, 1990); Harley Shaiken, 'Lean Production in a Mexican Context', in Babson, *Lean Work*, pp.247–59; and Jorge Carrillo, 'Flexible Production in the Auto Sector: Industrial Reorganization at Ford-Mexico', *World Development* Vol.23, No.1 (January 1995): pp.87–101.

14. Shaiken, 'Lean Production in a Mexican Context', pp.255–6; Matt Witt, 'Archbishop Condemns Ford for "Persecuting" Mexican Unionists', *Labor Notes*, October 1990, p.7.

15. Union density figures from Stephen Herzenberg, 'Towards a Cooperative Commonwealth? Labor and Restructuring in the U.S. and Canadian Auto Industries' (Ph.D. diss., MIT, 1991), p.230.

New Manufacturing Strategies and Labour in Latin America

JOHN HUMPHREY

INTRODUCTION

In the past few years, considerable interest in 'Japanese' production management and the reorganization of work has been evident in Latin America. The liberalization of the Latin American economies, involving both an opening-up of previously protected economies to imports of manufactured goods and an increased emphasis on manufacturing exports, has forced companies to recognize that many products have not been meeting the standards of price, quality, delivery, variability and innovation required for international markets, and that even where success has been achieved in export markets, this has often been achieved through cross-subsidization from domestic sales. In this context, 'quality mania', or more generally an interest in Japanese methods, is sweeping the continent. While talk is always easier than practice, there are signs that some significant shifts are taking place in parts of Latin American manufacturing.

This article considers the implications of such changes for labour. It considers whether or not the development of industrial production based on Just-in-Time and Total Quality Management (JIT/TQM) is likely to lead to an improvement in labour–management relations at plant level and also to changes in relations between companies and unions. Given the history of authoritarian management and conflictual labour relations in Latin America, will the possible spread of JIT/TQM have a liberalizing effect? Information will be taken from studies on Argentina, Brazil, Chile and Mexico. I attempt not only to provide answers to the questions posed above, but also to discuss the extent to which it is not possible to provide clear answers at the present time.

The article contains three further sections. Section Two outlines what is meant by 'Japanese methods' and why they might be expected to change relations between capital and labour. Section Three examines changing patterns of production organization and labour use in Latin America. Section Four considers how these changes are affecting capital–labour relations.

JAPANESE MANAGEMENT AND LABOUR

Three particular aspects of Japanese management are important for the consideration of changing relations between management and labour.

John Humphrey, Institute of Development Studies, University of Sussex.

- Improving the flow of products. Just-in-Time can be defined abstractly
  as production of the right quantity with the right quality at the precise
  moment it is required. The ideal factory is one where the product
  undergoes a continual process of transformation from the moment its
  component elements enter the plant until the point at which it is
  dispatched to the customer. Factories may be divided up into 'mini-
  factories' specializing in particular product lines or in particular
  components or sub-assemblies. Within these mini-factories, cellular layouts may be adopted. These arrangements may require multi-tasking and
  flexible deployment of labour (workers doing different production jobs
  and moving between them as required) and polyvalence (workers
  carrying out quality control and routine maintenance work in addition to
  production jobs), as well as increased emphasis on the reliability of both
  the quantity and quality of work performed. If cells and low stocks put
  a premium on producing at the right time, increased emphasis will be
  placed on routine maintenance, which may be carried out by the workers
  operating the machinery and equipment. This shift is usually referred to
  as Total Productive Maintenance (TPM). It may be coupled with the
  allocation of workers responsible for major and corrective maintenance
  directly to the production departments where they work.

- The definition of JIT just given already includes a reference to quality.
  JIT will not work if quality is poor. TQM is an approach to quality which
  seeks to trace quality defects back to their source and to continuously
  monitor quality in production. Part of this process involves control of
  quality by the operator. If the aim of the Japanese system is to produce
  'right first time', then the role of quality control is modified. Checks are
  still made, but increasing responsibility is put on to workers to produce
  correctly the first time and monitor the results of their own work. At the
  same time, managements put much greater emphasis on the tracing back
  of quality problems to their source and the correction of factors which
  give rise to poor quality. Increased pressure on workers to produce right
  first time is reinforced by the use of cells, internal clients and reduced
  stocks. Quality problems are noticed more quickly and more easily
  attributable to those responsible for them.[1] The responsibility given to
  the worker can take many forms: visual inspection, 100 per cent testing
  by means of fixed gauges or measurement, as well as the possible use of
  Statistical Process Control.

- Trial-and-Error. JIT/TQC involves a continual search for improvement,
  kaizen. Part of this improvement is found through practical
  experimentation on the shop floor. Engineers work closely with those on
  the shop floor, and workers and supervisors are involved in resolving
  problems and searching for ways of improving methods. Pressure to do
  this is applied systematically by the use of targets for quality and
  productivity improvement. Management retains responsibility for
  making major improvements, but the search for quality improvements,

stock reductions and more rapid throughput of parts and products is never-ending, and involves attention to detail and continuous minor improvements. In many cases, these minor improvements can only be located by the direct production workers, as only they know the work they do in sufficient detail. Their understanding is mobilized through small groups, with names such as quality circles, improvement groups, *kaizen* groups. The continual transformation of production and the activities of small groups may put a premium on team working and/or rotation of jobs. Workers who are familiar with a range of jobs can both adapt to changes in work practices and contribute better to small group activities.[2]

In some accounts of Japanese production management, emphasis is placed on the rupture between JIT/TQM and 'traditional' Fordist principles. Other accounts have questioned this contrast, arguing that 'Fordism' and 'Japanization' are idealized constructs which overemphasize both the unity of each and the contrasts between the two (Elger and Smith, 1994). In this article, the three aspects of the Japanese model outlined above are seen as tendencies which alter the way production is organized, which may be adopted to a greater or lesser extent in different plants.

The new demands placed on labour by these principles put a new emphasis on human resource development. For Japanese management to work it appears to be the case that labour has to be capable of performing a wider range of tasks, more able to take responsibility and initiatives, have a broader understanding of the production process and work together with other workers in teams. Nothing, apparently, could be in greater contrast to Taylor's account of Schmidt, the handler of pig-iron, whose only virtue was his willingness to do exactly as Taylor instructed him (Braverman, 1984: 102–6). Labour under JIT/TQM has to be trained and motivated. Labour, it is argued, is a key factor in competitiveness. Firms which can direct labour's efforts to the needs of the company, unleash its potential and obtain its involvement will be in a stronger position than those that cannot. Instead of control and discipline, the key words are now motivation, involvement, commitment and participation. A committed labour force can help to keep quality high, improve existing processes and more quickly introduce new ones, leading to better productivity, quality, flexibility and speed of innovation. The point is summarized by Mertens:

> 'The new beliefs [of management] start from the idea that it is workers who know best the problems arising in production, for which they can provide elements for improving both product and process. This requires the establishment of relations of confidence and co-operation, based on a system of values and reciprocity in terms of effort. The transformation of management culture has consequences for the content of labour relations, which will tend to be directed by concepts such as involvement, trust, values and reciprocity' (1992: 30–31).

These changes appear to imply shifts in labour relations and, possibly, union relations. According to Gitahy and Rabelo:

> 'In addition to retraining programmes, firms are also making progress towards more rigorous recruitment systems, in which schooling becomes a key variable, and in the direction of a new pattern of labour management based on more democratic and participative systems' (1991: 3).

For the analysis of Latin America this seems to imply two possibilities: either companies transform their labour–management relations as a precondition for successful JIT/TQM, or they continue in the old, authoritarian style and fail to implement JIT/TQM, with dire consequences for competitiveness. The situation in Latin America is, in fact, considerably more complex than this, as will be shown below.

ARE LATIN AMERICAN FIRMS USING JIT/TQM?

Big shifts in the economic policy have been responsible for the current wave of interest in quality and productivity in Latin America. Latin American economies have become more integrated into the world economy and more open to international standards of performance. In the four economies considered here – Argentina, Brazil, Chile and Mexico – the process of liberalization has been very different. In Argentina, a radical shift in policy by the Menem government has caused considerable dislocation of industry. In Brazil, a more gradual liberalization has taken place, while in Chile liberalization was abrupt, brutal and much earlier than elsewhere in the continent, and the interest in quality and productivity comes in the context of a revival in manufacturing industry and improved performance relative to imports in the domestic market and in export markets. In Mexico, NAFTA has delayed the full impact of liberalization on the non-border economy for some time, but in the past decade new, export-oriented industries have grown up in the North, creating a pronounced heterogeneity in industrial structure.

The ideal model of JIT/TQM associates the introduction of Japanese-style management with improved conditions for labour. Production labour should be more competent in a broader range of more demanding tasks. The polyvalent, multi-skilled, responsible and problem-solving workers have to have more skills and be motivated in a different way to the semi-skilled worker typical of Fordism. There is case study material which point to both increased training and multi-skilling, and, at least in the initial period of manufacturing, better relations between labour and management. In terms of multi-skilling, the example of Ford-Hermosillo is perhaps extreme. The plant's organization of work is summarized by Shaiken as follows:

> 'The plant employs many Japanese-style techniques – work teams, continuous improvement (*kaizen*) groups, job rotation, and a few

classifications ... At [the plant] all workers – skilled and production – fit into a single classification in which all jobs pay the same wage. Groups of 10–25 workers form teams to elect facilitators to co-ordinate production for two-month terms, after which they return to the line (the teams may no longer elect facilitators, according to reports from the plant in the summer of 1993). The actual tasks workers perform are similar to those in a conventional plant, but workers are expected to learn all the jobs on a team and normally rotate through them' (Shaiken, 1994: 59)

Ford-Hermosillo, for example, has been much studied, along with other auto plants in the North of Mexico (Carrillo, 1990; Shaiken, 1990), but other cases can be found in Latin America. Fleury and Humphrey (1993) describe a number of cases of firms which have developed broad-ranging restructuring along JIT/TQM lines, partly in response to liberalization and the threat of import competition.

One of the firms studied by Fleury and Humphrey was a Brazilian-owned manufacturer of components for cars and trucks. The plant had been restructured into cells, and in many cases this involved teams of 3–4 workers operating a set of 6–8 machines arranged in a U-shape. The workers in each cell were responsible for production, quality control, machine setting and adjustment and routine maintenance. In order to reflect these developments the company had introduced a new occupational structure, as shown in Figure One.[3] There are now six occupations for production workers. Access to each depends on a mixture of training on-the-job and formal training in the company's training centre. While the initial two days of training is largely motivational and introduces new workers to concepts such as Quality Control Circles, kanban and total quality, the content becomes increasingly technical. An operator/setter, for example, has to be able to prepare all the machines in the cell and be capable of carrying out routine maintenance on them. This involves courses in basic hydraulics and pneumatics, as well as extensive on-the-job training. The firm had originally expressed the ambitious aim of having all its workers on Grade Six by 1996. The level of pay for this grade is equivalent to that of an experienced toolmaker. In practice, by mid-1995 one third of the labour force had reached Grade Four, and just 6.5 per cent had reached Grade Five. However, it is clear that the logic of cellular manufacturing had lead this firm towards the aim of having all workers able to perform a range of complex functions in one or more cells. A new occupational structure was then created to provide the structure and incentives needed to make polyvalence work.

In order to provide the training required in-house, the company expanded its Educational Centre built in 1983. This is now housed in a purpose-built building in the middle of the plant site. It has a number of tutors, and it also has recourse to the Industrial Training Agency, the Serviço Nacional de Aprendizagem Industrial, SENAI, where more advanced

FIGURE 1

WORKER DEVELOPMENT PLAN, FIRM TWO

Grade One: Operator
Integration
Training for QC
Kanban and Cells   Two days
Safety
Total Quality Philosophy
Cleanliness and Tidiness
On the Job Training   6 months

Grade Two: Semi-Skilled Operator
Product Knowledge   8 hours
Measurement   20 hours
On the Job Training   6 months

Grade Three: Skilled Worker
Reading and Interpretation of Designs   40 hours
Basic Statistics   8 hours
Total Quality   8 hours
On the Job Training   12 months

Grade Four (3 options):

Operator Setter		**Quality Assurance Worker**		**Zero Defect Worker**	
Machine		Statistical Proces		Minor Machine	
Preparation	8 hours	Control	8 hours	Maintenance	8 hours
Lubrification	8 hours	Graphs and Charts	12 hours	Care of Tools	6 hours
Care of Tools	6 hours	Quality Systems	4 hours	Lubrification	8 hours
Basic Pneumatics	40 hours			Tool and equipment	
				maintenance	8 hours
				Basic Hydraulics	40 hours
				Basic Electrics	40 hours
				Basic Hydraulics	40 hours
				Basic Pneumatics	40 hours
On the Job		On the Job		On the Job	
Training	12 months	Training	12 months	Training	12 months

Grade Five:
Any two of the Grade Four skills.

Grade Six:
All three of the Grade Four skills

Source: Company documents and interviews.

courses are provided for skilled workers, but much of the training is carried out by the plant's own staff. An instructor is attached to each manager, and workers are trained to teach other workers. The aim of the plant was to have more than 100 hours off-the-job training per employee in 1993. This compares with levels found in Japanese auto plants (Office of Technology Assessment, 1992: 15).[4] This kind of commitment to improving educational standards and training is probably a key indicator of a radical shift in work organization along the lines discussed in the previous section.

Such changes by themselves may imply important shifts in labour–management relations. A commitment to training in the case of Brazil, for example, makes hire-and-fire policies uneconomic. Expecting workers to take initiative and responsibility must curtail some of the more authoritarian labour practices found in factories. At a basic level, the introduction of new manufacturing strategies can provide real improvements for labour in situations where labour–management relations have been authoritarian and labour has been too weakly organized at plant level to resist oppression. Leite quotes a woman worker at a Brazilian plant:

> 'The [supervisors] are, I would say, more human now. They talk to you. They say "Look, why did this happen. Let's try and improve it a little. Let's make sure it doesn't happen again." So now they talk to us normally, just like I'm talking to you. Before you were shouted at enough to make you cry, right in front of you.' (Leite, 1993: 16–17).

Other informants cited by Leite describe how their opinions count for more and they are encouraged to make suggestions rather than ordered to keep quiet and do as they are told. Such a basic change does clearly indicate how bad conditions were in the plant – although quite typical for Brazilian industry – and how important it is for workers that such basic shifts in attitude take place. This does not mean, of course, that firms using new production methods no longer exercise control, but they do so in a more careful and orderly manner, and they lay more emphasize on 'self control' (*auto controle*), by motivating the individual and mobilizing peer group pressure, as will be shown below.

For every case of broad adoption of JIT/TQM principles, however, there are many cases of failures to adopt JIT/TQM, or more importantly, the use of specific and limited JIT/TQM techniques in response to the crisis caused by liberalization (Roldán, 1993). This is the limitation of the case study approach. Case studies provide little idea of the extent of JIT/TQM use. They show that it is impossible for some firms in Latin America to restructure internally, and that even changes in supplier relations are possible. But the results of case studies are so varied they do not allow an overall picture to emerge. Worse still, firms themselves change so rapidly that what was true at one point in time no longer holds a year or so later. Some of the most characteristic features of Ford-Hermosillo described by Shaiken (1990), such as rotation of workers between production and maintenance tasks and the election of team leaders did not last into the 1990s.

In this situation, more general assessments of the spread of JIT/TQM in Latin America are of great use, whatever their shortcomings. A study of 185 firms in the metalworking industries of four countries by the Programa Regional del Empleo para America Latina y el Caribe, PREALC, provides important information, and some of the results are presented in Table 1. The survey considered the use of techniques which change the work performed by labour – SPC, teamworking, and the integration of inspection and maintenance tasks with production work. It shows, firstly, that there are considerable variations in the use of JIT/TQM techniques within countries, between countries and between techniques. Brazilian firms claim the greatest use of such techniques, followed by Mexico. Overall, in all of the countries, a minority of firms were using most of the techniques, even though one would expect larger firms in the metalworking industries to be among the first users of JIT/TQM. The transfer of inspection tasks to production workers was most common among the firms studied, but the use of other techniques varied considerably from country to country. As might be expected, in all four countries, firms are expected to do more in the future than in the past, although expectations in Argentina lag considerably behind those of other countries.

TABLE 1

INDICATORS OF REORGANIZATION, METALWORKING INDUSTRY, FOUR
COUNTRIES (% OF FIRMS RESPONDING 'YES')

	Argentina	Brazil	Chile	Mexico
Programmes Adopted 1990–92:				
Maintenance tasks transferred	10	42	13	16
Inspection/quality tasks transferred	29	53	50	48
SPC	0	43	0	36
Work teams	19	26	30	38
Programmes Planned 1993–95:				
Maintenance tasks transferred	12	43	27	36
Inspection/quality tasks transferred	48	72	57	68
SPC	6	55	20	54
Work teams	23	57	40	44
Workers' aptitudes:				
Difficulties in assuming responsibilities	70	94	83	83
Difficulties in taking initiatives	63	84	79	67
Basic Education Issues:				
Workers unable to concentrate	66	65	64	63
Lack of capacity for abstraction	54	49	41	54
Cannot learn new skills and abilities	42	69	64	56
Difficulties in reading and writing	33	65	39	51
Limited verbal skills	30	54	45	44
Skill:				
Poor middle management	58	77	70	78
Workers cannot operate new equipment	42	60	53	57
Scarcity of skilled production labour	78	67	79	76
Scarcity of technical and professional staff	33	75	68	69
No. of companies surveyed	52	53	30	50

Source: Abramo (1993)

This use of programmes altering the nature of production work which are commonly associated with JIT/TQM is, however, combined with considerable doubts about workers' aptitudes, basic educational standards and skills. Most firms complain that workers have difficulties in taking responsibility and initiative. The kinds of abilities which a basic education might be expected to provide, such as the ability to concentrate, a capacity for abstraction, capacity to learn new skills, the ability to read and write and verbal skills, are all deficient. In addition, firms face problems with labour supply at all levels.

It is clear that use of JIT/TQM techniques is not necessarily blocked by these labour supply problems. Brazil, which has the worst indicators for basic education, also has the highest use of programmes which extend the activities of production workers. What does this imply for the spread of JIT/TQM?

Firstly, problems with educational standards are not a barrier to the use of JIT/TQM, but firms may have to invest heavily in education and training to improve labour's skills and capacities. This is evident in Brazil. Firms developing JIT/TQM have often developed adult education programmes for their labour forces, literacy and numeracy programmes, and intensive training programmes, not only in technical skills but also in such basic skills as communication and group discussion.[5] This means that smaller firms which may lack the infrastructure and resources to invest in education programmes, and which may not be able to pay higher-than-average wages to secure the better-educated labour, will be at a severe disadvantage.

Secondly, there is a clear risk that firms will adopt their work organization to the characteristics of their labour forces. Instead of making heavy investments to make JIT/TQM possible, they will instead opt for production practices which need less input from labour. Firms become locked into cycles of labour capacities and work organization which reinforce each other. Poorly-trained and educated labour is confined to tasks which do not develop capacities. Carvalho (1994) has expressed concerns about work organization and education in the Brazilian petrochemical industry.

This does not mean that firms will not adopt JIT/TQM at all. It will affect the nature of this adoption. As was argued in the previous section, firms operating processes such as assembly of simple parts can develop low-stock, high flow, high quality production without using systematic job rotation, team-working or multi-skilling. Beyond this, however, it is possible that firms using more complex operations will use variants of them which do not require increased skills and responsibilities compared to more traditional work organization. Leite (1993) provides an example of this. She describes how management at a large North American transnational in Brazil adopted a production system developed by Goldtratt, which required less of a revolution in factory organization and culture than kanban and less inputs from workers (1993: 4–8).

This problem has been put in a different and more general form by

Kaplinsky (1995), who distinguishes between techniques and system:

> 'The various elements of production organization introduced by the
> Japanese in recent decades can be seen in either the limited context of a
> specific production technique – potentially applicable across a range of
> production systems – or as an integral component of the new production
> system itself. For example, specific techniques have been developed to
> reduce inventories (Just-in-Time, JIT) and to ensure better quality
> procedures (Total Quality Control, TQC). These can be implemented as
> stand-alone changes in procedure, often within the context of large-
> batch production of standardized products; alternatively, their
> introduction can be co-ordinated and be linked to the use of a battery of
> additional techniques to enable the flexible production of diversified,
> high quality products. To operate effectively and to approach the levels
> of achievement attained by many Japanese firms (and some Western
> imitators), there is little doubt that these JMTs must be adopted as part
> of a wider, co-ordinated package of measures. Nevertheless, even when
> introduced in a fragmented manner, the competitive returns can often be
> high' (Kaplinsky, 1995: 58).

Firms which do not develop education and training policies to overcome the
problems outlined in Table 1 will not go on to develop other areas such as
kaizen activities or multi-skilling. They may obtain significant improvements
in performance in the short term, but they will not develop continuous
improvement. One of the limitations of studies like that of PREALC is
precisely that it cannot distinguish easily between systemic and non-
systemic uses of JIT/TQM.

Low levels of schooling and training are one important factor which
limits the spread of JIT/TQM, operating as an obstacle which can only be
surmounted by the larger and better-organized firms. However, four other
factors may also inhibit the spread of the kinds of labour practices which
might transform labour–management relations, and they will be mentioned
briefly:

* Firms may simply not have the managerial competence needed to
  develop JIT/TQM. They introduce specific techniques such as cellular
  production or kanban in limited parts of their plants because they do not
  have the technical or organizational capabilities for wholesale change.
  Roldán (1993) analyses cases of limited adoption in the Argentine case.

* In sectors with limited competition, established manufacturing strategies
  will continue to be viable. While it is now clear that the principles of
  JIT/TQM are widely applicable in manufacturing industry, and in other
  sectors (banks, telecommunications), the pressure to adopt new
  manufacturing strategies is very uneven.

* In plants using simple production processes, the principles of production
  flow and quality-at-source may be achieved without resort to methods

such as team-working or multi-skilling. In North America, organization by team-working or job rotation are found much more extensively in Japanese transplants in the auto industry than in the electrical industry (Kenney and Florida, 1992b). A similar pattern can be seen in the case of Northern Mexico. While quite extensive use of JIT/TQM is apparent in the motor industry (Ramirez, 1993), the same is not true for the electrical industry, particularly in the maquiladora plants. Kenney and Florida find little evidence of 'Japanese' practices in Japanese maquiladoras, and they attribute this to the fact that working practices are very standard, educational levels are low and turnover is high (Kenney and Florida, 1992a: 21–22). Shaiken and Browne's study of 13 Japanese plants also finds limited use of 'Japanese' techniques, such as team-working, quality circles, multi-tasking, low stock production and *kaizen* (Shaiken and Browne, 1991). The plants are competitive, providing good quality and productivity and gaining market access (1991: 48), so the organization of work does not appear to be a problem. Attention to design and the detail of manufacturing processes, combined with intensive use of traditional quality control and some linked *kaizen* practices may be a recipe for success.

• A very different problem is apparent in Mexican auto plants. Managements may wish to introduce JIT/TQM along the lines of Hermosillo in their plants in central Mexico, but labour conflicts prevent them from doing so. Carrillo's (1995) study of the contrast between Ford's Hermosillo and Cuautitlán plants shows clearly how management was unable to make rapid changes in the latter plant, situated in Central Mexico. Similarly, the work of Abo and his team on hybridization shows a large difference in the use of Japanese work organization in Nissan's plants in Northern and in Central Mexico.[6] The implications of this point will be considered below.

For many reasons, JIT/TQM use is likely to be very patchy in Latin America. But it is still legitimate to ask what might be the impact of JIT/TQM on labour in the plants which do adopt it. The question has been put clearly by Leite:

> 'Are Brazilian industrialists really opting for systemic modernization based on job enrichment and more democratic labour relations? Up to what point will the position taken by the managements found in the studies by Gitahy and Rabelo and Fleury and Humphrey be extended to at least a significant part of Brazilian industry (if not the whole of it), or will it be restricted to a small number of technologically advanced firms? Is the current stage of research sufficient to allow us to talk of a new tendency among firms in relation to the management of labour? And, finally, if we assume that firms are in fact more inclined to adopt systemic modernization ... it is necessary to ask to what extent these transformations are leading to more substantial changes in labour

relations, particularly in terms of the adoption of a more democratic and participatory model of industrial relations' (Leite 1992: 21).

The remainder of this contribution will attempt to answer this last question.

NEW MANUFACTURING STRATEGIES AND LABOUR RELATIONS

Better treatment for workers at plant level, and the emergence of less authoritarian labour relations has led to some expectation in Latin America that a new 'modern' and less authoritarian era in relations between companies and unions might also emerge. So far there is little sign of this. On the contrary, three tendencies, none of them favourable to the union, can be perceived: the continued marginalization of weak unions, an attack on the rights of established unions, and the creation of a new, weakened unionism in new regions of production. None of this is unfamiliar to those with a knowledge of unionism in Japan. Toyota, for example, smashed a combative union in the early 1950s and replaced it with a subordinate, company union. Japanese transplants abroad, too, have become less and less willing to recognize unions. Costa and Garanto (1993: 107) show that in Europe, the rate of recognition of unions in Japanese plants established in the early 1970s was about 80 per cent. For plants established in the late 1980s, this rate had fallen to under 40 per cent. When unions are recognized, they are subject to restrictive conditions. Oliver and Wilkinson refer to no-strike deals, binding arbitration and agreements on flexibility (1992: 288–96).

The first situation mentioned above was continued marginalization. Briefly, unions in Brazil and Mexico have continued to find it difficult to develop constructive relations with managements, even when they show themselves willing to cooperate and to accept, even support, new manufacturing practices. Managements still fear the unions and do not want to risk involvement. Firms see the new manufacturing practices as a means of marginalizing the union threat further. Better working conditions and better and more direct relations between management and labour on the shop floor is seen as a means of making the union redundant. Clearly, however, the marginalization of the union is a key element in labour control. In Brazil, the development of profit-sharing schemes to motivate and reward workers is markedly different in plants with strong and weak unions. In plants with weak unions, bonuses are tied to individual or sectional performance, according to highly specific performance criteria and personal appraisal. The bonus scheme is part of a sophisticated and personalized system of control. In the strongly-unionized periphery of São Paulo, the unions have negotiated plant-wide schemes linked to general performance indicators (production, quality and absenteeism), and also successfully fought for a lump-sum bonus, which is more valuable to low-paid workers.

Where unions have been strong, firms developing new manufacturing strategies have often tended to seek to undermine union power, and for obvious reasons. Union power has often been constructed around negotiated 'rigidities' which protect workers from arbitrary managerial power and give workers a firm basis from which to negotiate. Managements wish to sweep these rigidities away. Strong unionism in Latin America has, in addition, been constructed behind protective trade barriers, and as these are dismantled, companies wish to make wholesale changes in production.

At the national level, formerly strong labour systems have been under attack. In both Argentina and Mexico, legislation has undermined previously held union rights (Catalano and Novick, 1992; Garza, 1993). At plant level, there have been many well-publicized attempts to smash union power. In Argentina, management at the Acinder steel plant:

> 'declared a lock-out, decided to dismiss all the personnel and re-hire them, obliging each worker to accept the new work methods. At the same time, the firm de-recognized the local union leadership as its interlocutor ... and attempted to begin negotiations with the national leadership of the UOM, which refused the invitation. As the workers at the plant united behind the union, the firm began mass recruitment of new workers among the unemployed in southern Rosario' (Novick and Palomino, 1993: 324).

In this case, organized resistance from workers and the union forced the company to retreat. In the case of the Ford plant at Cuautitlán in Central Mexico, management succeeded in sacking the plant's workers en masse during a strike in 1987 and then selectively re-hiring them under quite a different labour contract. In this case, the company had some support from the national union (Carrillo, 1995). There have been other cases of open conflict between management and organized labour at plants in Central Mexico, as firms seek to redefine work methods and labour–management relations.[7]

Forcing through radical changes in working practices might be expected to engender conflict between management and labour and opposition from unions. However, it is also clear that in new plants, managements have tried to either marginalize or subordinate unions. Once again, this is seen most clearly in the North of Mexico, where in the maquiladoras, unions are hardly recognized at all, and in the new non-maquila auto plants, the unions are in a greatly weakened position compared to Central Mexico (in the past at least). Garza (1993: 156–7) lists a number of areas in which contracts at Ford Hermosillo, GM Ramos Arizpe and the electrical maquilas give great freedom to the companies, including defining work methods, hiring of temporary workers, recruitment, overtime and internal mobility of labour. In the past, the union would have had a say in these issues. Similarly, Carrillo (1995) outlines the efforts Ford has made to establish new contracts in its Northern plants, separate them from the Central plants and define a wide degree of discretion for management. According to Carrillo (1995: 92–3):

> 'The Hermosillo agreement was a development of one first tried out by Ford at its Chihuahua engine plant, and it allowed the company a

wide degree of freedom in plant organization. The firm carefully restricted the union's role at Hermosillo, so that the free operation of the principles of responsible autonomy might be achieved. The union was left with practically no powers to interfere in production because work teams had wide powers to resolve day-to-day conflicts and interpret plant regulations. The result was that the local union representatives at Hermosillo never enjoyed the autonomy and influence which had once been enjoyed by representatives in Central Mexico, because of a structural lack of power to negotiate changes in the workplace. The company retained exclusive decision-making powers over such issues as the level of employment in the plant, recruitment and the content of training.'

Carrillo links the company's attitude to the union and the form of contract it negotiated with the CTM to the flexibility in work organization desired by the company. This flexibility concerns not only the right to reorganize work and encourage team-working, which unions might find acceptable. The application of JIT/TQM and *kaizen* also contains a spirit of continuing pressure and ceaseless demands for improvements in performance which are much less acceptable to unions. Work in JIT/TQM plants may be more interesting and varied, and workers may find that it is more meaningful, but it also more stressful. Berggren sums up the experience of Japanese auto transplants in the United States as follows:

> 'High quality products produced by a high quality workforce under a dedicated management offering job security and equal treatment, while at the same time demanding virtually unlimited performance, excessive working hours and the subjection to harsh conduct and discipline codes – the work experience of the transplants really seems to be a contradictory one' (1993: 31).

Work is more meaningful and more stressful. On balance, workers may prefer it like this, and there is little to suggest that given the choice workers would wish to return to the Fordist management style. However, the balance of meaning and stress is one which can be negotiated. Managements will push for more until they meet with sufficient resistance for them to stop. This resistance may be collective (stoppages, strikes, negotiations) or individual (poor quality, turnover). Not having a union helps management to impose a tough bargain.

Some of the apparently more attractive aspects of JIT/TQM can be used to this end. Team-working is a good example. Shaiken's description of work organization at Ford Hermosillo highlights this point:

> 'The [plant's] teams are structured both to capture the loyalty and good spirits of people who work together and to generate peer pressure to improve production when necessary. The work group makes many decisions normally taken by managers in a traditional plant, such as when to rotate jobs or who to send to training classes.

In addition, the teams mete out discipline for absenteeism. If a member is absent, a facilitator may have to work on the line or other members may have to be pulled out of training classes, hence considerable peer pressure can exist for people not to miss work' (Shaiken, 1994: 60).

The control over individuals is exercised by the team, which in turn, is subject to performance targets. Küsel (1990) describes a similar pattern of team pressure in the General Motors plant in Ramos Arizpe in Northern Mexico.

Similar patterns can be observed elsewhere. In Brazil a firm had built a sophisticated plant on a greenfield site, well away from the strong union with which it had been in conflict at the company's main site. The plant was technically advanced, and work was organized around teams. The plant offered job rotation and also promotion based on the systematic acquisition of skills and experiences. In principle all workers could be promoted from the bottom rungs of the ladder to the highest positions in the factory. As part of the process, the firm had introduced annual assessments of performance based on three items: the training courses workers had taken, the development of their operational skills and their attitude and behaviour (such as contributions to the suggestions scheme, effort, absenteeism and team spirit). A very good score meant promotion, but a poor score led to dismissal. At the same time, the firm was considering devolving responsibility to teams for accepting new team members and dismissing team members whose performance was not satisfactory. If management were to go ahead with the scheme, team members would be free to expel a worker from team, with the consequence that this would mean the worker would be dismissed from the firm. This was in a context where the team itself was set clear targets for quality and productivity, and in which the team suffered sanctions being applied for failing to meet them. Management talked of intervention in a team which failed to meet its targets. 'Intervention' was also used in Brazil to denote the suspension of an elected trade union leadership by the Ministry of Labour and its replacement by Ministry appointees. The pressure placed on team members by their peers could be intense. Individualized appraisal and rewards, combined with group responsibility and pressure, can be a powerful means of control.

The success of JIT/TQM depends in part on combining new and more efficient working practices with increasing intensity. For inefficient companies, using new manufacturing strategies can lead to great improvements in efficiency without increasing intensity of work. For many Latin American companies, *any* attention to manufacturing will produce big dividends because they have been such inefficient producers in the past. However, in order to reach international standards of competitiveness, intensity of work is also required. Work is both smarter and harder.

For this reason, firms may make great efforts to deal with worker grievances as a means of nipping discontent in the bud and preventing unions from organizing in plants. This strategy is very clear in Brazil. As Leite (1993) has observed, managements seek to anticipate the union as a means of marginalizing it. In Brazil, managements fear the unions because they cannot be excluded completely from the scene. The Brazilian labour system still guarantees unions formal rights of representation and gives unions a role in collective bargaining. Managements associate union activity with militancy and opposition to change. Therefore, they try to pre-empt union demands by offering wages and conditions which are attractive to workers. In fact, one of the motivations for management adoption of Quality Circles, Improvement Groups, better and more open relations between management and labour ('open-door' access to senior management, 'morning coffee with the boss', registers of workers' state of spirit, collective gymnastics) is precisely to catch worker discontent before the unions can mobilize around it.

This is why one sees what are apparently open and co-operative relations between management and labour within plants and a strongly hostile attitude to the union. Most of all management want to relate to workers as individuals, or as teams which are oriented towards the management problematic, not as a collectivity with the right to express different interests. This combination of, on the one hand, valuing workers through practices such as openness to individual grievances, recognition of the contributions workers can make to efficiency and investment in training, and on the other, intensified control, individualized appraisal and reward and hostility to collective organization is new in Latin America. There is the risk that the initial attractions of JIT/TQM will allow firms to marginalize collective organization and develop strong control systems, leaving workers defenceless in the face of demands for increasing intensity of work. In this context, the need for a countervailing power and organization is more necessary than ever, and unions will continue to have an important role in protecting workers from the worst excesses of management power.

NOTES

1. It should be noted that, while the focus here is on direct production workers, all of the innovations described here will only work well if considerable attention is paid to such factors as design for manufacturability, simplification of layouts and increasing the reliability of production processes. In fact, changing labour–management relations is only part of the process of introducing JIT/TQM. Firms should also change management structures, improve engineering capabilities improve design, etc. and these non–labour issues are just as important for overall performance.
2. The importance of small group activities does not in any way diminish the role and efforts of managements in seeking improvement. Most commentators agree that workers are involved in making minor changes, which frees management to plan major innovations.
3. Toolroom and maintenance workers are not included in this scheme.
4. Because training is so important for promotion in Firm Two, access to it must be transparent. The courses already taken by workers and plans for the coming year were on public display in each cell's meeting area.
5. See Fleury and Humphrey (1993), Gitahy and Rabelo (1991) and Posthuma (1991).
6. Information from a presentation at the 2nd Gerpisa meeting in Paris, June 1994. More generally, see Abo (1994).

7. See, for example, Pries (1992) for the case of VW at Puebla. One exception to this tendency might appear to be the agreement between unions and firms in the auto industry (Cardoso and Comin, 1993). But in this case the agreement focuses mainly on output, prices and employment, and not on the internal regulation of the plants.

REFERENCES

Abo, Tetsuo, 1994. *The Hybrid Factory*. New York, Oxford University Press.

Abramo, Lais, 1993. Las transformaciones en el mundo del trabajo, escolaridad y calificación en un contexto de cambio tecnólogico', Paper presented to 5th Workshop on Planning Policy and Education Management, Santiago, October.

Braverman, Harry, 1975. *Labour and Monopoly Capital*. New York, Monthly Review.

Berggren, Christian, 1993, 'Lean Production – The End of History?' in *Des Realités du Toyotisme*, Actes du Gerpisa, No.6.

Cardoso, A., and A. Comin, 1993. 'Câmaras setoriais, modernização productiva e democratização das relações de trabalho no brasil', paper presented to 1st Latin American Congress on the Sociology of Work, Mexico City, November.

Carrillo, Jorge (ed.), 1990. *La Nueva Era de la Industria Automotriz en México*. Tijuana, COLEF.

Carrillo, Jorge, 1995. 'Flexible production in the auto sector: industrial reorganization at Ford-Mexico', *World Development*, Vol.23, No.1.

Carvalho, Ruy de Quadros, 1994. 'Capacitacão tecnológico limitada e uso do trabalho na indústria brasileira', *São Paulo em Perspectiva* Vol.8, No.1.

Catalano, Ana, and Marta Novick, 1992. 'Relaciones laborales y sociología del trabajo: a la búsqueda de una confluencia', *Sociedad* 1(1) (Buenos Aires).

Costa, Isabel da, and Annie Garanto, 1993. 'Entreprises japonaises et syndicalisme en Europe', *Le Mouvement Social*, No.162.

Elger, Tony, and Chris Smith, 1994. 'Introduction', in T. Elger and C. Smith (eds), *Global Japanisation?* London, Routledge.

Fleury, Afonso, and John Humphrey, 1993. 'Human resources and the diffusion and adaptation of new quality methods in Brazilian manufacturing', Research Report 24. Brighton, Institute of Development Studies.

Garza, Enrique de la, 1993. *Reestructuración productiva y respuesta sindical en México*. Mexico City, UNAM/UAM.

Gitahy, Leda, and Flávio Rabelo, 1991. 'Educação e Desenvolvimento Tecnológico: o caso da indústria de autopeças'. DPCT/IG/UNICAMP, Textos para Discussão, No.11.

Kaplinsky, R., 1995. 'Technique and system: the spread of Japanese management techniques to developing countries', *World Development* Vol.23, No.1.

Kenney, Martin and Richard Florida, 1992a. 'Japanese Maquiladoras', University of California Davis, Program in East Asian Business and Development, Working Paper, No.44.

Kenney, Martin and Richard Florida, 1992b. 'Japanese styles of management in three U.S. transplant industries: autos, steel and electronics'. Paper presented at workshop on Japanese Management Styles: an international comparative perspective, Cardiff, Business School, September.

Küsel, C., 1990, "La Calidade Tiene Prioridad Número 1.' Restruturación del proceso de trabajo e introducción de conceptos japoneses de organización en la industria automotriz mexicana', in J. Carrillo (ed.) *La Nueva Era de la Industria Automotriz em México*, Tijuana, El Colégio de la Frontera Norte.

Leite, Márcia, 1992. 'Modernização Tecnológica e Relaçõ es de Trabalho no Brasil: notas para uma discussão'. Paper presented to Seminar 'Work and Education', São Paulo, Fundação Carlos Chagas.

Leite, Márcia, 1993. 'Cambio tecnológico y mercado de trabalho.' Projeto Regional PREALC/OIT/ACDI, Relatório Final.

Mertens, Leonard, 1992. 'El desafio de las relaciones laborales en la nueva competividad,' *Critica & Comunicación*, Vol.8 (Lima).

Novick, Marta, and Héctor Palomino, 1993. 'Estrategias empresariales frente a la reestructuración económica y respuesta sindical: un caso Argentino', *Economia & Trabajo*, Vol.1, No.2.

OTA, 1992. 'Worker training: competing in the new international economy'. Washington DC, Congress of the United States, Office of Technology Assessment.

Oliver, N., and B. Wilkinson, 1992, *The Japanisation of British Industry*, 2nd edition, Oxford: Blackwell.

Posthuma, Anne, 1991. 'Changing production practices and competitive strategies in the Brazilian auto components industry'. Unpublished D.Phil dissertation, University of Sussex.

Pries, Ludger, 1992. 'Contexto estructural y dinámica de acción del conflicto en la Volkswagen de México en 1992', Mimeo, El Colégio de Puebla

Ramirez, José Carlos, 1993. 'Recent transformations in the Mexican motor industry, *IDS Bulletin*, Vol.24, No.2.

Roldán, Martha, 1993. 'Industrial restructuring, deregulation and new JIT labour processes in Argentina: towards a gender-aware perspective', *IDS Bulletin*, Vol.24, No.2.

Shaiken, Harley, 1990. *Mexico in the Global Economy: high technology and work organization in export industries*. University of California, San Diego, Centre for U.S.–Mexican Studies, Monograph Series 33.

Shaiken, Harley, 1994. 'Advanced manufacturing in Mexico: a new international division of labour?', *Latin American Research Review*, Vol.29, No.2.

Shaiken, Harley, and Harry Browne, 1991. 'Japanese work organization in Mexico', in G. Székely (ed.), *Manufacturing Across Oceans and Borders*, University of California San Diego, Center for U.S.–Mexican Studies, Monograph Series No.36.

Volvo – A Force for Fordist Retrenchment or Innovation in the Automobile Industry?

KAJSA ELLEGÅRD

A 'VOLVO MODEL'?

The Volvo car has a good reputation for its safety, reliability and quality. The Volvo Car Company is known as a solid but relatively small producer of rather exclusive cars, and famous for its efforts to humanize industrial work in plants with innovative production systems – what has been called the 'Volvo model' or 'Volvoism'.[1] In this article the question: What does the Volvo model or 'Volvoism' stand for? is dealt with.

The aim of the article is to discuss innovative efforts within the Volvo company in terms of a model of change, illustrating the Volvo-model concept and discussing the difficulties encountered in attempts to spread the innovations within the company.

People in the international car industry and many researchers relate the Volvo-model concept to some specific operations of the Volvo company, and two car assembly plants within the Volvo Car Corporation are the main exponents of the Volvo model, namely the Kalmar plant (inaugurated in 1974) and the Uddevalla plant (inaugurated in 1989).[2]

Volvo has several car plants in Sweden and worldwide. Does the Volvo-model concept fit all plants? I will argue that the plants in Kalmar and Uddevalla have had little to do with the mainstream performance of other Volvo assembly factories, and that the innovations of the Kalmar and the Uddevalla plants were looked upon with great scepticism by many middle managers and by many production engineers in the older assembly plants. In addition I will argue that local pockets of innovative efforts appear now and then within Volvo, partly inspired by the ideas realized in Kalmar and Uddevalla. Some of them were flashes of innovation only, others work on a long-time schedule for adapting new ideas to their own operations.

One problem is that in debate the Volvo-model concept emanates from the characteritics of the two smaller Swedish assembly plants (Kalmar and Uddevalla), but the concept is used in such a way that it seemingly embraces the Volvo company as a whole. Thus, without redefining it, the Volvo-model concept is of little coherence in charaterizing the development of the Volvo company as a whole.

An additional problem related to the Volvo-model concept is that the two small plants in Kalmar and Uddevalla were very different from each other in terms of layout, learning and work organization. Therefore it is not a

Kajsa Ellegård, Göteborg University

helpful idea to use the same concept in order to characterize these two fundamentally different plants.

If the Volvo model is to be a useful concept in research it must be redefined. First, rather than being a general concept generated from the characteristics of only two specific plants, and second, rather than being a concept bundling two very different plants together, the Volvo-model concept should be general and relate to the company as a whole. Thereby, of course, the concept will be more difficult to handle as there are many internal differences within Volvo. In addition to this general concept there must be special concepts defined for charaterizing the specific production systems of the different plants.

I would like to define the Volvo model in the following way: The Volvo model is a concept characterizing the willingness of Volvo, when new production facilities are about to be planned (either completly new or renewed), to allow people in project groups to develop new production systems not necessarily located in the body of mainstream ideas. The result is that people's unique creativity has been let free, and recurrent innovations have been made when new plants are built. The Volvo-model concept, thus, implies a company's trust in the project groups' abilities. This implies flexibility and an orientation towards trying out new solutions to production-related problems. Of course the overall goal to yield higher profits must not be put aside. One point to note is that the acceptance of innovations may vary a lot in different parts of the company and in different plants. This is simultaneously a driving force and a drawback, and I will return to it later.

Some scholars have introduced new concepts to denote the specific characteristics of the production system in the Uddevalla plant, in order to avoid amalgamation between Volvo as a whole and the specific plant. For example, the term 'Uddevallaism' has been introduced by Freyssenet and Boyer[3] and the concept 'Reflective Production System' by Ellegård, Engström, Johansson, Medbo and Nilsson.[4] 'Uddevallaism' has an advantage as it relates directly to the specific plant where the new production system was actually born, thus indicating differences with the Kalmar plant, but at the same time, this is a disadvantage, as it does not imply a general application of the same production system.[5] A useful concept to denote the new production system must be a general one, related to general principles and not directly pointing to a specific plant.

What are the characteristics of Volvo, using the redefined Volvo-model concept to describe the development of the company?

HISTORY AND CHANGE

History is a powerful force influencing decisionmakers, often unconciously. Thus, a convenient handling strategy emanates from what is known from experiences in the past, as many things can then be taken as given.

In the auto industry, the past is embodied in the existifng plants and in the minds of the managers and employees. Therefore, it is often difficult to make radical changes to an existing organization. There are at least three occasions when big changes may be introduced: first, if the company experiences a very threatening situation (either societal or internal factors may force the firm to change), second, if the company is very profitable, and third when a new investment is to be made to replace older equipment. Ford, once was forced to find a more effective way to produce cars, as his aim was to take the lead among all car manufacturers selling their cars on a rapidly expanding market. The Japanese car makers, later on, were forced to make something more effective than post-Fordism in order to beat the western car makers on the world automobile market.

However, during the post-Fordist era in the US, radical changes were scarce within the automobile industry until the industry as a whole was severely threatened by the Japanese success in the 1980s. Protectionist tendencies were met by the Japanese who invested in transplants.[6] The strategy chosen by several US auto firms was to organize production in joint ventures with different Japanese auto makers, and to start car production in regions within the US where there was no tradition of automobile production. In this respect, the strategies of the US manufacturers and the Japanese manufacturers were amalgamated and a new starting point was defined. The NUMMI plant of GM and Toyota is one of the most successful plants where the western and the Japanese traditions are working in a joint direction enriched by new social principles of workers participation in decision-making.[7] The principle of a serial flow on an assembly line with short cycles, repetitive work tasks, however, remained unchanged.

There are consequently large differences between the social principles in, on the one hand, the Toyota plants in Japan and the GM plants in US and Europe, and on the other hand the NUMMI plant.

This reveals dual strategies of the large and successful companies. The power of history, on one hand, is embodied in the existence of the old social principles in older production facilities in the original location. The old factories very often are located at the original growth point of the firm, close to R&D, design, marketing and headquarters of the firm, and they are, of course, strongly identified with the history and success of the company. Thereby the power of what there already is, is intrinsic, and smaller peacemeal changes within the existing plants may be the only successful strategy for changes.

The firm's willingness for innovation and renewal, on the other hand, is revealed, for example by the greater steps taken when a new plant is built on a different spot. Examples of this kind of renewal are the Toyota Miata plant on the Japanese island of Kyushu and the GM/Toyota NUMMI-plant in the US. Within Volvo the innovative willingness is shown by the Kalmar and Uddevalla plants.

In such new factories there are no immediate signs of intertia where human manners, habits and values are taken for granted. Newly recruited people are open-minded regarding their opinions of work content and organization, at least if they have not been employed in the same company before. They are creating the culture of the new plant, a culture which will be the basis for the new traditions. These newly shaped traditions will obviously differ from the traditons of the older plant.

Just as profitability is one cornerstone of industrial success, growth (or at least maintaining the position within the industry) is another. This fact also emphasizes the power of history. If a fundamental change is to be implemented in a firm with only one or two plants manufacturing the main portion of the firm's production volume, it is vitally important that the change is successful. There is an obvious risk of losing market share if production does not increase as expected, when the market demand calls for it. However, it is not common to make significant changes in a new plant established for reasons of capacity alone. Letting history be in power of change, therefore, is a guarantee for slow and moderate changes, which are more easily carried out. In the short term neither profitability nor the firm's position in the industry is threatened if such a careful strategy is pursued.

A MODEL FOR CHANGE

The process of change discussed above, can be illustrated by a model (inspired by the school of time-geography, developed in the academic discipline of Human and Economic Geography[8]) taking a sequential, processual and contingent approach on the time dimension: past, present and future are parts of the whole. See Figure 1. Past, present and future appear very differently in the illustration. What has happened in the past can be described by a continuous trajectory (of the firm or the plant), because what has happened cannot be undone (though, of course it may well be re-evaluated). The present situation is described by a point: the position on the time dimension just NOW, simultaniously located somewhere on the dimension of change. Finally, future alternatives are described by possible alternatives – seen from the perspective of the present. See Figure 1. There are two different worlds of possibilities. One is the space of possibilities delimited by technique, organization knowledge and skills, in the illustration the 'total world of possibilities', and the other is the 'space of perceived possibilities', as they are experienced by the actors. The space of perceived possibilities may vary a lot from one individual to another.

Figure 1 shows the time dimension (vertical) and a dimension of change (horizontal) with two directions (A and B). What has happened in the past is described by the trajectory **p–a**. The position at present is described by **a** and the future possible positions of the firm are described by the area between the demarcation lines **a–b** and **a–c**. The firm can (NOW, at **a**) decide to start a process of change in any direction (A or B), though only one at a time. The trajectory from the bottom of the diagram **p–a** shows that in the past the firm did change its position, though moderately, in the B-direction. The lines **a–b** and **a–c** denote the outer limit of the possible changes within reach (given that the change starts *now* at position **a** in the diagram), and the lines **a–d** and **a–e** denote the area within the possible world of change that are perceived as possibilities by the majority of the actors in the firm. The difference between the outer demarcation lines (**a–b**, **a–c**) and the inner lines (**a–d**, **a–e**) shows the inertia of the firm.

One of the few really certain things already known about the future is that in every position (now), there are many future possibilities and it is difficult for one individual (perhaps impossible) to identify and perceive them all. Among the totality of possibilities (the angle between **a** and **b**, **a** and **c**), some possibilities are perceived as alternatives by the majority (the angle between **a** and **d**, **a** and **e**) to choose between.

The company level is, however, a complex level for characterizing the path of a firm. It might work if focus is put on what has happened in the past, but if we are interested in the future the divergence or convergence between the perceived alternatives of different decision makers, thus must be identified. Within one and the same firm there may co-exist people with different opinions and people who perceive the possible solutions in the future in very different ways. If one of the most powerful managers identifies a potential solution outside the space of perceived possible changes by the majority of decisionmakers, they may perceive the area somewhere in the **a–b–d–a** or **a–c–e–a** sectors in Figure 1. Then he or she must be strong enough to convince other decision makers that it might be a profitable alternative. A large change might appear relatively rapidly.

This kind of breaking through the 'wall of perception' set up by history (**a–d** and **a–e** in Figure 1) is not common. Henry Ford was one leader of this kind, taking an innovative step to introduce the assembly line into what before had been largely craft production. Not many people had to be convinced about the potential of the assembly line (the idea of radical technical change) or the reduced working hours and higher wages (the radical social changes). Ford's idea of combining the assembly line with one product model (T-Ford) remained successful for nearly two decades (1908–1927). In 1927 Ford was convinced by his son to change car model, as their competitors had done. However, the principle of the assembly line survived.

Another powerful manager who identified possibilities beyond the borders of what most people perceived as possible is the former Volvo CEO, P G Gyllenhammar. He started his career in Volvo in the early 1970s and he was the source of inspiration for the Kalmar (early 1970s) and Uddevalla factories (middle of the 1980s). Both plants went far beyond the space of perceived possibilities imagined by the majority within Volvo. In the next section I shall provide a short history of Volvo, consider the so called 'Volvo model' and relate this to the model of change as described in Figure 1 below.

VOLVO HISTORY IN BRIEF

Volvo was founded in 1926. Cars were produced in an old ball bearing plant in Lundby, Göteborg, on the west coast of Sweden. From the beginning

FIGURE 1

A DYNAMIC ILLUSTRATION OF CHANGE IN A FIRM

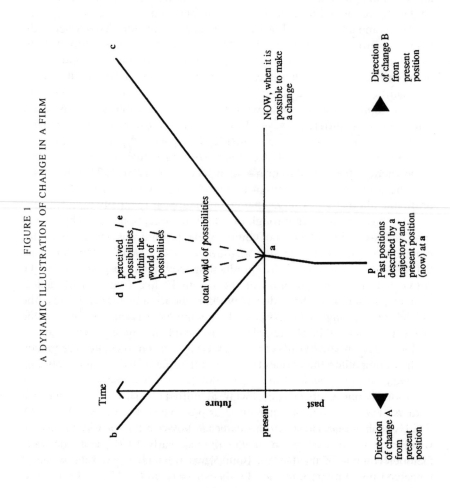

Volvo planned to start a flexible production system, which meant that production could easily be shifted from a passenger car to a small truck by means of using the same chassis. Production was organized on an assembly line,[9] but of course, in the small scale plant, during the late 1920s, the work as such was extremely craft dependent.

Still in the 1950s there was only one Volvo factory producing cars. By that time, however, Volvo began to expand greatly. The car market in Sweden increased enormously and the Volvo car became extremely popular amongst Swedes. In addition, a new Volvo strategy was created in the 1950s, not only to greatly expand exports but, in addition, to begin exporting cars to countries with a large internal production volume. The main goal was to successfully enter the US market. This was looked upon as a brave decision just at the edge of the possibilities perceived by the majority of the actors in Volvo. Therefore production facilities had to be improved and capacity had to be increased in order to adapt to the expectations of this optimistic environment.

The Torslanda Plant and other Pre-Kalmar Factories

As a consequence of the expansionist strategy, a new car factory was built in Torslanda, Göteborg, in the early 1960s. It was a complete factory, with a body-shop, a paint shop and an assembly shop. The Torslanda plant was planned during the late 1950s and it was formed in accordance with the leading production techniques of the time: the ideal was the assembly line with its serial flow. There were short cycle work tasks, balanced by the MTM-system.[10] The work content did not demand skills other than basic manual ones which were sufficient for the simple tasks required to fulfill the simple orders given by supervisors.

A few years later in the early 1960s, a plant was built in Gent, Belguim, as a result of the Volvo strategy to produce cars inside the borders of the European Economic Community (now the European Union). The factory in Gent, was constructed according to the same production system principles as the mother plant in Torslanda.

Early on Volvo decided to start production in Canada in order to easily export to the large US market, and in South East Asia, in order to enter a high potential market area at an early stage. Thus, in the late 1960s and 1970s, small factories for manufacturing passenger cars where built in Canada, Thailand, Malaysia and Indonesia. All these small factories assembled cars from imported components which were sent there in knocked down kits from the Torslanda plant in Göteborg.

The production facilities in the Torslanda plant were still modern in the early 1970s, but a great deal of the labour force disliked working there. In the late 1960s and early 1970s there were recruitment problems, strikes and other disturbances to production. Problems did not only appear in the assembly plant, but in the body shop as well and there were many discussions within the company and amongst the blue collar trade unionists.[11]

The Kalmar Plant

Volvo had a new CEO, P G Gyllenhammar, in the early 1970s. He showed from the beginning a strong appreciation of the social dimension of work, and this was an important factor for the further development of Volvo and what is called the 'Volvo model'. P G Gyllenhammar had to deal with workers low commitment to work and their low degree of work satisfaction at the Torslanda plant. As a consequence of the problems related to this and other labour market factors in Göteborg, a decision was taken to open a new final assembly factory in Kalmar. The social dimensions of work were highlighted in the planning of the Kalmar plant. One goal was to humanize work, and thus team work was introduced on the shop floor.

In terms of the model of change, PG Gyllenhammar in the early 1970s identified a possible route for change, far beyond 'the perceived space of possibilities' held by the majority within Volvo. This is principally illustrated in Figure 2. The prevailing wisdom within the auto-industry at the time was that the superiority of the assembly line was obvious, and this opinion was common among most Volvo managers. PG Gyllenhammar, however, was powerful enough to legitimize the innovative steps taken at Kalmar in the rest of the Volvo organization. The whole Volvo corporation gained from the worldwide positive publicity about the Kalmar plant. Therefore, the Kalmar plant, as a physical exponent of a new model, was accepted in the Torslanda organization, though there were not many supervisors and production leaders who themselves wanted to (and still fewer who tried to) implement the new type of organization.

The group planning the Kalmar plant took two radical steps. One step was taken on the social dimension to humanize work. The ideas of a strict hierachical, vertical division of labour and short work cycles were seriously put into question. In the Kalmar plant, work was performed in cooperative teams, and the cycle time was extended from 2 to 15–20 minutes. Another step was taken on the technical dimension, moving from the inflexible assembly line. In the Kalmar plant, the assembly line literally was broken into sections. During the assembly each car was transported throughout the plant on a self-monitoring platform, a so called auto carrier.[12] Workers could stand on the platform and do their assembly work whilst the carrier moved slowly through the team's area in the factory.

All work was organized in teams. Considering the period, this was an extremely radical organizational principle to apply to the shop floor. Each team in the plant had its own geographical area in which team members performed their extended assembly work tasks. Each team had its own rest-room near the work area. The physical and social environment was greatly improved in comparison with the older Torslanda plant.

The Kalmar plant was innovative in the 1970s. Some internal critics expressed their opinion that the plant was a PR gimmick, and that the plant never had any real chance to be profitable. But workers and managers felt it was a profoundly better kind of work place and Volvo gained a lot from the publicity worldwide.

FIGURE 2.

THE LOCATION OF THE IDEA OF THE KALMAR PLANT IN THE CONTEXT OF THE MODEL OF CHANGE.

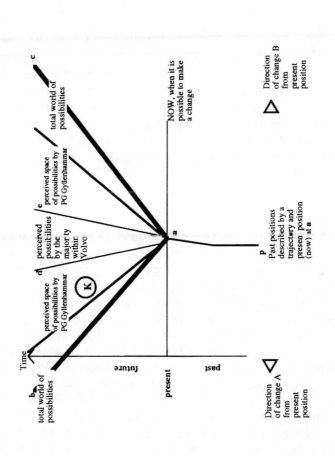

Note: **K** is the point within the total space of possibilities percieved by PG Gyllerhammar, but not (yet) by the majority within Volvo.

The Uddevalla Plant

The market for Volvo cars was expanding greatly during the early 1980s and capacity levels were achieved. At the same time, there were difficulties in recruiting people in Göteborg to the Torslanda plant. Until then only limited efforts were made to spread experiences from Kalmar to Torslanda. The efforts were some experiments, involving only a few people.

In the mid-1980s, it was expected that the number of young people in the Swedish labour force would decline dramatically by the mid-1990s, and traditionally young people have been the recruitment base for Volvo. This factor favoured a location outside Göteborg. Therefore, Volvo decided to build a new factory which could appeal to the potential labour force, not only young male workers, but also females and older people.

Now the second innovative Volvo factory was born. It was located at Uddevalla, planned and put into production during the late 1980s. The original intention was that the Uddevalla plant would be a complete factory, but eventually it was decided to build an assembly plant only. The goals formulated for the project group making up the plans for the plant were: a plant where profitability should be reached by flexibility, efficiency, quality and good working conditions. These were rather conventional goals within Volvo. At the Uddevalla factory fundamental changes were made on the technical as well as the social dimension. However, one important social innovation for the industry was the fact that female participation was in the order of 40 per cent.

The assembly line was completely abandoned and small teams, working parallel to each other, were responsible for the assembly of complete cars (one team made a complete car). Technically, there were new principles implemented for material handling and as a consequence the product flow could be highly parallelized. Complete cars were assembled while the car body was standing still in the same place at the same station.

A central issue was how to learn the extended work content required where only a handful of workers were needed to assemble the complete car. The answer was to adopt a holistic learning strategy. Skilled workers were to teach newly employed workers how to assemble cars. Beginning with the assembly of one quarter of a car, each individual could aspire to take the masters examination by building a complete car on his/her own. Employees did not only learn how to build cars, they also learnt how to perform several supporting tasks, such as maintenance, production engineering tasks, personnel tasks, economic tasks and so on. The teams planned their own production and were able to make plans in pursuit of their own educational needs. At Uddevalla, work was truly organized in integrated work teams.[13]

The term 'Reflective Production System' was coined by researchers to describe the new production system developed during the planning of the Uddevalla plant. It means that the work content demands skills other than only obeying detailed orders. Workers have to reflect over their work during the work process in such a way that the product reflects the workers performance back to him/her, which makes it possible for workers to improve upon working methods.[14]

The performance of the Uddevalla plant was good and improving all the time. The quality and productivity index showed a favourable curve, and people working there were proud of their job.[15]

Volvo suffered severely from the worldwide fall in demand for cars in the early 1990s and the two innovative assembly plants in Kalmar and Uddevalla were closed.

DIFFUSION OF THE INNOVATIONS OF NEW PRODUCTION SYSTEMS THROUGHOUT VOLVO

The two innovative Volvo plants were successful and quickly became 'the model factories of Volvo' to the outside world. Was there any sense of pride within Volvo in response to these innovations? Did the existence of the innovative assembly plants broaden the perspective of people within Volvo? Was the scope of innovation, or in terms of the model of change, the 'space of perceived possibilities', enlarged? Did people discover potential for other Volvo plants to develop in the same direction as Kalmar and Uddevalla?

The new social principles introduced in the Kalmar plant (team work and extended work cycles), together with the self-monitoring platforms to move the body during assembly work, allowed the workers to feel more satisfied with work in the plant. In contrast to the Torslanda plant, there were no problems with strikes and disturbances at Kalmar. This ought to have been a valuable argument for implementing the new system in the old plant too.

Influences on Assembly Shops

Were there influences from Kalmar in the assembly shop of the Torslanda plant? In the large assembly plant there were a few experimental areas set up in the late 1970s. They were, however, geographically isolated and they were soon 'killed' by tradition and the lack of willingness to adopt the new form of social organization. In 1980, however, a small copy of the Kalmar plant was started in a separate building in the Torslanda area, in order to assemble the start up series of the Volvo 700-model and the plant survived for about five years (it was called TUN). The most significant effects of Kalmar in the late 1970s and early 1980s became rooted in the minds of some managers and shop stewards in the Metal workers union. Efforts were made 'from below' to organize the work in teams in the assembly plant. Despite the lack of a strategy, common to all sections, some departments in the Torslanda assembly area were organized in 'teams' by the middle of the 1980s. In Torslanda, people were located next to the assembly line and they did rotate; that is, work tasks were rotated with a workmate on another workstation several times a day. However, this situation was far from the integrated teams that were fundamental to Kalmar.

In conclusion, there was no common strategy for changing the direction of the Torslanda assembly shop towards the system developed at Kalmar.

Influences on the Body Shop

The Kalmar assembly plant, however, inspired managers and trade unionists in the stamping and the body welding shops in Torslanda to begin thinking in new directions with respect to the organization and content of work. Great improvements were made in the stamping shop in the late 1970s and in the new body welding shop producing the 700-series bodies built in 1980.

The labour related problems associated with high turnover rates, strikes, high sick leave and the difficulties in recruiting young workers, which characterized the Torslanda plant in the 1960s and 1970s, were not isolated to the assembly shop. The stamping shop, the body welding shop and the paint shop experienced the same types of problems. Automation was the first response to these problems. In these factories a process of automation started when new techniques for stamping, welding and painting were adopted.[16] The first robot was installed in the early 1970s in the welding shop, and the first robot welding line was installed in the late 1970s in the same shop. What was intriguing, though, was that the process of automation increased the need for committed workers for reasons of ensuring maintenance, quality and total productive maintenance (TPM). The automation process was thus an important argument for improving working conditions so as to increase workers commitment. Improvement began by extending work content – both horizontally (job enlargement) and vertically (job enrichment), ergonomics and by introducing self-controlling, integrated work teams. The new body shop in Torslanda, built in 1980 was completely reorganized according to integrated team work principles.[17] The employees were much more satisfied with their work than the employees in the old body shop, where the new work content, new organization and new technical layout was not introduced until the late 1980s.[18]

An interesting fact is that in the project group, responsible for planning the Uddevalla factory, there were several people from the body shop in Torslanda, among them the project leader and one metal work trade unionist. Their chain of inspiration was: ideas from Kalmar inspired their efforts to improve the body welding shop and after that they developed their ideas further for the Uddevalla plant.

One reasonable assessment of these developments is that for decades Volvo was an innovative firm as far as the quantity and quality of innovations is concerned. However, when it comes to the diffusion of innovation in production systems, the lack of a common strategy is a profound drawback. Consequently, the diffusion has depended upon the commitment by individuals to the ideas rather than a strategy adopted on the part of the company.

A Volvo Strategy Presented in 1990

When it comes to the Volvo Car Corporation as a whole since 1990, a strategy, the so called KLE-strategy, for organizing work in a common way in all Swedish Volvo plants (Torslanda, Kalmar, Uddevalla making cars and in the other Volvo plants making engines and gear-boxes) has been developed. The aim at of this strategy is to make all employees familiar with the circumstances of the industrial firm – Volvo – and its main goals. KLE stands for Quality (K), delivery at the right time to the customer (L) and total economy in the operations (E). All the plants within Volvo in Sweden (and subsequently in the international operations as well) are to be organized in KLE-teams. This process is continuing today and many of the basic social ideas have been taken from experiences at the Kalmar and Uddevalla plants, and are now being implemented in the Torslanda plant, the only Volvo car manufacturing plant in operation in Sweden today. The experience of working in a technical system where the assembly line was abandoned was, however, not spread to the assembly shop in Torslanda.[19] One consequence is that the potential of the alternative technical system from Uddevalla may not be utilized in the KLE-teams in the Torslanda assembly shop.

The most successful implementation of integrated team work in KLE-teams in the Torslanda plant today is found neither in the assembly shop nor the body welding shop, but in the paint shop. It has been further developed from the ideas of integrated teams in Kalmar, from the new organization of production in the body shop and from the planning and operations of the Uddevalla plant.[20] The reason for the successful implementation in the paint and body welding shops is that the openess for new ideas in these shops has been high for decades. Additionally, there already existed many experiences from new forms of organization and techniques. In the assembly shop, where the majority of employees are working, the implementation of KLE-teams has been much slower. Some KLE-teams work successfully, while others struggle in their initial phases.

In Figure 3, the process of diffusion within the Volvo Car Corporation is briefly described in a two-dimensional diagram. In the figure the time dimension is indicated by arrows. At the endpoints of the social dimension there are 'Direction of social change towards unskilled monotonous work tasks' and 'Direction of social change towards skilled and well educated workers and integrated work teams' respectively. The technical dimension comprises 'Direction of change towards space compact operations' and 'Direction of change towards automation' as endpoints. There are different orientations shown by the development of some different Volvo plants and work shops. The situation portrayed makes it clear that there have been several trajectories within Volvo.

CHANGE AND SUCCESS

Naturally, the immanent force of industrial success is profitability. Profitability, though, appears in different concrete forms at different times and in different regions. During the early decades of the 20th century the force for success was embodied in Fordism as it developed in the rapid

FIGURE 3

THE DEVELOPMENT OF EFFORTS TO MAKE A PROFITABLE AND HUMANE PRODUCTION SYSTEM
WITHIN THE VOLVO CAR CORPORATION SINCE THE 1960s

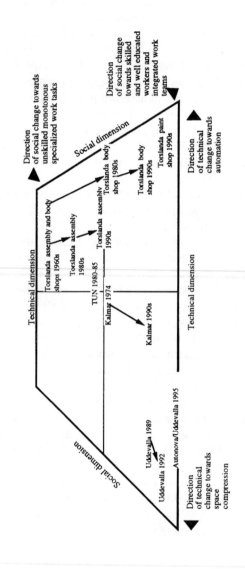

industrialization process of the US. The Fordist innovation is characterized by a strong vertical and horizontal division of labour, with production on an assembly line according to the principle of a serial flow.

However, since the 1980s the innovative production organization of the Japanese auto firms has outrun the modernized Fordism in the automobile industry. The profitability of the Japanese production system organization is generated by strong integrative efforts within the total production system: subcontractors are bound to deliver components just-in-time to the final assembly units, where products are manufactured as specified by customers, and finally, the customer can be convinced that his satisfaction will be eagerly measured by the autofirm in order to improve the production system. On the shop floor, however, the assembly lines still prevail.[21] The Japanese success was experienced by all auto makers in the US and Europe in the 1980s, and since then most of them have made strong efforts to copy what they deem to be the key points of the Japanese production system.

Clearly, in any society, the structural prerequisites for successful industrial innovation differ greatly from one time to another in ways which have as much to do with societal factors as those internal to the firm. Societal factors are for example income level, social infrastructure, size of labour market, unemployment rates, ideals of a good life, the educational level and the education system. Some internal factors are for example, skills of the employees, work organization in the firm, layout, the nature of the technical equipment, the implementation of new techniques and the factory level of integration between design, product development and production. Of course it goes almost without saying, the demand for the product on the market is fundamentally crucial to success.

Fordism was born and grew in a society where the educational level was low, where many people were looking for jobs to earn their living, and where the market demand for cars was growing rapidly. Mass production of identical cars on assembly lines in a very standardized manner was a successful means of meeting the growing demand and meant a breakthrough for industrialization in that period. Workers without special education could be recruited and instructed on how to perform the standardized, short cycle work task. Craftsmanship production, the predecessor of industrialism, had by that time no potential for increasing production to meet the rising demand. One important explanation is that the mass production ideals, advocating standardization and a high division of labour, were the opposite of craftmanship ideals, where planning, organization of work, production operations and control of the job were integrated parts of a whole job for one craftsman.[22] The profitability of Fordism in the early 20th century was thus much higher than the profitability of the old craftmanship production system.

The Japanese made huge efforts when they rebuilt their nation after the second world war in the 1950s. The employees wanted to participate in rebuilding their country and to take it to a leading position in the world. Long working hours, short holidays and high speed assembly lines are well known characteristics of these efforts.[23] The organization of the efforts gave rise to a new successful production system, the so called Lean Production System. The term 'Lean Production' was invented by western journalists and researchers when the phenomenon of the Japanese auto makers competitiveness in the 1980s was identified.[24] A successful way was opened to improve the performance of mass production, by strictly organizing the production chain in an integrative way (design, preproduction, production, marketing and after sales) and by coordinating the different parts of the chain, all aiming at the common goal of becoming competitive on the world market. The wage system encourages the workers to participate in quality circles and kaizen activities. Recently, though, there are signs of worker opposition within the Japanese firms.[25] Difficulties in recruiting young people and high rates of labour turnover are two problems which affect the smooth operation of the Japanese system. Another big problem for the Japanese firms is that the value system denoting what is required to live a good life in Japanese society has changed from one generation to the next. Young people of today want to have more time for leisure and personal concerns. The value collision between the generations, and the problems in the firms emanating from these changes, is shown by the recent problems of the Japanese automobile industry operating in Japan.

Fordism and Lean Production have the assembly line with its serial flow in common. Thus, for about nine decades, the innovations of Taylor as they were implemented first by Ford, and later on in a refined and improved fashion by the Japanese auto makers, have shown their strength and profitability in the auto industry worldwide. Therefore, over the last hundred years the assembly line together with a particular form of the division of labour prevailed as the means to profitability.

The easy conclusion would be that profitability can only be reached as a result of a firm strategy for the implementation of change, either by radical, innovative steps, as shown by Fordism when new technical and social principles were implemented, or by refining existing principles, as shown by Japanese Lean Production.

However, in this article I have presented an example of implementing new technical and social principles in order to increase profitability that relates to a minor section of a firm. The societal factors in Sweden, together with the internal factors at Volvo, made a break from the assembly line production system with its short and monotonous work tasks necessary. This occurred first in Kalmar and later in Uddevalla, and the openess to new production organization systems within Volvo made it possible to consummate this break. A new production system, named the Reflective Production System, was first developed in the planning of Volvo's assembly plant in Uddevalla during the late 1980s.[26]

To conclude, a Volvo-model concept, related to the level of the Volvo Car Corporation, shows that there has been an open atmosphere to new ideas in the company at the top level and innovative ideas were stimulated from there, for example in the new plants in Kalmar and Uddevalla.

However, simultaneously there was no strategy for spreading the innovations within the company and resistance to the new ideas within the operative units was strong. Therefore the diffusion of internal, Volvo-generated innovations, was taken on solely by individuals or groups of individuals who were already committed to the ideas. This meant that the production systems of Kalmar (since 1974) and Uddevalla (since 1986) were spread by chance rather than by any strategic planning process.

Since the early 1990s, however, a Volvo strategy was developed to organize all production operations in KLE-teams. This idea emanated from the positive results of team work in the car assembly plants in Kalmar and Uddevalla and in the engine factory Skövde.

The KLE-strategy has been implemented at the Torslanda plant where the assembly line still prevails. The KLE-strategy has its best potential in highly automated shops (such as body welding and paint shops) and, if adopted in labour intensive shops (such as assembly shops) the most promising result from the KLE-strategy is to be found in a plant without an assembly line.

The Volvo model, as it is defined in this article, was unique because for two decades it allowed people with ideas in project groups making up the plans for new plants, to develop an alternative to the mainstream. However, the lack of a strategy to spread the positive results from the innovations was a drawback. In 1992, only two years after the formation of a Volvo strategy for spreading the experiences from Kalmar and Uddevalla, these two model-plants were closed. Since then, Volvo has had no unique alternative to assembly line production where passenger cars are manufactured. The KLE-team strategy has been implemented throughout the Volvo Car Company, but there are no fundamental differences between the technical and social organization of the Volvo assembly plants and the plants of other auto makers. Volvo seems to have chosen a mainstream route, trodden by others, when it comes to layout and technique. However, Volvo might still have an advantage in the social relations of the firm.

There is one great exception when it comes to assembly plants, and that is Autonova AB, the reopened automobile plant in Uddevalla, where Volvo has a 49 per cent share. In Autonova AB, the principles of the Reflective Production System once developed within Volvo and the Uddevalla plant are being further developed. So, Volvo still has a joker left in the pack...

NOTES

1. Berggren (1990) and Berggren (1995). Freyssenet and Boyer (1994).
2. These exponents of the 'Volvo model' were, however, closed down during the world wide crises in the auto industry during the early 1990s. The Uddevalla plant was closed in 1993 and the Kalmar plant in 1994. One formal reason given for closing the two plants, exponents as they were of the 'Volvo model', was their lack of body and paint shops. Close proximity between body, paint and assembly shops was regarded as a decisive factor. The bigger Volvo plants of today are more conventional assembly line plants. The plant in Uddevalla, though, is now re-opened. A body shop is established as well as a paint shop, in addition to the assembly shop. The new Uddevalla plant is named Autonova AB and Volvo owns a minority

of the shares. Tom Walkinshaw Racing owns 51% and Volvo the rest.
3. Freyssenet and Boyer (1994).
4. Ellegård, Engström, Johansson, Medbo and Nilsson (1992).
5. In addition,Uddevallaism relates to a plant that was closed, though it is now re-opened.
6. Shimokawa (1995); Berggren, Björkman and Hollander (1991).
7. Adler and Cole (1995).
8. Time-geography was developed by professor Torsten Hägerstrand in Lund university, and it was presented to an international audience in 1977 when an edition of the Journal of Economic Geography was focussing on recent trends in Sweden. See also Hägerstrand (1974), (1984) and (1985); Thrift (1977).
9. The bodies on the assembly line were pushed manually from station to station.
10. MTM, method-time-measurement, is a method for defining the work content of a work task in a synthetic way. There are mean values for the time needed to perform a number of basic movements of the human body. The time use for such a movement is measured in TMU (time measure units), and the time use for basic movements are added until the cycle time is filled with work content.
11. Agurén, Hansson and Karlsson (1976); Ellegård (1986); Berggren (1990).
12. Agurén, Hansson and Karlsson (1976); Agurén, Bredbacka, Hansson , Ihregren and Karlsson (1984); Berggren (1990).
13. Nilsson (1981); Ellegård (1989).
14. Ellegård, Engström, Johansson, Medbo and Nilsson (1992).
15. Ellegård (1995).
16. Ellegård (1995b).
17. Ellegård (1995).
18. Ellegård (1986).
19. In one pre-assembly area, however, parallel assembly work stations were implemented (door assembly).
20. Ellegård (1989).
21. Jones, Roos and Womack (1990).
22. Nilsson (1981).
23. National Defense Council for Victims of Karoshi (1990).
24. Jones, Roos and Womack (1990).
25. Nohara (1995).
26. Ellegård, Engström, Johansson, Medbo and Nilsson (1992), and Ellegård, Engström and Nilsson (1990).

REFERENCES

Adler P. and R. Cole (1995) 'Designed for Learning: A Tale of Two Auto Plants in Å Sandberg (ed.)'Enriching production: Perspectives on Volvo's Uddevalla plant as an alternative to lean production' (Aldershot: Avebury).

Agurén, S., R. Hansson and H. Karlsson. (1976) Volvo Kalmarverken. Rationaliseringsrådet SAF-LO. Stockholm.

Agurén, S., C. Bredbacka, R. Hansson, K. Ihregren and H. Karlsson (1984) Volvo Kalmarverken efter 10 år. Rådet för utvecklingsfrågor SAF-LO-PTK. Stockholm.

Berggren, C. (1990) Det nya bilarbetet. Konkurrensen mellan olika produktionskoncept i svensk bilindustri 1970–1990. Arkiv avhandlingssserie. Lund.

Berggren, C. (1995) 'The fate of the branch plants – performance versus power', in Å. Sandberg (ed.) Enriching production. Perspectives on Volvo's Uddevalla plant as an alternative to lean production (Aldershot: Avebury.

Berggren, C., T. Björkman and E. Hollander (1991) Are they unbeatable? Royal Institute of Technology, Stockholm.

Ellegård, K. (1986) Från operatör till yrkesarbetare. Sammanfattning av forskningsprojektet 'Erfarenheter av arbetsorganisationsutveckling vid en ny jiggfabrik. Choros 1986:8. Dept of Human and Economic Geography, Göteborg University, Göteborg.

Ellegård, K. (1989) Akrobatik i tidens väv. En dokumentation av projekteringen av Volvos bilfabrik i Uddevalla. Choros 1989:2. Dept of Human and Economic Geography, Göteborg University, Göteborg.

Ellegård, K. (1995) 'The creation of a new production system at the Volvo automobile assembly plant in Uddevalla, Sweden', in Å. Sandberg (ed.) Enriching production. Perspectives on

Volvo's Uddevalla plant as an alternative to lean production. Aldershot: Avebury.

Ellegård, K. (1995b) *Automation and Inertia.* Paper presented at the Third International Workshop on Assembly Atuomation in Venice, Italy, Oct 1995.

Ellegård, K., T. Engström and L. Nilsson (1990) *Reforming industrial work – Principles and realities.* The Swedish Work Environment Fund, Stockholm.

Ellegård, Engström, Johansson, Medbo and Nilsson (1992) *Reflektiv Produktion. Industriell verksamhet i förändring.* AB Volvo. Falköping.

Freyssenet, M. and R. Boyer (1994) *The emergence of New Industrial Models. Hypotheses and final results.* Second English draft. (Paris: Gerpisa).

Hägerstrand, T. (1974) *Tidsgeografisk beskrivning. Syfte och postulat,* in Svensk Geografisk Årsbok Vol.50. Lund.

Hägerstrand, T. (1984) 'Escapes from the cage of routines. Observations of human paths, projects and personal scripts', in J. Long and R. Hecock (eds) *Leisure, Tourism and Social Change.* Dunfermline College of Physical Education.

Hägerstrand, T. (1985) 'Time-Geography: focus on the corporeality of man, society and enviroment', in *Science and Praxos of Complexity.* The United Nations University.

National Defense Council for Victims of Karoshi (1990) *When the 'Corporate Warrior' dies.* MADO-SHA.

Nilsson, L. (1981) *Yrkesutbildning i nutidshistoriskt perspektiv.* Acta Gothoburgensis. Göteborg University. Göteborg.

Nohara, H. (1995) *Towards a New Division of Labour in the History of Industrialization?: The second stage of the Toyota Production System.* Paper presented at the Troiséme Rencontre Internationale du Gerpisa 'Les nouveaux modèles industriels'. Paris.

Shimokawa, K. (1995) *Japanese Car-makers and Globalisation: Management and Transplants in North America and Europe.* Paper presented at the Troiséme Rencontre Internationale du Gerpisa 'Les nouveaux modèles industriels'. Paris.

Thrift, N. (1977) *An introduction to Time-Geography.* Catmog 13. Study Group in Qualitative Methods of the Institute of British Geographers.

Womack, J., D. Jones and D. Roos (1990) *The machine that changed the world. Rawson Associates.* (New York: Macmillan).

Competitivity of the Automobile Industry: The French Way

JEAN-PIERRE DURAND
Translated by Teresa Hayter

The French automobile industry is now one of the most successful in the world. It has had considerable success in resisting the pressures of other European or Japanese competitors in its home market. It has moreover been able to penetrate other European markets, including those that are reputed to be the most difficult, such as the German market. The Renault Clio was the best selling foreign vehicle in Germany in 1993. In addition, the two French companies PSA Peugeot-Citroën[1] and Renault SA have made profits continuously since 1987 (except PSA in 1993) while PSA in 1991 and Renault in 1992 were declared the most profitable manufacturers in the world. In 1991, with a profit rate of 3.5 per cent , PSA was well ahead of Toyota (2.9 per cent). These results, even though they appeared more precarious in 1995–96, are based on the major restructuring carried out by the two manufacturers following the crisis they experienced in the first half of the 1980s, which nearly caused them to disappear altogether.[2]

These upheavals are mainly the result of desperate efforts made by each company to survive and to adapt to a market in which the principles of flexible mass production replace those of straightforward mass production. To the requirement of a growing diversity of products were added concerns about quality which, for example, was not the strong point of Renault, while costs had to fall dramatically, in particular in order to cope with depressed markets. It was therefore not the threat of Japanese imports which caused the transformation of the French automobile industry (imports had been restricted to 3 per cent of registrations in France since 1977), as was the case for example in the United States. The need for radical transformations was based primarily on the need to deal with the manufacturers' massive losses (12.4 billion francs in 1984 in the case of Renault, which had debts amounting to 55 per cent of its turnover in 1985). In a search for solutions to their problems, the manufacturers made numerous visits to Japan, to understand why Toyota in particular was so successful. They brought back ideas for production methods (sometimes transformed into 'recipes') such as Just in Time, Total Quality Management, Total Productive Maintenance or *Kaizen.* They also brought back ideas about production goals (the reduction or absence of buffer stocks, the number of vehicles produced per employee and per year, the time it should take to design a vehicle...) and models for organizing their relationships with suppliers.

Jean-Pierre Durand, University of Paris-Evry.

In fact it was impossible to put all these ideas into practice immediately in France for a number of reasons. First, Toyota's engineers and managers set up the 'Toyota system' through a process of trial and error over several decades (cf. the writings of T. Ohno and of Shingo). The system was made up of organizational adjustments whose coherence was only made explicit and reconstituted *a posteriori*. The French manufacturers could not reconstruct this coherent system in a few years. The consultants who assisted them (especially at Renault) were often more concerned with their own interests than with the concrete results of their actions, and they introduced 'Japanese methods' without a systematic concern with the coherence on which their success is based. Second, the differences between French and Japanese employment relations mean that a particular type of organization of work, production, quality, and maintenance which is successful at Toyota may not work at Citroën, Peugeot or Renault. A system of organization cannot be separated from its context, and in particular from the nature of the employees' involvement in work, the system of wage determination, skill levels or the ability of trade unions to block a reform which appears to them to run counter to the interests of the workers.

Thus the teams of engineers visiting Japan brought back concepts, ideas and goals rather than solutions. The survival and then the success of the French automobile industry derive from the ways in which these ideas were put into practice in the real life situation of the companies, and especially of the shopfloor. It is possible to speak of a French Way , which links the trauma of a drastic reduction in the number of employees (and especially of shopfloor workers) to a general commitment to an experiment whose positive results are widely accepted.

This 'French Way' of modernization was largely based on the weakening of militant trade unionism. This weakness had existed for a long time at Citroën, where company unions occupy a dominant position. It is now prevalent at Renault where, after the closure of Billancourt and the long struggle of its chairmen Georges Besse and Raymond Lévy against the *Confédération Générale du Travail (CGT)*, the latter lost its majority in the Company Committee and in most of the company's plants. At the same time, this does not mean that militant trade unionism has disappeared. Social movements, sporadic work stoppages or longer strikes (as at Peugeot in 1989 or at Renault in 1991) show the relative dynamism of militant trade unionism. On a day to day basis, workers who are supported by one or more trade unions continue to resist or to refuse changes which are against their interests. The situation is therefore ambivalent. Trade unionism is still present but an intelligent management can obtain the acceptance of reforms which would have triggered strikes in the 1970s. A particular example is continuous working, that is, the continued functioning of production lines (assembly, welding) during breaks, thanks to the rotation of the workers who look after the machines.

In summary, the considerable increase in productivity was largely the result of management's ability to suppress pockets of resistance, both by weakening the militant trade unionism of the 'Golden Age', and by convincing the workers and certain trade unions of the urgent need to work in different ways and with greater efficiency, in order to secure the survival of their company and thus to save jobs. In spite of all the differences that exist with the Japanese context, a profound transformation of the employee relationship in France is taking place and is moving in the same direction. The majority of wage earners carry out the tasks which are assigned to them in the way they have been told to do so because there is no reason – and no possibility – to do otherwise.

At the same time, and this is the other particular feature of the French Way, management, especially at Renault but also at PSA, has carried out a large number of experiments, either at headquarters level (for example in the central engineering department) or at factory or even shopfloor management levels. These experiments are generally intended to improve productivity or quality.

Subsequently management was able to graft onto these practices, and onto the sense of commitment to the company, the goals imported from Japan, in particular those of quality and above all those of productivity growth. Thus it is incorrect to speak of a 'Japanization' of the organization of work and of the company in France. In reality, Japanese methods were profoundly distorted when the experiments were generalized. But the goals of quality and productivity persisted, were shared and were quite often attained, even though this was achieved through the detailed working out of solutions which were closely linked to the French organizational fabric, rather than through radical upheavals inspired by Japanese methods. For example, French factories usually had difficulty in eliminating internal buffer stocks on a production line (especially in the engine shop) or between two lines, since these run at high speeds (easily 50 per cent or 80 per cent faster than those I have encountered in Japan) and have therefore not been made totally reliable. However, thanks to strong commitment by employees, to a degree of pressure at work, and to sometimes acrobatic behaviour which is far removed from extreme Japanese rigour (Total Productive Maintenance, the five 'S's, total quality approach…), the results in terms of quality are good, and those in terms of productivity much better than in the previous decade.

In this contribution we shall therefore examine the nature and content of the syncretism of Japanese organizational techniques and the French social fabric: what is the French Way of achieving the modernization of the automobile industry? What are the foundations of its successes in quality and profitability? In order to answer these questions, we shall first analyse the conditions in which recovery took place in the 1980s and then several particular situations among French manufacturers, especially on the shopfloor. Finally, we shall show what remains to be done to secure the future of the automobile industry. While benchmarking remains essential (within Europe but also in relation to Japan and to Toyota in particular), it seems that the solutions will be more and more French ones, based on general principles which go beyond Japanese methods, since the issue at stake is the continuous growth of productivity, the fundamental goal in a period of stagnation of capitalism.

THE 1980S RECOVERY

After the losses of Renault and of PSA Peugeot-Citroën, the results of the two groups for recent years are as follows:[3]

TABLE 1

FINANCIAL RESULTS OF FRENCH AUTOMOBILE GROUPS
(Net profits in francs billion)

	1988	1989	1990	1991	1992	1993	1994	1995
Renault	8.83	9.28	1.21	3.07	5.68	1.07	3.63	2.14
PSA	8.84	10.30	9.25	5.52	3.37	-1.41	3.1	1.70

Renault has considerably reduced its debt, which fell from 55 per cent of its turnover in 1985 to 10 per cent in 1992. The state, which at the time owned practically the whole capital of Renault, contributed to the absorption of the debt through supplying capital,[4] in spite of the complaints of M. Jacques Calvet, chairman of the PSA group and main competitor in the French market, and the investigations of Brussels.

The two companies have been able to contain foreign penetration into France (at about 40 per cent), helped by the agreements to limit Japanese registrations to 3 per cent in France from 1977 onwards. In parallel the two groups, thanks to a distinct improvement in their products, improved their export performance. Exports now account for 66 to 68 per cent of PSA's turnover and it occupies third place in the European market, hoping to overtake General Motors; Renault was in fifth place in 1994.

The Foundations of Recovery

As with all the manufacturers in other European countries or the United States, industrial and financial recovery was based on improvements in quality, new design concepts and cost reductions.

As far as quality was concerned, Renault succeeded in transforming its image as a general producer, relying mainly on the lower and middle sectors of the market and producing vehicles of average quality. By creating a Quality Institute in 1988 Renault imbued in its personnel the idea of the importance of quality, in particular through intense programmes of training for final assembly operators. From the point of view of the design and manufacturing of vehicles, simultaneous engineering and project by project management techniques reduced delays in launching vehicles and somewhat improved the manufacturability of products. Both automobile groups also rationalized the use of components, beginning with vehicle platforms. For example the PSA group uses common platforms for its two

Peugeot and Citroën makes, as the following diagram shows:

TABLE 2
THE STRUCTURE OF THE PEUGEOT-CITROEN RANGE, 1982–96[5]

Market segments	Low	Medium 1	Medium 2	High	Single body
PEUGEOT	205 / 1983	309 / 1985	405 / 1987	605 / 1989	
	106 / 1991	306 / 1993	406 / 1995	"Z-8" / 1999	806 / 1994
	Saxo / 1996	ZX / 1991	Xantia / 1993	"Y-5" / 1999	Evasion / 1994
CITROEN	AX / 1986		BX / 1982	XM / 1989	

Note: Arrows indicate common platforms.

But it was from the point of view of reductions in manufacturing costs that the results were the most spectacular, even though they are still inadequate. First the manufacturers rationalized their relationship with suppliers, by reducing their number (800 in 1995 compared with 2,000 in 1985 and 600–700 in the near future) and by creating Assured Quality Suppliers (AQF) procedures which guaranteed total quality in all the parts delivered, often at reduced prices. In addition, the manufacturers no longer order parts but demand complete systems (braking systems, windscreen cleaning systems, for example) from the suppliers. This extended integration and partnership with the company guaranteed increased productivity and quality, since the goal of quality was shared and taken account of from the beginning of the process.

Second, both automobile groups considerably reduced slack time and modernized their productive equipment through massive investment, as soon as they had more or less sorted out their finances after the crisis of the early 1980s. For example Peugeot PSA, which was investing only around 4 billion francs in 1983, invested 7.3 billion francs in 1987 (7 per cent of its turnover) and 15.1 billion francs in 1990 (15.1 per cent of its turnover). But productivity increased mainly through a reorganization of work which had as its aim a massive reduction in wage costs. According to Jean-Louis Loubet the share of employee costs fell from 27.8 per cent of turnover in 1984 to 18.8 per cent in 1990 (8). Peugeot and Citroën lost nearly 60,000 employees in a decade between 1981 and 1990, or 27 per cent of their total workforce. Peugeot's management claims that the average yearly growth in productivity for the last decade was 7 per cent. It sets its factories annual goals of 12 to 13 per cent growth, often attained.

As for Renault, it too considerably reduced its workforce which fell by

31,000 (14.5 per cent) in only two years, between 1984 and 1986. The Flins factory increased its production from 1,600 vehicles per day in the mid-1980s to 1,650 vehicles per day at the beginning of the 1990s with 25 per cent fewer employees; but the average age of employees in this factory (47 years) is much higher than that of Japanese firms in Britain (30–31 years).

The principle ways in which the workforce was reduced in France were early retirement, aid for immigrants to return to their country of origin (an individual grant which might range from 40,000 to 80,000 francs) and the encouragement of voluntary redundancies (with an even more substantial bonus than the above and with various aids for setting up businesses). Today, the tools for dealing with variations in volume (flexibility in volume) are the use of over-time, temporary work or fixed term contracts in periods of high demand (or the launching of new models) and the use of 'technical unemployment'[6] in periods of depression.

The competitiveness of the French automobile industry is also based on the rather low level of wages compared to those of Northern Europe, the United States or Japan. During the last decade, a raising of the skills level of the workers looking after automated equipment was accompanied by reclassifications and wage rises. But these personnel are few in number. On the other hand the growth in wages of the great majority of workers with low levels of skills has been rather slow in the last decade. The trade unions themselves have had great difficulty in putting forward wage demands at a moment when job losses and 'social plans'[7] are prevalent. According to a CGT trade unionist questioned on the issue, 'the fear of losing one's job is much greater than before'. A CGT pamphlet (published in March 1994) reported that an employee of Renault-Douai (a factory in the North of France, near Lille) had been refused a loan by the DIAC[8] because his wage was too low! And the pamphlet pointed out, in conclusion, the contradiction between the growth in the productivity of work and the impossibility of buying the product manufactured by that worker.

The Price of Success

The industrial, commercial and financial successes of the French automobile industry have a considerable social cost (job losses and low wages, for shopfloor workers in particular). One might therefore ask why employees remain as involved and as motivated as they are today. In response to the same question, asked in relation to the automobile manufacturers of Japan, we answered[9] that 'Corporate Welfare' was a sufficient condition: remaining in a big Japanese company guarantees good social coverage, a pension and high wages which allow employees to be better housed and to provide their children with a good education (especially in evening classes or *juku*). In order to stay in the big companies Japanese employees submit themselves and conform to the standards of behaviour and productivity set by management. It seems that in the West and in France, the fear of losing one's job (the pressures of unemployment) acts as a functional equivalent to the threat of leaving a big company in Japan and its Corporate Welfare.

Thus compliance with the standards set by the company becomes obligatory for keeping a job in France, beyond a certain age, or for obtaining promotion and building a career for younger people. This is the more so as the automobile industry generally speaking pays its employees better than many other sectors. Among the standards to be respected by employees, clearly the most important are an absence of protest and trade union militancy. At the same time this situation, which is not new but which constitutes a new imbalance in the the relationship between capital and labour, does not mean that the company has become a concentration camp where a permanent and omnipresent form of social control of work holds sway, as a whole school of sociology maintains. The new standards and the pressures to respect them are in fact fairly willingly accepted by most of the employees who remain in the companies (hence the diffficulties experienced by militant trade unionism). They are all the more easily accepted as they are reconstructed and reinterpreted in daily working practices so as to make them more acceptable and make life at work bearable, though monotonous and repetitive. This constitutes a possible reinterpretation of the work of M. Burawoy on 'making out' in piecework, which argues that employees, especially older employees, play at reinventing the social rules of the game of work relationships to make them more liveable and agreeable. The employees' commitment to their work rests in part on such foundations, and on the local and constantly repeated reinterpetation of the standards prescribed by management into rules of the game which mark out and regulate the activity of the operators.

In summary, the achievements of the automobile companies, and in particular those of the individual shops, rest on this new eqilibrium in the balance of forces between capital and labour which favours consensus and work satisfaction, and in which protest does not really have a right to exist. This is what we shall now look at in a number of concrete situations within French manufacturers.

CONSENSUS, QUALITY AND PRODUCTIVITY IN FRENCH MANUFACTURERS

The transformations carried out since the mid-1980s were concerned both with production techniques and with the organization of work. The ways in which these transformations were put into practice – which clearly have social effects – are at the heart of the concerns of this study. We shall deal successively with the cases of Citroën and Renault.

Citroën and the Plan Mercure

From 1980 onwards, aware of the deterioration in the social climate and of their backwardness in relation to Japanese firms, Citroën's factory managers suggested to the company's head office that they should jointly consider possible reforms to improve the performance of the company. Thus the initiative for change did not come in the usual way from head office, but from 'operational' personnel, that is from those who were directly responsible for production and who wished to transform the productive system.

This discussion lasted for more than three years. It brought together those who had initiated it and the head office's functional directors in order to work out the generic principles of the transformations which were to be carried out. These were eventually translated into a plan of action,[10] the *Plan Mercure*. This title comes from the name of the hotel in which the discussion group's bi-annual seminars were held; it also relates to the fact that the god Mercury is the god of commerce. Since Citroën hoped to transform itself from a 'manufacturer' to a 'seller' of cars, this was an affirmation of the priority to be given to customers over the internal relations of the company. The *Plan Mercure* was then explained to supervisory staff through numerous meetings, which affected more than 5,000 people.

The *Plan Mercure* addressed both technical and social matters. From the technical point of view inspiration came essentially from Toyota and from the teachers Shingo and Ohno, since the goals were to accelerate and intensify production flows within factories and between factories and suppliers. At Aulnay, near Paris, where the AX and the ZX are manufactured, die changes for new production runs now take place in less than 15 minutes, which allows work to be carried out with small batches and reduced stock. The same goal led to a considerable increase in the periods of availability of machines, in particular through preventive maintenance promoted through a reorganization of work (see below in relation to modules). Finally, the concept of freeing the flow of goods makes bottlenecks caused by quality defects unacceptable; quality checks are therefore carried out while products are moving by operators (self-assessment) and quality defects are continuously evaluated through failure marks which position negatively certain sectors of production (and their men!) in relation to others. This systematic self-assessment has made possible the total, or almost total, elimination of rectifiers at the end of lines, and a reduction of the associated costs.

The originality of the way in which these ideas were adopted in France is that stock reduction and the adoption of Just-in-Time methods were a goal to be pursued; they were not applied immediately as the advocates of Toyotism recommend, with their aim to show up the weak points of the productive system with a radicalism which sits ill with Citroën's culture of adaptation. On the contrary, caution required that, while maintaining the goals of Just-in-Time, the main problems of availability and quality should be resolved first. The reduction of buffer stocks and the introduction of Just-in-Time methods were therefore introduced in stages so as not to make the flow of products vulnerable, until these goals were attained.

To meet the challenge of the *Plan Mercure,* the social organization of production was substantially changed. First the hierarchical chain was shortened through scrapping two layers, those of setters (who, in France, traditionally performed both a technical and an elementary managerial function) and shop managers. The new hierarchical chain includes the operators, the AM1 (level 1 supervisors), the AM2, sector managers and factory directors. If necessary, and for technical problems, the AM1 and AM2 are joined by Production Assistants (ADP) who are area technicians. The number of operators directed by each AM1 gradually fell from about 30 to an average of 18 in a decade, as a result both of job cuts (the workforce at the Aulnay factory has an average age of 41 years) and of the desire to reduce the gap between the AM1 and the operators. The goal is to have one AM1 per 15 operators, with this number varying between automated and manual sectors (around 15 in final assembly and up to 25 in the components factories; this figure has fallen to 7–8 on the assembly lines at Aulnay).

At Aulnay, in the assembly shop (with an average level of robotization) maintenance always takes place off the line, unlike in the Rennes factory (for the medium to upper Xantia models and the top of the range XM) where it is integrated into the production line, since the workforce there appears to be more flexible than at Aulnay. In the assembly shop at Aulnay, the operators, who over a few years have significantly improved their skill levels, deal with breakdowns which require less than 15 minutes' work; beyond this point they call the maintenance workers who are at the end of the line. On manual jobs,[11] the operators change jobs fairly frequently so as to diversify tasks, even though these tasks are in fact quite similar to one another and are equally repetitive. In the Rennes factory, there is little rotation of operators and multi-skilling only applies to a small percentage of the operators; those who are multi-skilled on three tasks do not have any additional status, which limits multi-skilling; they clearly have a higher level of autonomy and a better understanding of the manufacturing process. Multi-skilling favours promotion, which remains an advantage for the most dynamic operators.

The responsibilities of the AM1 have increased compared to those of the former foremen: on the one hand they are responsible for their budgets (for tools, spare parts...), on the other hand the results they obtain in terms of quality and volume have an effect on their careers (but not on their immediate pay; there are no productivity bonuses such as exist at Toyota). The AM1 have a computerized information display in their area and follow daily production levels; they are responsible both for the management of production and for the management of personnel.

Once a year the AM1 carry out individual interviews, based on an evaluation programme, with each of the operators in their section. Normally each AM1 has attended a training session for these interviews organized by the Human Resources Department. According to one AM1, the idea is to make the operators talk so that they evaluate themselves; then during the interview the AM1 present the results of the preceding year: attendance, participation in quality circles, quantity and quality of the suggestions made, satisfaction in relation to the declared objectives. The interview is also intended to oblige the management hierarchy to engage in discussion with the operators, both to make clear to them what is expected of them and to show them which development paths are available to them; it is on this basis that training is proposed to those who are interested.

The AM1 generally have at their disposal a production assistant (ADP) for technical problems. The role of the AM1 has clearly moved away from the resolution of technical problems, as was the case in the former system and in current Toyotism, towards management functions (administrative and productive) and responsibility for the motivation and management of personnel. The ADP are responsible for areas such as setting up production runs, and managing and setting up tooling; they have no hierarchical authority.

The AM2 – the rough equivalent of the former shop managers – work during normal hours and direct the AM1 of two teams, or a total of four AM1. They have a minimum of two years of higher education and satisfactory shopfloor experience. Their functions are also largely administrative and if they are successful they have the support of a production technician. On the other hand the sector managers who are in charge of four AM2 (or between 300 and 500 operators) often have a more technical role since they also, in most cases, are responsible for maintenance in their sector.

From 1985 Citroën set up quality circles, which are voluntary. They bring together between 5 and 6 operators, those most interested in their work. They meet for one hour every two weeks (multi-skilled workers fill in on their jobs). The quality circle always includes the same operators who may however invite others to join them, according to the problem treated. Discussion is about working conditions, safety, production and of course quality. The quality circles are generally led by an AM1, or even by an ADP. Depending on the personality of the leader, the circles may discuss particular problems in a rigorous manner over several meetings, or they may become the place in which social bonds are created in the team; sometimes a great variety of questions are debated, including life outside work.

The operators perceive that, through the quality circles, they may be able to modify and improve their jobs. Suggestions are debated there and this is one place in which they can be formalized with the support of the AM1, the ADP or a technician, since the operators are not adequately trained to be able to do this themselves. Subsequently the suggestions are dealt with by the AM2 and by the relevant technical services, who evaluate them and decide whether to put them into practice. The bonuses for suggestions range from 250 to 7,500 francs and each factory formally announces the prices paid for suggestions at an annual ceremony.

Beyond the suggestions and the quality circles, which concern up to 50 per cent of the workers in certain shops, Citroën has created under the *Plan Mercure* 'modules', which constitute an original way of resolving manufacturing problems. Ad hoc modules may be set up, for example when a piece of machinery is bought, but the spirit of the *Plan Mercure* is to create permanent modules to improve the processes of production. Each module brings together the AM2 of the area under consideration (as leader), any other AM2 who are concerned, the production technician, the maintenance technician, an engineering technician and a representative of the relevant peripheral services. The module meets every month or every two months, with each participant carefully preparing for the meeting, to discuss a particular technical problem and questions of productivity, quality or reliability. As can be seen, the operators are absent from the modules, given that they are technical meetings which go beyond their level of skills; it is the AM1 who make the links with the operators and with the quality circles on the matters with which they are concerned. While the quality circles and suggestions appear to be above all tools of social integration, with limited technical concerns and effects, the modules are considered to be the solution for the technical integration of the different participants and services which used to exist in a splintered form. Even if the module does not meet frequently 'it is permanent and permits the everyday management of the relations between manufacturing and functional tasks'.[12] In this sense it is strategic, since the traditional organization of production suffered greatly from its compartmentalization.

In the analysis of Citroën's transformations, an attempt can be made to distinguish between what is imitation and what is local creation. The general application of the Just-in-Time system can definitely be described as imitation, with all the consequences this entails, as at Toyota, in the rigourousness required in matters of equipment reliability and immediate quality at different levels. The second type of imitation is undoubtedly in the new importance attached to the technical integration of services (manufacturing/functional) to resolve problems and to improve the performance of the industrial system. The modules constitute a kind of diffusion and dispersal throughout the various parts of the factory of the job of determining organizational methods, in the same way as this occurs in the Japanese automobile companies and at Toyota in particular.[13]

The third form of imitation is the yearly individual evaluation of operators by their direct superior in the hierarchy, which deals mainly with the goals set for them and their participation in suggestions and the quality circles. But is this an imported idea or is it rather the systematization of a practice which already existed? In fact, supervisors have always had an important role at Citroën and to some extent had the same coercive functions as at Toyota. Promotion to supervisory jobs required membership of the SNIC,[14] the company union which appears even less capable of putting forward claims and of defending the interests of workers than most of the company unions in Japan.

According to one AM1, membership of unions, including the SNIC, is low. The SNIC is considered to 'sit on the fence too much' and to 'put forward "realistic" wage rises which seem too low to a lot of employees'. What is most striking is that no soothing speeches are made about 'teamwork' in its Japanese version (formalized by the advocates of 'lean production'). In the same way, there is only a minimum of displays of performance indicators on the shopfloor, unlike in most European factories which use them as an obvious barometer of the the workers' level of commitment. Finally there are no, or very few, daily or weekly information meetings where supervisors attempt to motivate their workers.

In other words, apart from the imitations and imported techniques referred to above, employee relations at Citroën remain profoundly traditional, with a form of work organization which is typically Fordist (with the traditional Fordist work team, and no attempt to introduce group working). Which does not mean that there is not strong social integration, as in Japan, thanks both to the nature of the dominant trade unions and to the very effective role played by supervisors, most of whom belong to the company union. It is these supervisors who hold together the team and who influence daily events through informal and yet effective means, thus enabling Citroën to avoid having recourse to the devices which are part of the Japanization process.

Renault and Cumulative Experiments

After the crisis and the financial losses of the early 1980s Renault's management decided it needed to carry out fundamental reforms in the company's culture. It recognized that even in prosperous periods (such as 1991–92) there was a need to make preventive changes designed to cope with future crises; this is why the period 1984–85 is described as a creative crisis.

Renault management considered it necessary to change mentalities in the company and prepare for an uncertain future by putting an end to certainties, established structures and fixed or rigid forms of organization. It appeared as though a culture of instability was being deliberately created. I shall take two examples to illustrate the current changes: that of the implantation of Just-in-Time systems (JIT) on the manufacturing lines of old gear boxes at Cléon, and that of the launch of a new vehicle in the assembly plant at Douai.

Instead of creating a new building to manufacture the new PK gear boxes at Cléon (in Normandy), management decided in 1988 to make extra space in an old workshop. At the time of the reconversion of the old production lines (and therefore of the old machines), management wished to introduce JIT. Its intention was that JIT should show up the technical and human weaknesses of the manufacturing lines so that the employees could compensate for them. We are thus at the heart of the application of the methodologies of the consultants who take their inspiration from Japan: the tensions of JIT were to enable quality to be increased and costs (especially labour costs) to be reduced, thanks to a continuous improvement in reliability.

To attain these goals, a number of new principles were applied: the transfer of gear box manufacturing from homogeneous machining units to line production, ordering single parts as they were needed, multi-skilling of the operators who were to be trained to carry out first level maintenance tasks, and collective responsibility. In reality, as is shown by a detailed study of Renault's achievements,[15] the changes brought about by the reorganization and by JIT fell well short of these goals:

- while buffer stocks diminished compared to the old system, the operators created new stocks (not foreseen in the plan) to cope with machine breakdowns or slow production changeovers;

- quality barely improved;

- the productivity gains were evaluated at 11 per cent , but maintenance costs (indirect costs) were slightly higher;

- there was no multi-skilling over the whole line (considered too complex for the operators), but 'homogeneous sequential sections' were created, similar to the old 'technological pools';

- the impossibility of moving to strict JIT led to a multiplication of regulations, the creation of small buffer stocks and greater complexity in the management of flows;

- the imposition of JIT from outside and the weakness of participatory measures (the supervisory staff did not believe in the reorganization) meant that the operators did not take ownership of the new organization; at the same time the more active role of the operators and especially of the setters allowed the elimination of one foreman's job;

- JIT increased pressures and stress;

- faced by these changes in their working conditions, the operators, who had temporarily lost their way in the organization, developed individual (and sometimes collective) strategies to protect themselves;

- the operators still had only a limited view of the line as a whole. Linked to an insufficient knowledge of the machines, this truncated view of the manufacturing process did not give them sufficient control over the information they received; their ability to anticipate was thus also limited.

We are here in a situation which is far from the situation described at Citroën, where the organizational changes linked to the implementation of JIT methods were introduced progressively, by stages. However the results are equally interesting. By completely different routes, learning about change was on its way. There was a real teaching effect and the conditions are now ripe for the introduction of a real JIT management system. The operators, the setters, the supervisors possess a 'vision of the process of production, of the product, of the machines, of the flows, of their relations with their colleagues and the hierarchy which is totally different from the view they had of them in the previous form of organization. They have found themselves essential actors in a new system, while their minds were still filled with the doctrines of the old organization (priority for volume rather than flows, the job station or the link in the chain rather than the line as a whole, volume indicators rather than the satisfaction of the client...). They have gone from a world where work was prescribed to one where it was less and less so, where it was necessary to react to unpredictable events, to know how to resolve problems...'[16]

At Renault, unlike in Citroën's culture of adaptation , the French Way of taking on competitivity objectives was the a priori transformation of employees' perceptions and understanding of their social environment (the rethinking of their relationships with others) in order to prepare them for future changes. This meant that, in this slow process, management now accepted the long term nature of social change, aware that it required time.

Another dimension of the French Way to a new productive model, closely linked with the transformation of mentalities and perceptions, is that of organizational experiments and step by step change, through the collective learning of those involved.

For example, the forms of productive organization put in place on the manufacturing lines for new engines at Cléon, and JIT on the manufacturing lines described above, were based on lessons learnt from the organization of integrated lines for the manufacture of the JB gearbox (installed at the beginning of the 1980s), which itself was inspired by organizational experiments in the manufacturing of crankshafts.[17] In the same way, in the second case concerning Renault to be examined here, the productive transformations accompanying the launching of the R19 in 1988 at Douai (in the North of France) were based on the results of experiments conducted during the manufacturing of the R9/R11 from 1980 onwards, which integrated professional maintenance workers in the manufacturing process.[18]

The launch of the manufacturing of the R19 was much better prepared and planned than the previous launches, thanks in particular to the setting up of a project group[19] which brought together several engineers and technicians. This project group first recruited the future operators and production technicians from the old shops. Not only were they better trained since they took part in the project before the launch took place, but they were motivated because this procedure made the project *their* affair. Finally, this practice permitted advance planning of jobs and careers.

The manufacturing of the test batches did not take place in as linear a fashion as had been foreseen on paper and did not attain its objectives. But the technical and organizational innovations which followed were facilitated by the fact that the operators, maintenance workers and supervisors already knew one another well and were committed to the project. The degree to which the team was able to respond to unpredictability and unforeseen events was proportional to its technical preparation and the internal quality of its social relationships. At the same time it became clear that the levels of achievement of the various categories of participants were directly related to the potential efect of their new role on their careers and professional advancement. For example the operators and especially the line charge-hands (generally formerly unskilled shopfloor workers said to have potential, that is capable of advancing technically) succeeded better than expected because they committed themselves totally to the challenge; for them it represented an opportunity to escape from their condition as life-time shopfloor workers. On the other hand, the maintenance workers and technicians failed to ensure the total reliability of the system in the designated time; their future in the new organization was less secure than that of the operators and line charge-hands because they saw themselves as being in competition with the latter in first level maintenance operations. Finally, the supervisors, coming from traditional manufacturing systems, failed to meet the demands of multiple functionality in their new role, by providing the lead in internal relations in the team and in training, both organizational and technical, for the new productive system.

Thus the first group, motivated by the prospects of promotion (financial but also symbolic) seemed destined to succeed while the others, even though they were equally committed to the project, were aware that their prospects were somewhat uncertain in the new organization. As a consequence the system reverted, provisionally, to the former form of organization, under which the maintenance workers rediscovered their autonomy and their identity through their differentiated status in manufacturing. It is true that this took place at the time when production of the new vehicle was being brought up to speed. Concerns with short-term production goals took on more importance than the structural improvement of the productive system; problems were not seriously addressed and palliatives were resorted to to keep up the planned rate of production. The statistical result was positive, since Douai broke the European record with a production of 1,500 vehicles per day after six months and 1,700 vehicles per day after a year. But in this organizational step backwards, the hopes that the line chargehands had placed in the original project were not met.

Further analysis suggests that this situation is even more complex, since the form of organization which became entrenched at these high levels of production was hybrid. Formally, the separation between maintenance and manufacturing sectors was maintained, but in practice exchanges between the two sectors were dense and fairly harmonious, on the basis of the introduction of techniques for improving and measuring performance. As a result of a number of concrete methodological innovations in work organization (such as 'Total Productive Maintenance') and new management tools (such as performance indicators and other measurements...), goals common to the different categories of workers were rebuilt and local leadership was reactivated.

This does not mean that these management tools and participatory methods were enough to motivate the shopfloor. On the contrary, it is because the introduction of these tools took place in the context of the long process started by the creation of the project-group that they were accepted and used, so that they promoted exchanges between competing categories of employees and helped them share the same company objectives.

The significance of this case is that, although the target-organization was never actually put in place, the cumulative effect of the experiments, and then of the process of trial and error, in fact allowed the company to get near to this objective without conflict or excessive traumas,[20] and to reach and then overtake it in a new cycle.

The French Way to the modernization of the automobile industry is not a carbon copy of 'lean production' or Toyotism. In the most determined and successful forms of implementation, it can be said that management:

- announces a target-organization or a guiding principle (which is to varying degrees inspired by what is known about Japanese productive realities);

- prepares the transformation of understanding, perceptions and mentalities through changes in concrete practices, that is through organizational changes which are limited and therefore acceptable;

- uses experiments which have already been carried out or conducts gradual and repeated changes, with advances and retreats, leading towards the target-organization.

In other words the French Way is that of gentle rationalization[21] – since all the Toyota techniques are in fact new rationalizations of old techniques –, by small steps, gradual and carefully assessed. It is perhaps here that its specificity and the basis of its success are to be found.

But these successes do not mean that we should not raise questions on the limits or obstacles encountered in the current transformations, and thereafter on their real nature and that of the 'new productive model'.

RENAULT: A HYBRID FORM OF WORK ORGANIZATION?

At Citroën and Peugeot, as we have seen, the organsiation of work remained quite traditional – which did not prevent it from being effective – and was based largely on the Fordist work team. At Renault, management decided at the beginning of the 1990s to adopt a system of Basic Work Units (*Unités Elémentaires du Travail* – UET). This was intended to be a break with the past, and to achieve more quality and productivity. The idea was to reorganize the work into teams with a maximum of 20 people (8 to 10 in services) managed by a unit leader, who was to be the first step in the hierarchy.

By looking at the origins of the idea of the UETs, it is possible to demonstrate the extraordinary complexity of the history of team and group working at Renault. These were sometimes inspired by foreign models, but on each occasion they were reinvented and influenced by the culture of the factory and even of parts of the factory. I shall then examine the concrete experience of the establishment of the UETs in order to show that their functioning is the result of permanent adjustments between the goals of management, the practice of the supervisors, the relative autonomy of the operators and the demands of production.

Renault was influenced by Swedish organizational methods. It set up semi-autonomous work groups at Douai from the mid-1970s onwards, in particular for engine dressing. At Cléon, at the beginning of the 1980s, final engine assembly took place on Automatic Guided Vehicles on which the operators installed themselves; each engine was accompanied on this guided vehicle by its 'picnic basket' which was filled with the parts that were to be assembled. The vehicle stopped at various job stations where operators used suspended electric or pneumatic tools (to improve ergonomic conditions). The loop, with seven job stations, lasted about 21 minutes and the work group was responsible for its internal organization; the operators could carry out the entire cycle of the 21 minute loop or a fraction of it, at their discretion.

In other factories, and especially at Le Mans, team working was organized from the beginning of the 1970s after a double phenomenon: the establishment of automated lines and strike action by shopfloor workers in support of a wage increase. The factory management was allowed by Renault's central management to recognise certain operators as 'authorized leaders of automated units', who thus became professional and therefore better paid workers. These led a small team of operators which had collective responsibility for production and its quality. The unit leaders carried out minor maintenance tasks which justified their new classification.

In the automobile assembly plants (Flins and Douai in particular), the installation of lines of welding robots also led management to reorganise work. It created work teams which were responsible for their own production and which therefore had the capacity to maintain the robots in working condition. Depending on the situation, they might or might not have recourse to an independent maintenance team.[22] Whatever the case, these teams had much greater functional autonomy than previously, essentially because the various participants in production had invented a scheme to cope with the technical demands of the robot lines.

In another Cléon shop where new manufacturing and gear box assembly lines were installed in 1980, a firm of consultants, given responsibility for the reorganization of work, proposed the establishment of operator teams directly inspired by the 'Japanese model'. Each team of operators (former unskilled operators trained to become skilled workers) was made responsible for the functioning of the line, for production, for the machines and for quality, with precise goals for the availability of equipment. The team leaders (who for a long time were called 'Super-operators', which demonstrates the force of the inherited culture and vocabulary) were made responsible for the leadership of the group and its external relations. As in the Japanese system, the team leaders take part in production once they have carried out their specific tasks.

In summary, when teamworking became the policy through the decision to create Basic Work Units (UETs) from 1992 onwards, the ground was not uncharted and a number of units of production or shops had experimented with teamworking, 'inspired' by Swedish or Japanese models, through inventing hybrid methods specific to their circumstances. This did not mean that the majority of shopfloor and salaried workers had experienced one or other of these innovations. For those who had had this experience for a protracted period, team-working had built a culture of collective responsibility and commitment. This team spirit also meant growing autonomy and responsibility for individual team members, and thus also an increase in skills and competence.

These various experiments, that is experiments which were not systematized but which fostered a growing culture of the collective spirit and the wish to 'work otherwise',[23] brought together certain principles which formed the basis for the 'Living Agreement' (*'Accord à Vivre'*) which was signed in 1989 by Renault management and all of the trade unions except the CGT. The 'Living Agreement' can be understood as a shared awareness on the part of the social partners, apart from the CGT, of the need to transform the company's professional relationships and work organization so as to improve its financial results and secure its survival. The 'Living Agreement' aims essentially to develop new forms of work which increase multi-skilling and productivity, through training for the workforce in general[24] and for shopfloor workers in particular, since the latter generally have a low educational level in French industry. The 'Living Agreement' also ensured that organizational transformations – and training – became part of the concerns about quality improvements of the Renault Quality Institute, set up in 1987.

The creation and then the generalization of the UETs after 1992 was one of the key aspects of the work reorganization. The organizational principles of the UETs were as follows:

- a single responsible employee placed in a short line of seniority (first level in the hierarchy, in charge of one UET, or exceptionally several UETs in the case of very small units);

- a maximum size of 20 people, depending on the technology to be applied, working together in the same time framework;

- a unit with a clearly defined product, with definite entry and exit points (principle of the client/supplier);

- physical management allowing, through performance indicators, the evaluation of the unit's competitivity;

- a bringing together and development of skills (multi-skilling and the integration of peripheral activities);

- a scheme of contractual participative organization (performance indicators, goals, progress plans known to all the unit's members, yearly interviews).[25]

The UET leader is on the first step of the hierarchical ladder, which clearly differentiates the UET system from the Japanese team or the Swedish (or German) work group. The team is quite large, which is another point of difference. The UETs, on the other hand, possess a functioning autonomy and evaluate their own performance through formal indicators, while their role and its boundaries are clearly identified through relationships of the client-supplier type; this brings them somewhat closer to the Japanese systems with their precise, multidimensional and permanent evaluations.

The establishment of the UETs could not be general or immediate. This is why six stages of development were planned, starting with the splitting up of each shop into UETs, with the identification of the main client and supplier, and moving to a structured organization functioning at full capability (with individual interviews, various meetings, follow-up of performance indicators). By demonstrating the extent to which it had achieved its goals, each UET could position itself in relation to the others. By multiplying the state of development of each UET by the number of UETs, the state of their development in the department or the factory as a whole could easily be measured. Finally, audit systems were created to help management to carry out this evaluation.

Two years after the start up of UETs at the Sandouville factory, its management reckoned that the establishment of the new work organization was 46 per cent complete. Sandouville claims to have initiated the UETs. From 1982, its management undertook simultaneously to 'broaden the outlook' of the supervisory staff through training in the leadership of work groups, to break down the compartments between services, to create quality circles and working groups for Just-in-Time production, to organize a contest on cleanliness (the 'five S's), to set up displays of performance indicators, up to the point of creating units, foundations for the future UETs. There are now only five levels in the hierarchy (operators, UET leaders, shop managers, department managers), as opposed to seven in 1985. The UET leaders have partly absorbed the functions of the setters (who should not be needed because of the operators' training) and those of the former foremen. They have the following functions:

- the management and leadership of the team,

- the provision of additional information on problems of quality in procedures and parts,

- relations with the engineering department,

- the organization of work (beyond the prescriptions of this department), in other words the assignment of operators to particular jobs (filling in for absentees, training for multi-skilling, rotation between jobs, checking of supplies, the malfunctioning of machines).

As a member of the factory management pointed out to us, 'all this takes place in a difficult environment; there are many demands on the UET leaders and some of them cannot cope with it!' The tendency is to recruit UET leaders from among employees who have two years of higher education, rather than among the operators. This is particularly because of the age of the operators (the average age at the Sandouville factory is 44), since it is generally considered that the best elements have already risen from the ranks.

In relation to the operators, management had already introduced a substantial socio-technical innovation: self-regulation of the line speed. On the assembly line, the operators moved forward the platform (on which the vehicle being assembled is fixed) to the next job station according to whether they had accomplished their tasks (within fixed limits, of course: the cycle time at that time was 1'49"). Through this form of self regulation, management considered that it had circumvented the permanent frictions and conflicts between supervisors and operators over working speeds (while previously these had been controlled through the speed of the line). According to our informant, this had been achieved through the transparency of self-regulation, since neither party could accuse the other of 'cheating': 'the mood has changed on both sides, with a return to greater confidence, and management has also made supervisors understand their mistakes: today rulings are negotiated and therefore accepted'.

At the same time, the self-regulated lines allowed work to take place at fixed stations, which is much less tiring for the workers, partly because the platforms position the cars at the right height. When self-evaluation (certifying that the work at that job station has been satisfactorily completed) gives negative results, the workers do not send the vehicle on to the next station and can call the UET leader, or more often the UET's technical assistants who deputize for the UET leaders in their technical functions. The technical assistants work in production for 50 per cent of their time; they assemble cars to keep their hand in, train the operators for multi-skilling and look after their machines. They receive about a hundred hours of training and are paid about 150–200 francs extra per month.

The operators have the benefit of an annual interview with the UET leader. This procedure also has similarities with the Japanese system, in which employees are very closely supervized, often with two interviews a year. But this similarity is formal since, in France, there are no open career structures in car manufacturing. In addition to the discussions on reciprocal expectations, the individual interviews are intended to distribute yearly 'career supplements' worth from 0 to 100 francs a month according to the merits of the worker.[26] Other forms of income may be added to the wage, such as those resulting from suggestions (*kaizen*) or linked to points won through 'Total Productive Maintenance', self-regulation or 'Statistic Process Control'.

As can be seen, the organization of work through the UETs remained traditional (which does not mean that it was not economically effective, as I have already said). The generalization of team-working appeared to have wiped out the benefits of the experiments which had been carried out at various places and times. It is of course always more difficult to generalize a success than it is to carry out a number of positive local experiments (positive because they were local?). It seems nevertheless that the creation of the UETs did not seek to build on the positive successes of the previous experiments, in the three following senses:

- in many cases the division into UETs was based on the old Fordist teams, thus failing to create technical units in the strong meaning of the words, that is sections of production which made sense to the operators as technical units autonomous from the others. Perhaps priority should have been given to the unity of the technical process in its antinomy, with the educational advantages that this would have entailed, rather than to the already constituted human group or the criterion of size;

- the considerable size of the groups (20 people) may have ensured that the team leader necessarily became the first step on the hierarchical ladder. In any case the UET reproduced precisely the Fordist team, while on the ground the UET leaders were often former foremen who, in spite of the training provided, lost few of the shortcomings inherent in the Fordist team. The restructuring could have provided the opportunity to create a more flexible leadership (see the role of team leader in Japan[27]), corresponding better to the new declared objectives;

- the UETs could have achieved much more if they had had more technical and management autonomy, that is if they had included men not engaged in direct production (maintenance, supplies, logistics, computing, quality). Instead, these technical services were themselves organized into UETs alongside the production UETs; the synergies and multi-skilling envisaged by the promoters of UETs were thereby reduced.

Perhaps this over-cautiousness in the the reorganization of work was the result of the fear of losing control, which tends to arise in any social innovation or change. For social conflict remains barely submerged at Renault. Even though the CGT lost its majority in the general company-wide elections at Renault, it retains considerable power in the local shops, where the cars are actually produced. The reform of work through the creation of UETs has been too 'top-down' with formal objectives (organization into UETs) which did not greatly disturb the existing organization. To go further in paradigmatic work changes would have meant granting much more autonomy to the base units, thus delegating more trust to the operators. This risk, it seems, management did not wish to incur, given the trade union divisions which exist in France and the attempts by unions to outbid each another which can result from them.

In fact the trade unions disagreed with one another on the question of signing the 'Living Agreement' and subsequently on the UETs. In 1992 CFDT-Renault stated the following in a pamphlet on the subject of the UETs:

> The CFDT has taken a position in favour of the changes in the organisation of work for two reasons:
>
> - First, they are unavoidable for the maintenance of an automobile

industry in France which employs several hundred thousand workers,

• Second, they may permit more interesting professional activity with continual evolution in job classifications.

But there is no question of maintaining a reactive attitude, merely adapting to the initiatives of Renault as they occur. On the contrary an offensive trade union attitude is required which demands and monitors the establishment of changes in work organisation.

The CGT, on the contrary, which claims that it was not consulted on the question of the establishment of the UETs since it did not sign the 'Living Agreement', points out and challenges the concealed objectives of the new organization of work: an increase both in flexibility and in productivity, without any resulting job gains, or wage rises for the workers who have jobs.

The interpretation of employee relations at Renault is thus complex from the point of view of the influences which the Japanese model may have had on Renault management. Even though 'lean production' has been the official political line of Renault since 1991–92 – it should be remembered that Raymond Lévy, chairman of Renault, wrote the preface of the MIT book[28] – the employment relationship has not (yet?) been Japanized in spite of management's efforts, in particular to weaken militant trade unionism.[29] In reality employee relations at Renault remain largely unpredictable. Even though the CGT has lost some of its power (in particular with the closure of the Billancourt plant) and its majority on the Central Company Committee, it retains a certain ability to mobilize the workforce over classification and/or wage demands. The CFDT, in its critical support for management decisions, oscillates between effective support and more or less radical denunciation of management's cautiousness in the introduction of the reforms. Finally FO, the second representative of the reformist position, feels obliged to maintain some pressure (particularly over wage demands) to increase its influence.

The situation in the factories is thus relatively tense but it is not explosive, as a result of the socio-economic context (the fear of unemployment), the weakening of militant trade unionism and the awareness of a certain degree of fragility in the company. As a result the supervisory staff play a pivotal role both in the application of the reforms and social change, and in the maintaining of social peace. In reality supervisors are solely responsible for establishing the UETs, whose ambivalent effects they are aware of. Thus if the UETs have significant autonomy, the role of supervisors may be at stake. On the other hand the multi-skilling which is part of the policy enshrined in UETs makes it much easier to replace absentees and considerably reduces the number of supply workers, so lowering labour costs, one of the variables on which the evaluation of supervisors is based. The implementation of multi-skilling and rotation between jobs is therefore viewed quite favourably, although a drastic reduction of the workforce makes it impossible to free operators to be trained and become flexible. Hence the emphasis placed by management and supervisors on the struggle against absenteeism; the latter fell from 10 per cent at the beginning of the 1980s to around 3 per cent in the mid-1990s in Renault as a whole.[30] It is well known that in the case of a 'Social plan' (see note 10) it will be the most frequent absentees who are the first to leave the company, while the career supplements (see above) distributed by supervisors are largely affected by the degree to which operators are present.

The unpredictability of employee relations is at the heart of managers' concerns. At times they use coercion. They also have recourse to integrationist policies such as those of the 'Progress Action Plans' which accompany the organizational changes and which, according to one manager, 'undermine trade union power by doing the job of trade unions'. This explains in a few words the specificity of employee relations in the automobile industry in France (with the variations between producers described above). They are unpredictable because of the continued existence of militant trade unionism and the failure to delegate trust. But they are also capable of creativity (hence the notion of progress plans) for mutual advantage when policies are pursued jointly and are based on trust (always for a limited period and needing to be constantly renewed).

THE FRENCH AUTOMOBILE INDUSTRY AFTER THE 'JAPANESE MODE'.

Japanese exports woke up the Western automobile industries, first in the United States and then in Europe. By offering lower prices for superior quality and variety ('options' are integrated into Japanese cars when they are initially assembled, for reasons of distance and transportation), Japanese exports raised international competition to a much higher level. It could be said that it is a classic case of the current phenomenon of the globalization of markets and economies.

It can then be asked what is the future of the French automobile industry: in spite of its achievements at the beginning of the 1990s, does its relative fragility, of which we have pointed out some elements, expose it dangerously to foreign competition? Or, on the contrary, will the French Way towards social experimentation, which allowed it to react positively to the big crises of the early 1980s, lead it to further successes?

After the total opening of European frontiers to Japanese competition in 1997, the level of penetration of Japanese vehicles is forecast at 16 per cent (excluding those built in the European Union), compared to 11 per cent today. In France, this penetration is expected to reach 9 to 12 per cent , compared to less than 12 per cent today as a result of the trade agreements. The risks French producers run of losing parts of their markets to Japanese vehicles are therefore real, but perhaps could be said to be at an acceptable level. What is at least as serious is that their market is being eroded, slowly but surely, by the other European producers, especially by German producers (including US producers in Germany) and to a lesser extent by Italian and even Spanish producers.

This erosion of French markets is counterbalanced by growing exports. But, as is well known, the costs of penetrating European markets is high, outside the producer's own strictly national space, in particular because of the price reductions that have to be offered. Renault wishes to become 'the best European generalist through the quality of its product and its service',[31] a formulation which PSA would not reject. The two companies are also attempting to increase their presence outside Western Europe, not only through trade,[32] but in production. In particular, PSA is establishing strong bases in emerging areas such as China (where it hopes to produce more than a quarter of the total number of vehicles manufactured locally by the end of the century) and India. The gamble is relatively costly for very uncertain results, but if these markets do take off, the profits could be considerable.

If we return to the French and European situation, matters are relatively simple. The image of French makes and cars has distinctly improved in a decade, especially as a result of improved and continuously increasing quality. But a dilemma remains for both groups. Should they retain high prices in France so as to keep high profit margins which feed into their financial results[33] with the risk of losing some markets, or should they reduce prices (and thus profit margins) to resist the pressures of foreigners, or even to reconquer market shares? This dilemma proves one thing, which is that French cars are too expensive in comparison with the competition.

There are two possible, complementary ways of reducing costs. The first is an improvement in the manufacturability of products. This will come from an increase in the effectiveness of simultaneous engineering which brings together research engineers, industrial engineers and factory technicians, to give joint consideration to manufacturing methods and the product itself. Enormous progress has already been achieved in reducting the development time of a vehicle (from its technical definition to its commercial launch). In particular, the French Way, with its accumulation of experiments, made possible a shortening of lead times while at the same time increasing substantially the quality of the final product.[34] Today, each manufacturer brings together small teams (from 300 to 550 people) called 'plateaux' or 'platforms' which decide on the best technical choices (for products and processes), while teams which are linked to them finalize the agreed solutions. The next stage is to simplify the products,[35] and therefore the industrial solutions, so as to reduce costs while maintaining standards of quality. The advantages already acquired in the matter of 'concurrent engineering' should make it possible to achieve such cost reductions on future models.

The second way of reducing costs concerns the process of manufacturing (at equal levels of manufacturability and automation). At Sandouville, our interviewee compared the Toyota factory in Great Britain, which manufactures 400 Carinas a day with 800 people, with the factory at Sandouville which manufactures 750 cars per day (Safrane and Laguna) with 7,500 people. The comparison is difficult because on the one hand the vehicles do not belong to the same sectors of the range and, on the other hand, Toyota remains an assembly unit without manufacturing support services, while Sandouville builds two types of vehicle and the lines were only running at half speed at the time for various reasons (commercial for the top of the range vehicle and bringing up to speed for the other).

Nevertheless the difference in productivity remains considerable. Given French traditions and the history of French automobile companies and factories, it seems difficult – and indeed not very desirable – to seek to reduce direct labour costs by increasing line speeds, as certain managers and organizers are thinking of doing. In particular it should be borne in mind that the average age range in the assembly plants is usually between 41 and 45 years in France, compared to 30 in Japan and in the Japanese transplants in Britain. Even if job stations have now been better designed at Sandouville, Flins, Sochaux or Poissy with the help of experts in ergonomics, work there, as it is abroad, remains in most cases physically harsh because of the positions of the employees and the repetitiveness of their movements (hence, from 38–40 years old onwards, the occurrence of back and repetitive strain injuries).

The second comment often made is on the large numbers of indirect workers who accompany the manufacturing process in peripheral activities (planning, supplies, logistics, quality, preparation, balancing, time measurement). This labour surplus through hypertrophy of the peripheral functions, together with the increasingly recognized need to make final assembly jobs more attractive, might lead the French manufacturers to a fundamental reconsideration of the idea of assembly work. The young workers recruited for the lines might hope to benefit from a career path (and thus from a substantial difference in their wages between the end and the beginning of their professional life in the company), by taking over fundamental aspects of the peripheral activities. This indirect work would increase the interest of workers in their work and would make it necessary to recruit more assembly workers because of the integration of indirect work into their functions, but would mean an overall reduction in costs (through a significant reduction in the number of indirect jobs[36]).

This big reform is the one way to undermine the foundations of Taylorism, since the workers would make a substantial contribution to the preparation and design of their own work. It is possible to envisage such a reform on the basis of the incremental experiments which are currently occurring in French industry. It would be an additional paradox to see the very Fordist French industry proposing a radically different organization of final assembly and taking its inspiration from Swedish reflective production, in particular through the lengthening of cycle times and a return to meaningful work (37). Although such a hybridization is not conceivable in the immediate future, the precepts of the 'Japanese model' are daily losing their attractiveness and force. The French manufacturers and their employees seem again to be facing their destiny on their own.

NOTES

1. The PSA Peugeot-Citroën group (abreviated as PSA) brings together Peugeot Automobiles, Citroën Automobiles and several subsidiaries (including Peugeot Cycles) which work mainly for Peugeot Automobiles and are mostly located around Sochaux.
2. I am grateful to Jean-Louis Loubet for his careful reading of this study and for the improvements and wise advice which he provided.
3. The two groups' good financial results in 1995 obscure much worse results in their automobile operations: PSA profits from these were only 0.5 billion francs, while Renault lost 1.7 billion. This situation was the result of a price war on the European market, with loss-making sales in Italy for example, and of manufacturing costs which were still too high.
4. Thus Renault was recapitalized to the extent of 20 billion francs, directly or through the cancellation of debts. According to PSA and Brussels, Renault received 28 billion francs between 1982 and 1994. Cf. Jean-Louis Loubet (1995), *Citroën, Peugeot, Renault et les autres. Soixante ans de stratégies* , Paris: Le Monde Editions, p.85.
5. Jean-Louis Loubet (1997), 'Lorsque Peugeot rencontre Ford, Sloan et Toyota ou trente ans d'histoire PSA Peugeot-Citroën' in Michel Freyssenet, Andrew Mair, Giuseppe Volpato (eds), Oxford: Oxford University Press.
6. On days of 'technical unemployment' the workers stay at home and are paid 70–90% of their normal wage. Part of the wage is paid by UNEDIC (the national fund for unemployment insurance) and the rest by the company, in the framework of an agreement which is specific to each company and is signed by management and the trade unions.
7. The 'Social Plan' is a procedure authorized by the state which has nothing 'social' about it since it is a case of dismissing employees. The social plan organizes training for the personnel concerned and seeks to 'redeploy' them to other companies or other activities; the oldest can leave in a process of early retirement financed both by the UNEDIC and by the employer, in the framework of an agreement signed by the state and the company.
8. A Renault subsidiary providing loans for the purchase of cars.
9. Cf. the final section in Robert Boyer and Jean-Pierre Durand (1996), *After Fordism,* London: MacMillan.
10. Cf. Sylvie Célérier (1990), 'Le Plan Mercure de la Société des Automobiles Citroën' in ECOSIP, *Gestion industrielle et mesure économique,* Economica. Xavier Mercure (1989), *Citroën, une nouvelle culture d'entreprise,* Paris: Les Editions d'Organisation.
11. According to an interview with an AM2, Jacques Calvet, chairman of PSA, is holding back robotization and automation in general in order to maintain flexibility in the volumes produced; the depreciation of robots carries on even in periods of weak demand, whereas operators can be put on 'technical unemployment'.
12. Sylvie Célérier, op. cit., p.347.
13. Cf. J.P. Durand and Joyce Durand-Sebag (1992), *The Hidden Face of the Japanese System,* Paris: D.T.T. Université d'Evry.
14. The *Syndicat National Indépendent Citroën* (Citroën National Independant Trade Union), a member of the *Confédération des Syndicats Libres* (CSL – Confederation of Free Trade Unions). At the Rennes factory the results of the 1993 elections to the *Comité d'Entreprise* (Company Committee) for the different trade unions were as follows:

    CSL (58%); CGT (30%); CFDT (6); FO (3%); CGC (2%); CFTC (1%).

    At Aulnay, the CSL and the CGT have approximately equal support, with a slight advantage to the CSL; but with the alliances between unions, the CSL generally obtains a majority of seats on the Company Committee.
15. G. Bauché, P. Charpentier, C. Lallemand, C. Martin, D. Tonneau (1991), *Réussir une organisation en juste-à-temps. L'exemple d'un atelier de mécanique chez Renault,* ANACT.
16. Ibid., p.156.
17. Cf. J.P. Durand, 'Usinage en continu et nouveaux savoirs professionnels' in J.P. Durand *et al.* (1986), *L'enjeu informatique: former pour changer l'entreprise,* Paris: Les Méridiens-Klincksieck.
18. Cf. C. Mahieu, 'Expérimenter et former pour gérer la production flexible' in J.P. Durand *et al.,* op. cit.
19. Cf. F. Charue and C. Midler (1992), 'Mutation industrielle et apprentissage productif' in G. de Tersac and P. Dubois (1992), *Les nouvelles rationalisations de la production,* Toulouse: Cépaduès-Editions
20. For a short critique of the concept of target-organization, see Part 2 of R. Boyer and J.P. Durand, op. cit.

21. Cf. 'Critique de la rationalisation douce' in *Futur antérieur*, No.10, 1992/2.
22. Cf. Michel Freyssenet in J.P. Durand, J. José Castillo, P. Stewart (eds) (forthcoming), *Teamwork: a Real Change or a Passing Fashion?* Oxford: Oxford University Press.
23. This was the slogan of trade unionists in the 1980s.
24. This was the purpose of the creation in 1990 of a 'jobs watchdog'. Consisting of a central organization which worked closely with the watchdogs for each unit, 'this joint consultation structure is responsible for identifying problematic trades at Renault, to establish the state of affairs and to follow its evolution. This work is then intended to enable the supervisory staff to propose, two or three years in advance, various solutions in the areas of training, mobility or redeployment. On their part, the employees can obtain a clearer understanding of their jobs and give thought to their professional prospects' (from the journal *Avec Renault*, March 1993). Several jobs sectors such as the commercial secretariat, maintenance and administration were analysed. The greater knowledge aquired led to the development of training programmes for the personnel concerned.
25. 'Les UET', *Les dossiers du progrès*, No.1, 1992.
26. Their distribution, as a percentage of employees, is as follows:

0 francs	30 francs	70 francs	100 francs
10%	5%	70%	15%

    The career supplements are added together from year to year but are nevertheless subject to a platform (about 1,250 francs for a monthly wage of 7,000 francs).
27. See on this subject R. Boyer and J.P. Durand, op. cit.
28. The original title of the book in English was in the past tense (*The Machine that Changed the World*) but became volontarist in French: *Le système qui va changer le monde* (*The system which will change the world*). This says a great deal about Renault's will to appropriate the concept of 'lean production' and its methodology.
29. During the period when Pierre Dreyfus was chairman of Renault, his desire to make this nationalized company a 'social show-case' led him to a kind of 'gentleman's agreement' with the CGT which played a considerable, though indirect, role in the policies of the company (which did not however prevent there being strikes on the initiative of the CGT, especially on wage demands). With the arrival of Georges Besse following the big crisis of 1984, the reduction in the CGT's influence, power and representativity in favour of the 'reformist' trade unions was one of the goals pursued in the interest of transforming the company's culture.
30. At Sandouville for example the rates were respectively 14% and 4%.
31. Cf. Renault's 'seven strategic goals'.
32. PSA's goal is to achieve a quarter of its sales outside Western Europe in the year 2000.
33. These are in fact lower for 1995 because of discounts offered for buying back old cars, in order to promote new car sales.
34. Cf. Gilles Garel (1994), *Déduction du temps de conception, concurrence et savoirs professionnels: le cas de l'emboutissage dans les projets automobiles*, Doctoral thesis, Ecole Polytechnic.
35. It appears that French vehicles offer better use value (especially in fuel economy, road holding, and safety in general) than their competitors' vehicles (especially the Japanese), but that this value is not apparent to potential buyers who prefer other more immediately visible facilities such as power steering, electrically operated windows, sunroofs, or air-conditioning. The French manufacturers may well have to challenge the 'engineers' power' which prefers an expensive *fine machine* rather than one dressed up in commercial attributes.

    The engineers could in fact regain their power through designing cars in *modules*, or coherent sub-systems which could be assembled onto cars belonging to different sectors of the range. Renault is especially advanced in this technique while PSA assembles the vehicles of its two makes on the same platforms (see above).
36. We are placing ourselves here in the context of international competition and of the search for lower costs. The question of the sharing of work, of its reduction and of a different distribution of wealth must also be posed, but it is posed at the macro-economic level and not *within* companies (see, for possible ways out of the crisis of employment in Europe, *After Fordism*, op. cit.).
37. Cf., for such an outcome, my chapter 'Volvo: l'innovation brimée' in J.P. Durand (ed.) (1994), *La fin du modèle suédois*, Paris: Syros. Cf., on the subject of reflective production at the Uddevala factory, K. Ellegard, T. Engstršm, L. Nilsson (1991), *Reforming Industrial Work. Principles and Realities in the Planning of Volvo's Car Assembly Plant in Uddevalla*, Stockholm: The Swedish Work Environment Fund.

Reactions to the Crisis: Job Losses, Shortened Working Week, Income Losses and Business Re-engineering in the German Auto Industry

ULRICH BOCHUM and C. DÖRRENBÄCHER

PRODUCTION AND EMPLOYMENT INCREASES IN THE 1980S

With a two-year delay the world-wide recession has caught up with German car manufacturers and their suppliers. At just below 3.9 million units, car production in 1993 fell to the level of 1980. The success story of the 1980s seemed to be over. During the 1980s, German car manufacturers set one record after another: between 1980 and 1985 production increased by 15 per cent, between 1985 and 1990 it went up a further 12 per cent. At just under 5.2 million units, production peaked in 1992, representing an increase of 34 per cent compared to the production level of 1980. Looking at these figures, one is somewhat surprised at the discussion on the German car manufacturers' lack of competitiveness that was initiated by the German employers. After the prosperous 1980s, the economic slump in 1993 came unexpectedly for many firms, even though the 1993 crisis of the auto industry was one of the best predicted of all times.

Many observers were surprised at the growing importance of this industrial sector, and everybody knew that things could not go on like this forever. Ecological arguments played a critical role in this assessment. It was also obvious that certain regions in Germany had become extremely dependent on car production and that job losses could be expected in times of crisis. The car boom triggered by German reunification concealed these problems at first. East German demand for West German cars was in effect an employment programme for West German companies: East Germans bought secondhand West German cars from West Germans, who in turn spent the money thus earned on a new car. Other European car manufacturers benefitted from German reunification in the same way. On the other hand, it meant the end of the East German car industry. Naturally, cars produced there were not competitive so that production figures in East Germany decreased from 186,000 units in 1990 to 19,000 units in 1991.[1] Volkswagen, GM/Opel and Mercedes-Benz took over the existing East German final assembly sites, in order to build up new capacities for the new markets in Eastern Europe. In 1993 145,000 units were produced at the newly established assembly sites in eastern Germany, and more than 250,000 units were assembled in 1994.[2]

Ulrich Bochum, C. Dörrenbächer, FAST e.V. Berlin.

Hopes that emerging markets in the east would allow this development to continue seemed justified. Volkswagen and Mecedes-Benz in particular had already established business links in East Germany and the Soviet Union before the collapse of socialism. Volkswagen supplied East Germany with a plant for the production of engines and as payment received engines manufactured there. Mercedes-Benz provided the Soviet Union with the technological know-how for the production of trucks, hoping for an expansion of their business. The reasoning was that should the Western markets be hit by an economic slump, sales in Eastern Europe could to some extent compensate for the losses.

In West Germany all car manufacturers expanded their production in the 1980s. Volkswagen alone built 500,000 more units in 1990 than in 1980, and manufacturers in the so-called luxury segment of the market broke the barrier of 500,000 cars. Even Porsche produced more than 50,000 cars in 1985 and due to the strong demand from the United States almost turned into a 'mass manufacturer'. With these figures under their belt, the German industry was hit all the heavier by the crisis in 1993: At Volkswagen and Opel production decreased by 25 per cent compared to the year before, Audi by 31 per cent, Ford by 30 per cent, and BMW by 12 per cent. Only Mercedes-Benz managed to increase their sales during the crisis by launching a new series.

As well as production, employment in the auto industry increased considerably in the 1980s. Between 1980 and 1992 employment in the narrowly defined automobile sector increased by 100,000. The employment volume of the entire vehicle industry came to 872,000 people in the late 1980s and thus accounted for 11.1 per cent of total industrial employment.[3]

At a time when industrial employment is losing some of its significance, this development seems quite remarkable. On the whole, the 1980s were characterized by the economic success of countries with high labour costs and strong trade unions, such as Sweden and Germany, as opposed to countries like the United States or the UK, who tried to regain their competitive advantages on the basis of low costs.

IS THERE A GERMAN PRODUCTION MODEL?

At the beginning of the 1990s the foundations of the German car manufacturers' success began to shake. The example of the highly efficient Japanese plant and work organization put re-organization processes on the companies' agenda. But which factors were responsible for the relative success of German car manufacturers until the late 1980s and with which factors should a re-structuring process start?

The specific (successful) German production model in the 1980s was characterized by high labour costs, high skill levels, strong trade unions and worker representation at the company level. Companies attempted to achieve a competitive advantage by pursuing a diversified, high-quality mass production scheme, reacting flexibly to customer wishes. This strategy was closely linked to industrial relations in the car companies. Roughly speaking, they consisted of three elements: binding wage agreements, worker participation and the protection of skill levels, as well as attempting to improve the general work conditions for employees.

This climate fostered a quick adaptation to the requirements of modern technologies. Mechanisms for the resolution of conflicts facilitated a cooperative, but, where necessary, conflictual relation between employees (works council and union) and the management.[4]

With the growing success of Japanese firms German manufacturers could not afford to keep up their strategy of leaving the highly competitive market for smaller cars to the Japanese, while concentrating on the more lucrative, but less competitive up-market sector themselves.[5]

The strategy of German manufacturers led to a continuous increase in the quality of their products (for example, more versions of the same model), which consequently pushed up prices vis-à-vis comparable Japanese products. Furthermore, the Japanese were by now beginning to offer the same quality for lower prices in the up-market segment of the market.

With the aim of increasing productivity, new microelectronic technologies and production automation were introduced on a large scale. Volkswagen's Hall 54', with an unequalled degree of automation of 25 per cent in final assembly, epitomizes this strategy. However, the system turned out to be less reliable than expected in the assembly operations. Buffers had to be established, emergency solutions were drawn up and personnel had to be on standby. Despite all efforts the process could not be completely mastered so that the hoped for savings never materialized and costs even went up.

In the late 1980s German companies pursued a technology-oriented productivity strategy. They did this despite the fact that the ensuing problems became more and more apparent, such as the high requirements with regard to training, as well as problems still occurring – despite all technological flexibility – when adapting production to new models.

As a result too much high skilled work was tied up in the ironing out of mistakes. This potential was thus not available for further reforms in the work process as such. The disappointment over the results of this technological strategy somewhat dampened expectations about further progress through the automation of production processes.

Efficient organization seems to be a serious problem for German industry – why else would they always be experimenting with new work structures, less hierarchical management structures and so on? As a result of disruptions in technological development many companies introduced some form of team work. A recent study shows, however, that many of the projects initiated were either abandoned after some time or somewhat watered down in their initial aims.[6]

At the newly built Opel plant in Eisenach, criticism of the global introduction of work teams is increasing. For the areas of body assembly, paint shop and final assembly a total of 203 teams with 6–8 workers each have been set up. Each group has a team leader, who is not elected by the members of the group, but whose post is advertised. The team leader is responsible for the framework conditions necessary to allow his team to achieve the production target, and if necessary, he works in the team. Team leaders in particular complain about stressfull working conditions according to the head of the works council. Obviously GM's target assembly time' of 20 hours for an Opel Corsa could only be achieved with a significant intensification of work processes: the work cycles for a certain number of operations were gradually cut from 152 to 110 seconds. These cuts, however, do not suffice. Meanwhile GM is aiming at an assembly time of well below 20 hours in order to keep up with Japanese and American plants. A survey among employees has shown that the increased pressure has had a very negative impact on the work climate.[7]

The Eisenach plant is well known as an example of one which has adopted lean production principles. In 1993 a third shift was introduced and another 1,000 employees were hired. Total employment now is 1,900. Opel carefully selected the workforce: mainly skilled male German workers with an average age of 34. Compared to other East German companies wages at Opel Eisenach are high but after some time questions will arise as to why Opel workers in West Germany earn twice as much. So a combination of lean production and low wages seem to be the key factors of success in Eisenach.[8]

A number of companies have introduced so-called individual work spaces removed from the assembly line, utilizing automated unmanned transportation systems. At the body-making stage certain last-minute welding, soldering and grinding activities (such as attaching the front and rear bonnets) were excluded from the assembly line. The unmanned carriers glide into boxes carrying the chassis and work teams carry out the remaining tasks.

Such concepts cut down on short work cycles as well as work-related stress. Job enrichment and advanced forms of self-organization within groups, however, could not be observed; changes only occured at the horizontal level (job enlargement). In the highly automated sectors of the stamping section and the construction of chassis, the teams responsible for a machine were supposed to rotate their tasks, but this attempt failed, too.

Recent studies on work process changes in the car industry put the share of system regulating activities at only eight per cent of production activity. System regulators are those workers who carry out supervisory tasks; in the chemical industry, for example, they account for 47 per cent of the work force. Despite their relatively small number in the motor industry, these employees are expected to play a key role in the reorganization of work and organizational structures, due to their important function in certain production processes. Despite strong technological pushes during the 1980s the car industry is still dominated by manual labour. More than two thirds of the work consists in activities characterized by their direct contact to the product, such as assembly, painting, grinding, welding, etc.[9]

Under these circumstances it comes as no surprise that the MIT report was taken as an incentive to improve internal organization and communication structures. For the management as well as the employees and the trade unions, individual interests are linked to the introduction of lean production. While the former are interested in running their plants at full capacity with more flexibility and work efficiency, the latter hope for more cooperative structures, and more responsibility.

After the publication of the MIT report on principles of lean production in the auto industry German auto makers tried to show their commitment to these principles. But right from the beginning the discussion on the MIT study was linked as well to companies' complaints over high production costs and labour costs in German plants. From this point of view the main problem of auto manufacturing in Germany is labour costs not the insufficient organization of production and work. The auto companies therefore emphasized, necessary' improvements in productivity and favoured short term cost reductions by reducing the work force as far as possible. The economic slump helped them to do this. So the concept of lean production in Germany is closely related to what companies think will allow them to regain lost competiveness. One could say that auto companies have tried to learn only two major principles of lean production: how to make people redundant and how to intensify the work of those who stay.

What about the unions and lean production? In general it can be said that unions' and employees' hopes for greater empowerment within work did not become a reality. When lean production was first discussed the unions and many works councils argued that the MIT report confirmed their criticism of management which did not take the opportunity for reforms of work processes and bureaucratic organization within the companies. At a conference in 1992 the powerful union IG Metall said that they would cooperate with managers in introducing lean production if this meant not only intensification of work, but more skills and democracy at work.[10]

But three years later it was apparent that lean production had led to a deterioration in working conditions. IG Metall argued that lean production, improving working conditions and more codetermination do not go together, and that stress and cost reduction targets now dominate work life. Particularly on the assembly line, efforts to humanize tayloristic working conditions had been abolished by companies who believed they decreased competiveness. For IG Metall and many employees, hope turned into disillusionment when they realized that lean production and economic crisis led mainly to improved productivity and left no room for better working conditions.[11]

To sum up the findings so far it can be said that the Japanese example has had some impact on the German car industry, especially with regard to expanding just-in-time processes in companies. On the whole, however, a complete adoption of the Japanese model seems highly unlikely. This is also true for the attempts to introduce lean production, a highly one dimensional perception which emphasized only the potential of employment reduction.

The next sections will show exactly what happened in German car companies in recent years and what kind of strategies individual companies pursued.

WHAT HAPPENS IN A CRISIS?

The crisis of 1993 has undoubtedly served to illustrate the existing weaknesses of the German car manufacturers and has made changes in the company organization processes essential. Tension between the collective bargaining partners has increased significantly. In the context of a debate on the production site in Germany, employers tried to save the German industry by setting up collective bargaining agreements on massive cost reductions. Between 1990 and 1994 about 125,000 jobs were cut in the car industry. These drastic cuts were dearly regretted when demand soared again in 1994. Extra shifts, working on Saturdays and overtime were the result for the remaining reduced work force.[12] At the Mercedes-Benz truck plant in Wörth, 3,000 out of 15,000 jobs have been cut since 1991. Yet in 1994 the reduced work force had to produce about 6,000 units more than the year before, a fact that created work intensification. The most important suppliers also considerably reduced work forces and were unable to meet the dramatically rising demand. As a result, short-term, often unskilled labour was employed and work processes either fell victim to rationalization or were intensified even further. Most of the jobs destroyed during the crisis were lost forever. Under these circumstances, the motivation and readiness to leave the trodden path and try out new forms of business organization might not be very pronounced. Product quality is likely to go down and repair work will probably increase. This development is diametrically opposed to the commonly touted ideals of lean production.

Cost cutting targets by reducing the work force not only caused problems in meeting rising demand in 1994 and 1995. Production increases heavily relied on car exports in the European and American markets, but pressure for further cost reductions was also triggered by a revaluation of the Deutsche Mark. In general, cost reduction through layoffs was compensated by the revaluation of the German currency against the US Dollar and other European currencies of about seven per cent in 1995.[13] Economic experts said that modest wage increases during the period of crisis must not endanger economic recovery. For the car industry this is a bitter result because it shows that job losses and income reduction do not pay off if changes in international financial markets cannot be mastered.

Below we choose four examples to illustrate the different reactions of companies to this challenge.

FIRST EXAMPLE:
BMW – SAILING THROUGH THE CRISIS UNHARMED?

To start with a positive example: BMW is a car manufacturer who sailed through the 1993 crisis without any discernible problems. The decrease in production was well below that of other German manufacturers, and between 1992 and 1993, 2,500 people (four per cent of employees) were laid off. Even though employment in 1993 is below the level of 1990, BMW has witnessed a continuous increase in employment over the 1980s and recently announced an increase in employment of 700.

With the takeover of Rover and the setting up of a production plant in the United States the year 1993/94 marks a turning point in the company development of BMW, in so far as it started a strong trend towards internationalization. Looking at the distribution of employment over different BMW production sites, a clear concentration of production and employment in the federal state of Bavaria can be observed. All important assembly sites were located in a triangle, all at a distance of no more than 100 km from one another. The Austrian site of Steyr with engine development and production was within reach of the Munich headquarters. The number of employees in foreign countries increased almost eightfold from a maximum of 5,000 persons to nearly 40,000 in 1994.

TABLE 1

BMW LOCATIONS

Location	Employee 1994	Product
Munich (+ Headquarters)	23,099	Final assembly 3 series stamping parts, engines (6 and 12 cylinders)
Dingolfing	17,528	Final assembly 5/7/8 series, axles, bodies, stamp. parts, ckd
Landshut	3,056	Plastic parts, other auto parts propeller shafts, light alloy cast
Regensburg	6,920	Final assembly 3 series cabriol.
Wackersdorf	500	Body-construction 3-cabriolet
Berlin	1,887	Motor cycles, auto-parts, camshafts
Eisenach	212	Tools, body-parts
Total German production staff	52,990	
Foreign Locations		
Rosslyn / RSA	2,920	Dkd-assembly operations
Spartanburg / USA	600	Ckd-assembly 3series
Rover / UK	33,000	Own brand
Steyr / Austria	2,100	Engines
Total foreign production staff	38,600	
Vehicle production BMW (1000 units)	1994	574,000
Vehicle production Rover (1000 units)	1994	487.000

Source: Annual reports

For a German manufacturer of large cars the decision to internationalize production is an unusual step. This holds especially true for BMW's decision to eventually supply the US market from its own production plant.

In September 1994 the first BMW left the assembly line in Spartanburg, South Carolina. By the end of the decade BMW is aiming at an annual capacity of 90,000 cars with about 2,000 employees.

It is interesting to note in this context that BMW is establishing organizational structures in Spartanburg which comply with the ideal of lean production which could never be realized in Germany. Low wages, no trade union representation of employees and less hierarchical management structures distinguish BMW production in the States from its German counterpart. Nevertheless, the BMW managers are taking no small risk by setting up a production plant in the United States – BMW simply cannot afford to build cars of an inferior quality there. Therefore, production will increase only slowly and employees are carefully chosen. For the 600 jobs on offer so far, up to 60,000 applications have been received.[14] Applicants were put through difficult tests and afterwards some underwent their on-the-job training at German plants. Production workers start with an hourly wage of 12$, which gradually increases to 16$. In addition, BMW provides full free health insurance, accident insurance, a savings scheme, to which the company contributes up to three per cent of annual wages, and attendance bonuses. With a top wage of 16$ an hour BMW does not come up to the 18$ an hour agreed between the Big Three and the UAW. Up to now, BMW has taken great pains to create a climate which will make worker representation superfluous.

With its decision to manufacture in the US, BMW is the first European car producer to dare cross the Atlantic again. After Germany, the States represent one of the most important markets for BMW, and one which in the long run could not be supplied from Germany without problems. There are several good arguments for shifting production to the US: the proximity to this crucial market, more flexible production conditions, lower costs than in Germany and substantial subsidies from the local administration. For the time being, Spartanburg is no threat to German production sites.

The decisive step towards an internationalization of BMW's corporate structures was taken with the decision to buy out Rover. This decision was met with surprise in Germany, but in the meantime it has become clear that the takeover provides BMW with an entry ticket to important segments of the vehicle market: small cars and four-wheel-drive utility vehicles. Furthermore BMW has not yet produced front-wheel-drive technology. Taking into consideration the information available so far, BMW's strategy after the takeover can only be called very sensible.[15] Evidence suggests that Rover's sales abroad will pick up rather than decrease. At the same time BMW has always stressed Rover's independence and is not planning to lay people off.

Since 1990 BMW has been trying to involve its suppliers in the development of new models at an early stage, setting up process-oriented project teams, designed to have a general view of the planning of a new car, from procurement of parts to final assembly. BMW's procurement policy regards about ten per cent of the parts bought from external suppliers as just-in-time-suitable. These ten per cent account for about 60 per cent of the cost of external supplies. Together with Audi, BMW has succeeded in setting up a logistical triangle between Munich, Regensburg and Ingolstadt, where a number of suppliers of just-in-time parts, who sell predominantly high-value parts are located: seats, bumpers, cable harnesses, exhaust catalysts, etc. BMW's most important supplier of tyres, Pirelli, is hooked up to the firm's information system and can thus produce and supply just-in-time. In the long run BMW is aiming at further reducing the number of suppliers from about 1,200 to 900.

The policy of BMW's management – even in times of crisis – can only be called very sensible. The company was the only German car manufacturer to make profits in the crisis year of 1993. Unlike its competitor Mercedes, BMW resisted the temptation to expand capacity during the car boom and thus did not have to resort to short time work. The company pursues a clever policy, often offering its clients new models or new engines. It thus managed to increase sales in the United States by 20 per cent in 1993. The development department with its 5,000 employees is located at one single location and has a model character with regard to working in project teams. BMW is also very advanced in so far as agreements on flexible working time is concerned: At the Regensburg plant, employees work a total of 36 hours in a so-called flexible working week, but the plant runs at full capacity for 99 hours. Various banks attest that BMW has the most favourable cost structure in the German car industry, and an excellent personnel management to boot. Up to now not a single agreement between the board and the works council has been cancelled, and there were no sudden cuts in wages, such as at Mercedes-Benz.

What also distinguishes BMW from its major competitor is the fact that the company has always concentrated on its core business, cars, and not undertaken costly excursions into other sectors. The portfolio of companies is still of manageable size. BMW has savings of about five billion DM, enough to undertake possible further acquisitons or to further develop the existing companies and the cooperation with Rover. The importance of a clever management policy in times of crisis for employees and their jobs cannot be overestimated. The example of other, less fortunate companies shows that mistakes in management and rash decisions aggravate crises. In contrast, BMW's relatively stable development in times of crisis and the relative stability of jobs can be attributed to flexible company structures which leave more scope for measures going beyond the classical instruments, such as layoffs, cuts in investment projects, and other steps taken at the expense of employees.

SECOND EXAMPLE:

MERCEDES BENZ – LOSSES, LAYOFFS, NEW CAPACITIES

The Mercedes-Benz AG represents the vehicle sector within the group Daimler-Benz. The Mercedes-Benz group comprises 12 manufacturing sites for automobiles and commercial vehicles, as well as 18 production and 25 assembly sites abroad. The company has four assembly sites in the car sector, three in Germany and one in South Africa. In 1993 the assembly sites in Sindelfingen (near Stuttgart) and Bremen were complemented by a third newly built in Rastatt. Among the domestic plants there is an intensive network for the production of aggregates, body parts and other components. With 45,000 employees Sindelfingen is the largest (integrated) automobile assembly site with a capacity of 1,600 units per day (compact class, S-class). There are close links to the Bremen plant: every day stampings for 500 units are exchanged between Sindelfingen and Bremen and 150 estate model chassis take the night express train from Bremen to Sindelfingen.

The structures of Mercedes-Benz's automobile production differs greatly from those of the commercial vehicle sector; the former is concentrated almost exclusively in Germany, whereas the latter is highly internationalized. This clear distinction was somewhat blurred during the crisis, in so far as Mercedes decided to build a new production plant for the four-wheel-drive sport utility car market in Tuscaloosa, Alabama. Like BMW in Spartanburg, Mercedes is planning on 65,000 units with 1,500 employees from 1996.[16] The production manager of this new plant used to hold the same position at the Toyota transplant in Canada. Unlike BMW, Mercedes-Benz will not use its US site for the assembly of kits, but produce from scratch. The entire plant layout is strongly influenced by the Japanese example.

The decision to internationalize the production of Mercedes cars is as unusual for Mercedes-Benz as it was for BMW. The reasons, however, are similar: proximity to markets, more favourable cost structures for planned exports (about 50 per cent of the vehicles are earmarked for export), and the trying-out of new forms of organization.

What the impact of this transplant on the German plants will be remains to be seen. In Germany, Mercedes-Benz was hard hit by the crisis. In 1993 the losses in operating business amounted to 1.2 billion DM and there was justified concern over this most important pillar of Germany's largest group. Simultaneously, there was increased pressure on employees, the planned expansion of capacities was cancelled and the production of Mercedes's new small car in Germany became doubtful:

- Mercedes had planned the building of a new plant for the production of light and medium weight trucks in east Germany, with an investment volume of one billion DM. The setback in the market for commercial vehicles invalidated this decision. Last but not least due to the intervention of the works council, who did not see the point of building new capacities when existing capacities were under utilized, the planned new manufacturing plant was turned into a mere assembly site.

- Mercedes is planning to build its new baby-Mercedes from 1997 at the newly built plant in Rastatt, which is at present not running at full capacity. The board played off low-wage locations, such as the Czech Republic, against the high labour costs at the Rastatt site. The works council had to make major concessions in order to have this model built in Germany; fewer jobs at the new plant than initially planned, as well as a general cost reduction by a one per cent cut in the wage increase for 1995/96, which is calculated against bonus payments. Simultaneously, an employment moratorium was agreed which foresees no redundancies in the near future.

- Since 1992, 38,500 jobs have been cut at Mercedes-Benz. The 14,000 jobs that were on the line for 1994 included some redundancies, but the works council warded these off by agreeing to lower wage increases. To Mercedes employees the threat of redundancies came as a real shock. The threat to shift production to other European sites intimidated employees and works council alike, even though the realization of this announcement never seemed very likely. After all, Mercedes has a new state-of-the-art plant in Rastatt, where after extensive consultation with the works council the introduction of new team-work structures was planned. The management thus took advantage of the weak situation of its employees during the crisis for cutting down wages. However the works council could not hinder the management's decision to locate the new production site of the Swatch Car to France.

- In order to make organizational structures at Mercedes-Benz more efficient, the number of hierarchical levels was cut down. Below the board, the management consisted of four levels of executive management: directors, heads of section, executive heads of department and, as executive organ, the heads of department. Communication between these levels was slow and had to observe the formal hierarchies. In the course of the reorganization one level of middle management was abolished, so that now there are three groups of executives below the board: a directorate, an upper executive circle and an executive circle. The new structure is said to have greatly improved the conditions for project and team work, but one has to bear in mind that a reorganization as such does not create a new management culture.

- In order to improve cost structures, Mercedes-Benz has initiated a number of projects with other companies and shifted tasks to supplying firms. In order to achieve better economies of scale with steering systems they set up a company for the production of these systems together with Volkswagen and ZF (the joint company is headed by the supplier ZF). Another example is the setting up of a company for the manufacturing and distribution of valve systems, which is headed by MWP (Mahle-Wizemann-Pleuco), another Mercedes-Benz supplier. Mercedes contributes its own valve production in Bad Homburg to this joint venture. The company will buy the six-cylinder engines for its planned Mini-van entirely from Volkswagen.

- In the factory more changes are under way that involve a direct exchange of production workers: At the Bremen site the supplier's workforce is taking over the production of car seats, using a hall on the manufacturing site. The 170 Mercedes workers responsible for this task before now either work for the supplier or have taken on new tasks in the plant.

On the whole, Mercedes' situation has stabilized over the year, last but not least due to the excellent sales figures for the new C-Class. The crisis has had a lasting impact, however, and Mercedes-Benz has had to come to terms with the fact that the golden times are over for good. The impact of the recent changes cannot be judged before the introduction of the new medium price range series in 1995. Mercedes's expansion into new sectors, such as small cars, may also carry no small risk.

TABLE 2

MERCEDES-BENZ IN THE FIRST HALF OF 1994

	First half 1994	First half 1993	Change (%)
Turnover Mio DM	34,675	29,075	+19,3
Employees 30.6.	200,528	213,315	-6,0
Cars			
Turnover Mio DM	21,164	17,232	+22,8
Sales (Units)	296,770	211,507	+40,3
Production (units)	302,076	209,351	+44,3
Employees (30.6.)	84,524	93,336	-9,4
Trucks			
Turnover (Mio DM)	13,511	11,843	+14,1
Sales (Units)	135,113	117,507	+15,0
Production (Units)	140,011	116,462	+20,2
Employees (30.6.)	82,582	86,862	-4,9

Source: Mercedes-Benz

THIRD EXAMPLE: VOLKSWAGEN – SUDDEN AWAKENING

Following the takeover of SEAT and Skoda, Volkswagen in the early 1990s initiated a restructuring programme, which was designed to test new organizational concepts. Even though VW had managed – against the current trend – to increase turnover, production and employment figures in the course of the 1980s, operational profits were down by 110 per cent between 1983 and 1992. The company produced record figures with regard to market volume and the tangible fixed assets, but made hardly any profit. The company policy seemed to be too concerned with expanding sales and investment, instead of increasing organizational efficiency.

This strategy is reflected in their attempt to generate new capacities and to build a number of future-oriented production sites. VW established additional capacities in east Germany (Mosel Plant), a new SEAT plant in Matorell (Barcelona), and together with Ford they set up a plant for Mini-vans in Portugal. In addition, there were new capacities at Skoda in Mlada Boleslav, in Mexico and in China. It was recently announced that, together with a local company, VW has set up a joint venture in Taiwan for the assembly of about 30,000 light commercial vehicles. Capacities there could be increased to 150,000 units.

Looking at the development of new capacity, it becomes clear that VW is planning to increase its production by almost 50 per cent. Most of the growth is taking place on the periphery of Europe and in China, but by building a new plant in eastern Germany, Volkswagen is also considerably increasing its capacity in Germany. This increases the competition with the traditional core plant in Wolfsburg. Currently, VW's bread-and-butter car, the Golf, is built at four locations: in Wolfsburg, Brussels, Mosel and in Mexico. With minor adjustments, it could also be built in Spain and in China.

The contradiction between market success on the one hand and low profitability on the other came to a head in 1993. After 1992 had seen profits of just under 600 million DM, operating sales accounted for a loss of 1.6 billion in 1993. 'We can only pray' was the comment of many newspapers when faced with this result. In this situation Volkswagen announced the cutback of about 30,000 at the six domestic plants for the period 1994/95. The board informed the company works council that less than 50 per cent of the planned redundancies were due to volume reductions. It was obvious that the classical instruments of short time work and early retirement were not adequate to deal with the present employment situation.[17]

TABLE 3

PRODUCTION SITES OF CAR ASSEMBLY AND PLANNED ADDITIONAL
CAPACITIES OF VW-GROUP

Location	Production 1990 1000 Units	Additional Capacity 1000 Units	New Plant
VW Germany			
Wolfsburg, Emden, Hannover	1,644		
VW Saxony Mosel	2	250	Mosel II
Audi AG			
Ingolstadt, Neckarsulm	430		
VW Brussels	206		
SEAT, Barcelona,			
Prat, Pamplona	533	400	Matorell
TAS, Sarajewo	37		closed
Skoda Czeck Rep.		340	M. Boleslav
VW Bratislava		3	Bratislava
VW /FSR, Poland		5	Poznan
AutoEuropa (VW/Ford)		80	Setubal
VW Mexico	214	150	Puebla
Autolatina	290		
VW South Africa	50		
VW Shanghai	19	150	Shanghai
FAW-VW	10	150	Changchun
VW/Ching Chung		30	Taiwan
Total	3,435	1,618	

Source: Annual reports, Press information

The works council and the trade union IG Metall were faced with the alternative of either walking open-eyed towards mass redundancies or acting in solidarity in finding a solution for the present employment dilemma. Two pieces of background information are necessary to be able to judge the situation. First, Volkswagen's employees work under a company wage agreement, which guarantees them incomes above the average for the industry; second, a gradual reduction of the weekly work-time during the 1980s had already proved to be a valuable instrument to limit job losses. As a response to the works council's demand for an employment concept the board published its Reflections on the further development of employment policy at Volkswagen. The core suggestion was a reduction of the weekly work time to 28.8 hours or four working days. This model was to be applied to all groups of employees from the board to workers and would come with corresponding cuts in monthly payments. In return the IG Metall and the works council demanded that there be no redundancies and that the agreement would only be valid for a limited time span. Furthermore, special regulations for trainees and older employees were negotiated, as well as a combination of full-time work and further qualifications.

IG Metall was determined that a 20 per cent reduction in working time could not entail a 20 per cent reduction of monthly wages. At the same time, such a big reduction of working time at such short notice could not be realized with full wage compensation. VW was expected to pay its share for the new work scheme, too.

At this final point negotiations hit an impasse. VW considered the setting of a time limit as their contribution; they argued that further financial sacrifices from them were unreasonable. Various talks finally led to an agreement on keeping wages at the level of October 1993. In particular, it was agreed that:

- the introduction of the 35-hour work-week, originally planned for October 1995, was advanced to the 1.1.1994 (with full wage compensation).

- the already agreed upon wage increase of 3.5 per cent for November 1993 was used to compensate for wage losses and thus converted into work time.

- in anticipation of the wage negotiations of August 1994 a wage increase of one per cent was granted.

- the usual annual bonus of 96 per cent of monthly wages and part of the holiday payment were transformed into monthly payments.

- VW contributed about two per cent.

This agreement granted Volkswagen's employees unchanged monthly wages. It was clear that agreed bonuses could only be turned into monthly payments for a limited time span. The most important result, however, was that about 30,000 jobs were thus saved.

The agreement was much discussed and talked about in Germany. Particular attention was given to the question of how far this agreement might serve as an example for other sectors or companies. In principle, the reduction of work time with partial wage compensation is a tool to avoid redundancies. However, VW was in a privileged position. Wages are not as high everywhere. In the context of German collective bargaining agreements, where employers always bring up the spectre of economic doom when a further reduction of work time is put on the agenda, the contract has had a positive impact. Furthermore, in the case of an upswing in the economy, which can already be observed at some VW locations, it allows management to be flexible by shifting employees between plants.

On the whole, Volkswagen's economic situation had stabilized by the end of 1994. However, despite the contract on the reduction of the weekly work-time, employment prospects are not guaranteed. The works council, too, explicitly ties the company's future success to further improvements in work productivity and further cost reduction. Certain Volkswagen departments deliberately seek the cost comparison with external suppliers. By in-sourcing production processes that were formerly given to external contractors they hope to get back jobs at Volkswagen. It is clear, however, that the financial losses tied to work reduction are regarded ever more critically.[18]

FOURTH EXAMPLE:

A SUCCESS STORY IN THE CRISIS? –

BUSINESS REENGINEERING AT PORSCHE

After years of being flooded with lean production concepts, the latest fashion is business reengineering. The term first cropped up in a study by the US business consultants Hammer and Champy,[19] published in 1993, and soon became the new corporate buzzword.

Particularly for companies who lacked competitiveness, business reengineering seemed to be a highly promising concept. The aim is not a continuous, step-by-step improvement of organization and production, but a radical renewal of the entire company. The intention behind this is not to proceed from 12th to 11th rank among the competitors, but to become the market leader, if possible on a global scale.

Such aims can only be achieved with radical measures: for the benefit of the customer, production time and cost are to be reduced drastically. Tayloristic thought and work processes do not aid in this context. Several related work processes have to be integrated and brought into an order that complies with customer demands. Specialists are increasingly making place for generalists, who, assisted by modern information systems, are in command of several working practices. Specialized departments are turned into process teams, who in the framework of clearly defined production goals are granted extensive decision-making rights in the carrying out of complex managerial tasks. Entire management levels are thus made redundant or will have to adapt to new tasks.

These changes are naturally not easy to implement, so the entire project needs to be carefully planned. It demands a leader from the top management level to initiate the entire reengineering process and to lend the project credibility within the company. Furthermore, it requires an reengineering team, consisting of concerned employees and external experts (business consultants, data processing specialists and customers). This team is designed to develop and implement the new concepts. A brainstorming session can serve to question existing production patterns. Additionally, successful solutions found by companies from other sectors or different countries have to be adapted.

Protest against the realization of reengineering projects has to be expected, not only from the employees, whose number is to be reduced, but also from the levels of lower and middle management, whose supervisory tasks will largely be taken over by the process teams, thus allowing less hierarchical management structures. This opposition is met by a strategy based purely on the acceptance of necessities, presenting changes as unavoidable and appealing to the employees' sense of fair play and ambition. Business reengineering concepts are presented as imperative if competitiveness is to be maintained. The vision is supposed to consist in tangible results, produced by the new concept. So much for the theory.

From the mid-1980s onward, exorbitant prices customers could no longer afford, the crisis in the triad (western Europe, USA and south-east Asia) and the fall of the American Dollar propelled Porsche into a crisis of unknown proportions. The number of cars sold fell from 53,000 in 1985/86 to about 23,000 in 1991/92. Business results deteriorated continuously. In 1991/92, for the first time in company history, Porsche made a loss.

This was the reason the Porsche management began to look for new ways forward. Having extensively studied production at Toyota, Mazda and Mitsubishi, the Porsche board decided to radically redesign existing production by 1996. The aim – or, in reengineering lingo, the vision – was to introduce new manufacturing processes which would result in less hierarchical management structures. This in turn would improve the price/performance ratio of Porsche models and allow the company to capture a market share of at least 20 per cent in the sports car segment, naturally making a profit.

Interim results show that so far Porsche`s reengineering concept seems to be working. By mid-1994 the restructuring process implemented with the aid of Japanese business consultants had led to 35 per cent reduction of assembly time and 25 per cent rationalization of the production process, compared to the figures for 1992. According to W. Wiedeking,[20] chairman of the board, not one Porsche worker in 1994 worked in the same position he had occupied 18 months before, and two levels of management had been made redundant. Space requirements have gone down considerably and the know-how acquired in the reengineering process is being used in an independent consulting department. Since May 1994 Porsche has been writing black figures again.[21]

However, Porsche's reengineering success has its dark sides – especially for the employees. No less that 30 per cent of production workers and 38 per cent of management have lost their jobs in the course of the reengineering process so far, about 2,500 jobs have been cut since 1990/91. The management is planning a further reduction of 300–500 jobs.

With the smug remark, 'We have picked the right ones', Wiedeking also confirmed that at least at the middle management level cuts were carried out not according to social, but on performance criteria. Among blue-collar workers, who had to bear the brunt of the cuts, Porsche tried to optimize performance via an extensive use of early retirement schemes.

For the remaining employees reengineering has not exactly meant a bed of roses, especially since Porsche has neglected to use the restructuring process for the introduction of innovative work concepts, such as semi autonomous work groups. So far, only a system aimed at continuous improvement (Kaizen) has been introduced under the name of Porsche Improvement Process (PVP – Porsche Verbesserungsprozeß). In tough negotiations the works council has achieved the concession that decisions on controversial suggestions for improvement have to be unanimous. This, however, does not apply to the introduction of entirely new production methods, which after all lie at the heart of business reengineering. These decisions will still be taken exclusively by management; corresponding investments are also their prerogative. This could be observed in the area of engine production, where management ordered the introduction of continuous assembly line production, which considerably aggravated the work conditions of affected employees.

The utilization of this and similar approaches can be held largely responsible for Porsche's productivity gains mentioned above. Other important factors were the reduction in the number of external suppliers and the increasing standardization of parts. In some rare cases (for example in the paintshop) efficiency was increased without simultaneously negative effects on working conditions. On the whole, however, performance pressure at Porsche has increased significantly due to the reengineering process, and it will probably increase even further, if the management carries out its intention of turning the entire production into continuous assembly-line manufacturing by 1996, with an intended work time of 8.75 hours per shift.

It is not exclusively blue-collar workers who are affected by mounting work pressure. The reduction from six to four levels of management has also induced certain changes, which particularly affected the production plants. By abolishing the level of foremen, management placed a lot of their tasks squarely on the shoulders of the Meister.

In the case of Porsche the reduction of control, which is allegedly a result of reengineered company processes, also turns out to be myth. With the introduction of continuous assembly line manufacturing, with every step planned down to the second, employees are more easily controlled. Furthermore, mistakes can now be clearly attributed to individual workers, which according to Wiedeking was one of the principal aims of Porsche's reengineering processes. Another innovation is information boards, where the individual performance of every employee is documented for everybody to see. Information is given for example on who masters how many and which steps in the work process.

Job cuts, increased performance pressure and easier control of employees are all indicators that the radical restructuring processes demanded by business reengineering concepts have a more negative impact on the working conditions of employees than the concept would make one believe. On the contrary, Porsche seems to be a case in point that business reengineering is merely a new social strategy to carry out old rationalization concepts. This point was impressively brought across by the Porsche chairman at an industrial engineering conference in Berlin. Asked how Porsche had managed to implement the restructuring process, Wiedeking answered: 'We involved the works council in all our projects, but with the number of topics they completely lost sight of what we actually implemented.'

CONCLUSION

Since 1993, the German car industry has faced a period of crisis. This led to serious questions about the future of the German model of making cars. German car companies reactions to the crisis show that there is a variety of ways to address the challenges. Radical shifts in the sense of 'reengineering' seek to turn companies upside down while other concepts seek change through compromise. This leads to reduced working hours but preserves established structures to a large extent. Again other companies initially increase foreign production facilities. Car companies used the economic slump to question the high labour-cost of location in Germany and threatened unions and works councils by moving production abroad. There is no doubt that German companies will increase their foreign production facilities but there is no evidence that internationalization of production is related to high labour costs in Germany. On the contrary economic recovery in 1994 and 1995 showed that exports were strong and companies were doing well on foreign markets.

In adopting lean production principles companies focussed on employment reductions and cost cutting measures. In this context the debate over new structures of work organization within the factories came to a halt. The major result of the 1993 crisis is that there is a shift to traditional approaches of increasing productivity by abandoning 'cumbersome' labour relations. So far, works councils and unions do not have much room to improve working conditions.

NOTES

1. *Verband der Automobilindustrie* (VDA), VDA Pressedienst No.3/1994.
2. *Auto 93/94 Jahresbericht VDA*, p.39.

3. Meissner, H.R., K.P Kisker and U. Bochum (1994), *Die Teile und die Herrschaft. Die Reorganisation der Automobiliproduktion und der Zulieferbeziehungen* (edition sigma), Berlin, p.34.
4. Streek, W. (1988) 'Successful Adjustment to Turbulent Markets: The Automobile Industry', WZB discussion papers FSI 88-1, Berlin, p.18.
5. Jürgens, U. (1994) 'VW at The Turning Point – Success and Crisis of a German Production Concept', in *Actes du GERPISA* No.10, *Des Trajectoires des Firmes aux Modeles Industriels*, Universite d'Evry-Val d'Essonne.
6. Endres, E. and T. Wehner (1993) 'Vom plötzlichen Boom der Gruppenarbeit' in *deutschen Automobilfabriken. Harburger Beiträge zur Psychologie und Soziologie der Arbeit*, TU Hamburg-Harburg.
7. *Manager Magazin* (1994) In a process of continuous improvement the team members eliminate everything that is not related to the value-added process.
8. See J. Buteweg (1995), 'Modell im Alltag', in *Die Mitbestimmung*, Heft Vol.7/95, p.26–29.
9. Schumann, M., V. Baethge-Kinsky, M. Kuhlmann, C. Kurz, U. Neumann, (1994), *Trendreport Rationalisierung. Automobilindustrie, Werkzeugmaschinenbau*, Chemische Industrie, Berlin, p.69f.
10. See Steinkühler, F. (1992), 'Für eine demokratische und soziale Unternehmensreform – gewerkschaftliche Antworten auf die "japanische Herausforderung"', in: *Hans Böckler Stiftung / Industriegewerkschaft Metall* (Ed.) Lean Production , Baden-Baden , p.18.
11. See IG Metall, Wachstum in den Stau, Arbeitsplätze im Rückwärtsgang. Diskussionspapier zur Konferenz der IG Metall zur Zukunft der Automobilindustrie May 1995 Frankfurt / M.
12. See *Der Spiegel* Nr. 49/1994, 'Schuften wie die Pferde'.
13. See DIW Wochenbericht 15/16 1995.
14. *Der Spiegel* No. 43/1994.
15. Unlike that of Daimler-Benz after taking over the Dutch airplane manufacturer Fokker. There it came to serious conflicts on future strategies and the reorganization of the firm.
16. Benz in'Bama,' Automotive Industries June 1994.
17. Peters, J. *et al.*, 'Nicht kapitulieren – trotz Krise und Rezession. Der Weg zur Sicherung der Beschäftigung bei Volkswagen', in: WSI-Mitteilungen No. 3/1994, p.165–71.
18. See the interview with a member of the VW works council in Wirtschaftswoche No. 49/1994.
19. Hammer, M./Champy, J. (1993), *Reengineering the Corporation*, New York.
20. At a Business Management Conference (Betriebswirtschaftertag) in Berlin in 1994.
21. Wiedeking was elected Manager of the year by the magazine *Top Business*.

APPENDIX

(Extract of an interview published in the newsletter *Porsche Intern* with four workers who work in the engine plant)

Intern: Has the rate of work increased since management introduced the continuous assembly line production?

Worker A: Yes, your performance has to be much higher now, yes definitely.

Intern: Can you imagine working like this for ten years?

Worker A: No I can't. I think you can work like this only for two or three years.

Intern: What do you think, how long can you stand that?

Worker D: Till you are forty years old I think. There may be some exceptions.

Intern: What kind of advantages did the company get out of this?

Worker A: Management could keep workers under better control.

Worker B: I would say that's the only thing, they wanted to keep workers under control.

Worker C: There is no time for doing something else, so they keep you under control all the time.

Intern: Can you imagine how to design engine assembly in a workers-oriented way?

Worker C: It was better before – just normal assembly line. You can train workers working on several jobs, they can even assemble a whole engine. We have seen it before, if you assemble a whole engine quality is better, because everyone is responsible for his engine.

Intern: ...and people did like it?

Worker D: Yes definitely, they liked it.

Worker B: Before, you could change jobs every week as well.

Intern: You don't have that anymore?

Worker A: No, sometimes you do the same job for half a year. That does not satisfy very much.

Worker D: Not only for half a year but for your whole life, if you can stand it.

Intern: The continuous assembly line dictates what you have to do from morning till evening. What is good and what is bad with this?

Worker C: What's bad is that the assembly line has the same speed all day long. In times before if you were not fit in the morning you could do something. Now you have to be fit right from the start, there is no relaxation.

Worker A: If you are not fit you better stay home, you can't come up with the speed. If somebody is helping out then your colleagues wouldn't like this too much either.

Worker C: I think the continuous assembly line will not work in the long run, because workers come in even if they are ill, so absenteeism will rise.

Worker A: When I come home, I'm knackered, I can't do anything. The whole family suffers then.

FIGURE 1

EMPLOYMENT IN GERMAN CAR COMPANIES 1980–1994
– According to Manufacturers – 1000

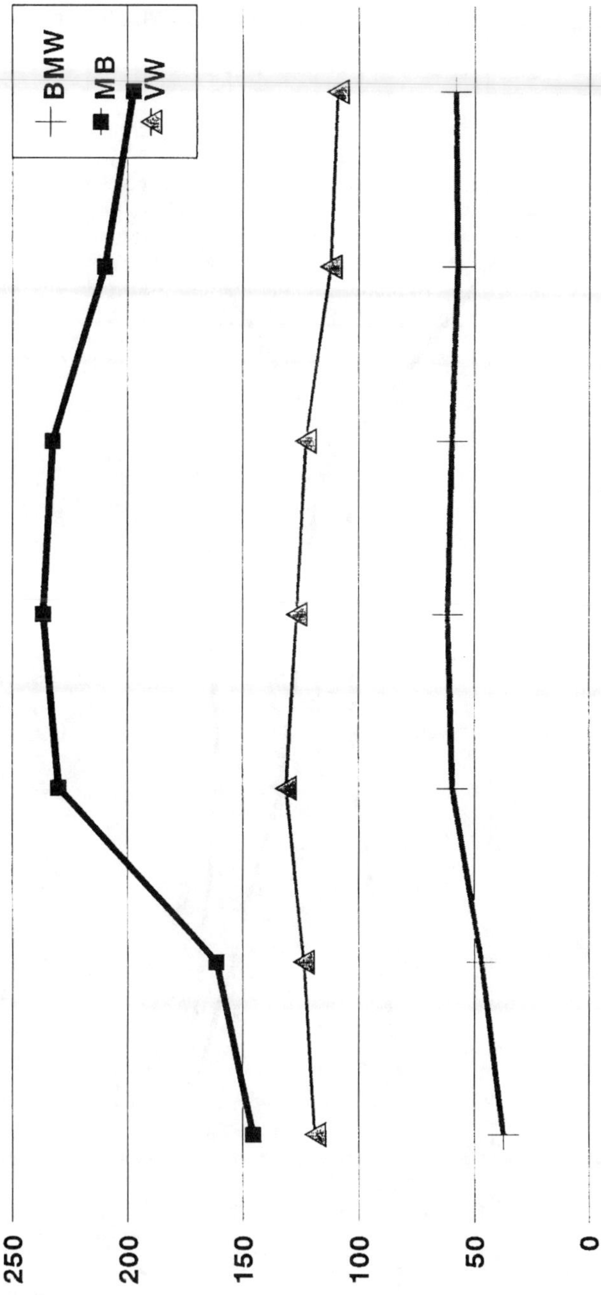

Legend: BMW, MB, VW

	1980	1985	1990	1991	1992	1993	1994
BMW	37	47	60	62	60	57	58
MB	146	162	230	237	232	210	198
VW	119	124	131	127	123	112	109

FIGURE 2
EMPLOYMENT REDUCTION AT DAIMLER-BENZ 1992–1995
1000 Employees

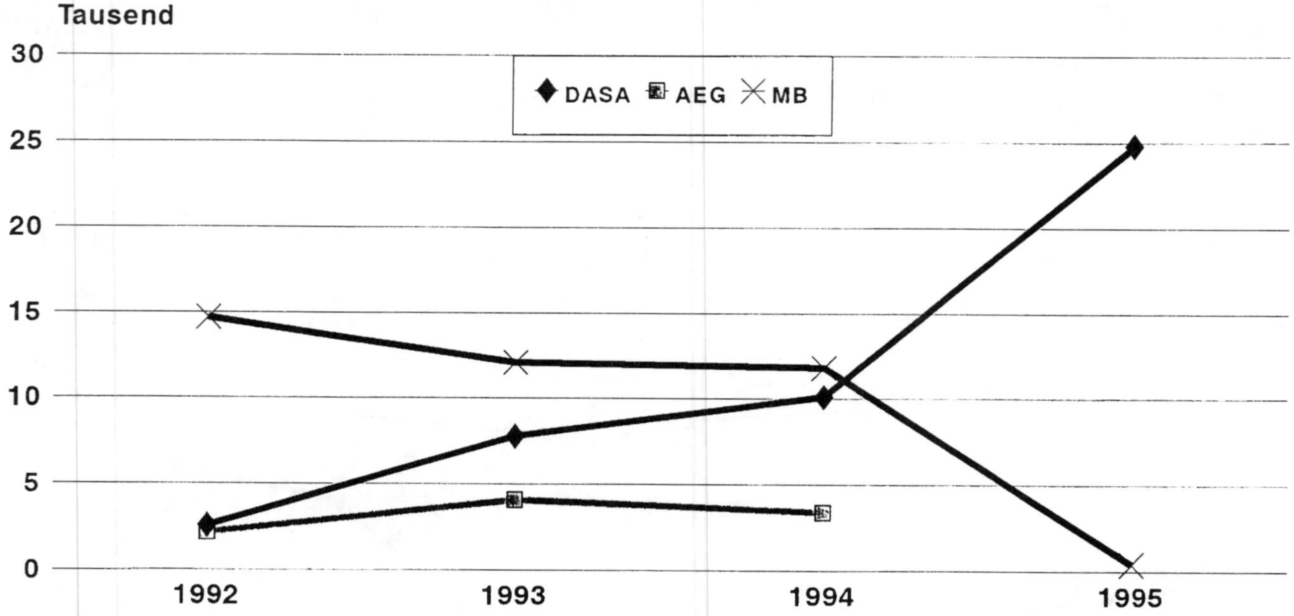

	1992	1993	1994	1995
DASA	2,6	7,8	10,1	24,8
AEG	2,2	4,1	3,4	0,4
MB	14,7	12,1	11,8	25,2
Total	19,5	24,1	25,8	

Source: Daimler-Benz

FIGURE 3

NEW MONTHLY WAGES (VW AG) 4-DAY WORKING WEEK
Reduction of Working Hours from 36 to 28.8

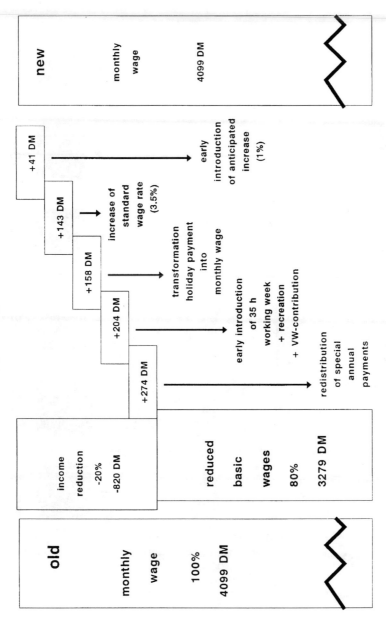

Source: IG Metall

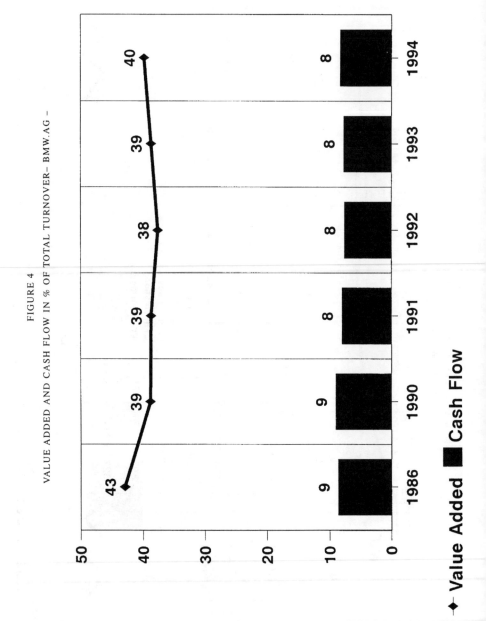

FIGURE 4
VALUE ADDED AND CASH FLOW IN % OF TOTAL TURNOVER– BMW.AG –

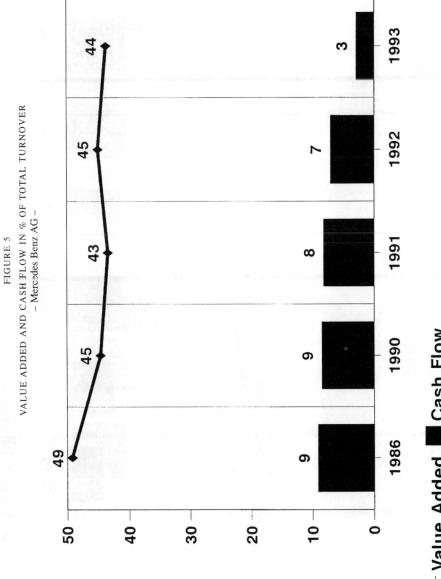

FIGURE 5
VALUE ADDED AND CASH FLOW IN % OF TOTAL TURNOVER
– Mercedes Benz AG –

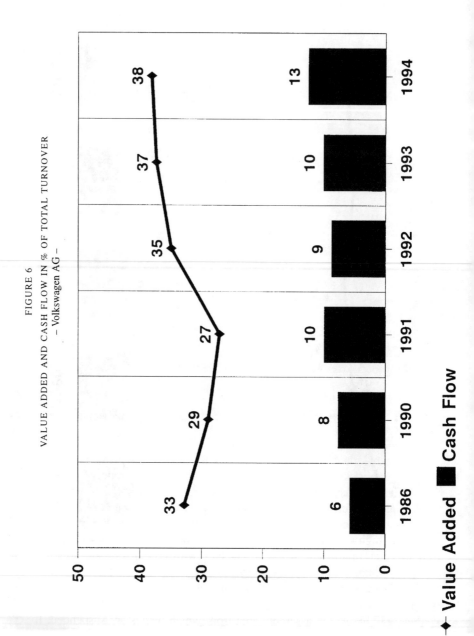

FIGURE 6
VALUE ADDED AND CASH FLOW IN % OF TOTAL TURNOVER
– Volkswagen AG –

Taylorism, Lean Production and the Automotive Industry

MIKE RAWLINSON AND PETER WELLS

INTRODUCTION

In this article we examine the nature of work organization in vehicle assemblers and component suppliers that are operating lean production systems. Unlike many other observers, as well as the proponents of lean production (Womack *et al.*, 1990), we do not concentrate on final assembly operations (Berggren, 1982 and to a lesser extent Garrahan and Stewart, 1992). We concentrate on manufacturing operations within car plants, as these areas of activity contribute more to the value of the vehicle and represent more of the capital input, labour input and value added in a typical passenger car. The assembly line is least amenable to automation, due to the nature of the materials to be handled; in particular soft trim items which present technical problems for handling, and the greater variety of parts which are fitted at this stage in the manufacturing process. It is for these reasons that the assembly lines of modern vehicle manufacturing plants remain labour intensive. The final assembly process itself can represent less than 15 per cent of the value added of a finished vehicle. We contend that the skill levels demanded on the assembly line are amongst the lowest in the major areas of activity in a car plant.

Historically, skill levels in the assembly operations of traditionally organized volume car plants (commonly termed 'Fordist' or 'Mass Production') have always been low. Despite this, in motor producing locations, such as Coventry (UK) and Detroit (US) during the post war era, jobs that in the rest of the manufacturing sector were considered semi-skilled were paid at skilled rates by employers, due to successful collective bargaining by trade unions. In some circumstances this created tensions between highly skilled craftsmen such as toolmakers and relatively highly paid manual line assembly workers. The Coventry Tool Room rate was used as a means of securing differential pay rates between the 'car workers' and the 'skilled engineering workers'. Such was the success of the car workers in eliciting high wages that phrases such as 'middle class by overtime' were used to refer to the car workers together with 'the Klondike' to their workplace (Standard Triumph Canley Plant).

The final assembly track is in fact one of the simplest machines in the modern car plant, comprising a moving track below the car bodies or an overhead rail above the assembly area from which bodies are suspended. It

Mike Rawlinson and Peter Wells, Cardiff Business School.

rarely embodies any significant area of technology, and has not differed greatly from the first vehicle assembly track at Ford's Highland Park. Indeed the moving conveyor was used in the meat processing industry in the US well before finding its way into automobile factories. The assembly line really cannot be used either for assessing changing levels of skilled jobs, or for assessing the impact of innovative production technology. We believe that such analysis should concentrate on the manufacturing activities within car plants, such as: the press shop, the body in white assembly shops, the drive train and power train plants. These areas have seen a progressive introduction of newer technologies which have brought their own idiosyncratic imperatives for the organization of labour and working practices. Therefore this article examines work organization in *manufacturing* and not *assembly* operations and in effect tells two stories, one about the comparison between so-called mass and lean production systems in the press shop, and one about the impact of technological change on both systems.

PRESSWORK

The Ford Model T and its production process examined by Williams *et al.* (1994) was in one important respect a high-volume craft-based design rather than a mass manufacture design. The Model T had a basic steel chassis frame, onto which was constructed a wooden framework that carried a rudimentary steel 'bucket type' body of several variants. In the US in the 1920s a radical new design paradigm was established by Edward Budd. In his approach, the body was entirely constructed of steel sheet parts, pressed as separate components and then welded together to form a monocoque or unitary body (unibody). The first application of this technology actually appeared on a 1928 Chrysler car, and it offered such great advantages for mass manufacture over separate chassis construction that all of the world's volume car manufacturers eventually followed suit and constructed their vehicles in this way. An additional benefit was the increased rigidity of the vehicle bodies compared with contemporary chassis-body constructions. When the first Budd system cars were manufactured press technology was in its infancy, having only been developed in the 1860s (Greyson, 1978). In presswork, flat sheets of steel are draw or pressed into shape through a series of operations between sets of forming dies held in the ram and bed of a large (general purpose) press. The process is also known as 'stamping'. The large and complex panels body panels demanded by the Budd system cannot be successfully formed by one operation; first a drawing operation is used to form the major panel shape, and then the semi-formed panels are fed into a succession of presses for trimming, hole punching and flanging operations. In the early years of application, when steel performance in the press was little understood and when die and press design were less advanced, the press operators were skilled staff:

> ... some of Budd's workmen developed a Stradivarius-like feel for

> how steel would act, and could adjust a huge press the hair's breadth
> necessary to correct a fault (Grayson, 1978: 355)

A typical car might have 250 to 350 pressed components of which 40 or so
would be large exterior body pressings. Unsophisticated die designs meant
that many parts required multiple die sets. As a result presses were arranged
in series known as Tandem lines – typically a line would have up to ten
presses. The output of such a line would be in the region of three to six parts
per minute. With the volume manufacturer the high costs of dies and presses
could be amortized over the long production runs, giving a significant
competitive advantage over craft constructed vehicle bodies. However, it
also resulted in the growth of very large press shops and a characteristically
segmented division of labour.

THE TRADITIONAL PRESS SHOP

Here we provide a charicature of a traditional press shop used by North
American and European vehicle assemblers so that the difference from the
approach adopted by Toyota may be more fully appreciated. A large press
shop would have up to 100 presses with perhaps eight main tandem lines
along with an associated tool room which manufactured, serviced and
prepared the die sets, stock rooms (steel inwards, parts outwards) and
management. Work segmentation is summarized below.

TABLE 1

JOB TYPES AND TASKS IN A TYPICAL VEHICLE ASSEMBLERS' PRESS SHOP

Category	Tasks	Number/Shift
Toolmakers	Make/repair dies	120
Die setters	Place and remove dies in presses	10
Stock control/storemen	Control steel inwards and parts outwards	8
Stock movement	Supply steel to press lines, unload steel inwards, remove parts from end of press lines to store, transfer parts to body welding shop	50
Press shop management	Allocate parts to tandem lines, establish schedules, maintenance regimes, etc.	25
Line supervisors	Oversee the operation of each line	10
Electrical maintenance	Maintenance	12
Hydraulic/mechanical maintenance	Press machinery maintenance	14
Crane operators	Overhead cranes to move dies, steel coils etc.	4
Quality inspection	Parts inspection on batches	10
Press operatives	Transfer/loading of parts along tandem lines	400
Ancillary staff	Cleaning	25
Total		688

Under this system of organization the line operatives were regarded as unskilled, their main task being to transfer steel between the presses and place it into the presses for forming. Dies required a great deal of skill to set in the presses, the slightest error in alignment could result in the part not being made or, even worse, in the dies being damaged. The dies could be up to 2m by 4m, weigh up to 30 tonnes, travel over 2m up and down and come together with a force of over 800 tonnes. The dies must come together at the same thickness of the steel, even an error tolerance of +/-0.1mm could prove disastrous: either the dies could 'crash' or the parts will not be properly formed. Specialists, often with separate Trade Union representation, dealt with the electrical, hydraulic and mechanical repair and maintenance, with material handling and so on. Changing a set of dies on a tandem line to produce a different part would take a full shift, as a result parts were produced in large batches and placed into storage in order to cope with the demand of 300 different parts or so for each vehicle from the body assembly shop. This form of organization was employed by virtually every high volume vehicle producer in the immediate post war period, including the Japanese manufacturers.

ORIGINS OF LEAN PRODUCTION: THE TOYOTA PRODUCTION SYSTEM

The Toyota Productions System (TPS) evolved over time as a number as specific engineering and organizational practices or techniques were incorporated. The basic building blocks of the TPS are *Jidoka* and just-in-time. The TPS is the basis for the 'ideal type' or 'stereo type' that has been termed Lean Production by McDuffie (1989) and Womack *et al.* (1990).

Just-in-time was developed by Kiichiro Toyoda, son of the founder of Toyota. It is much discussed in the academic and practitioner literature and so we will not dwell on it here. Generally just-in-time tends to be discussed in terms of inter-firm linkages and logistics management and inventory reduction by industrial geographers and business-related literature. The importance of just-in-time in manufacturing terms is the quality control aspect, in that parts are made sequentially in a flow process and defects are immediately visible.

Jidoka was developed by Sakichi Toyoda, the founder of the Toyota Group. It is largely ignored by labour process analysts, and indeed the *Machine That Changed the World. Jidoka* relates to the operation and features of machine tools; it is a concept of automation, or more accurately autonomation. *Jidoka* is the principle of equipping a machine to stop work immediately when there is a defect or abnormality. It is essentially concerned with building the task of inspection into the machine. If a faulty part is placed into a machine then the machine will detect the fault and will not operate. Combined with just-in-time, this results in defect-free production, and as parts are produced as they are needed there is no chance of an inventory of defective parts being built up. Essentially *Jidoka* embodies the skill of quality inspection into the machine tools and/or jigs and fixtures.

> At Toyota, a machine automated with a human touch [*Jidoka*] is one that is attached to an automatic stopping device. In all Toyota plants, most machines, new or old, are equipped with such devices as well as various safety devices, fixed-position stopping, the full work system, and poka-yoke foolproofing systems to prevent defective products... In this way, human intelligence, or a human touch, is given to the machines. (Ohno, 1988a: 6)

The benefits of *Jidoka* do not stop at the fool-proofing of production against defects.

> Perhaps the most fundamental effect of *Jidoka*, though, is the way it changes the nature of line management: it eliminates the need for an operator or operators to watch over each machine continuously – since the machine stops automatically when abnormalities occur – and therefore opens the way to major gains in productivity. (Ibid.:10)

Thus *Jidoka* does not only incorporate into production machinery relatively skilled operations of quality control, but it can also incorporate unskilled machine minding operations. This is an overt strategy and ultimately will help shape the skills composition of the workforce in manufacturing areas into semi-skilled general purpose operatives. The composition of work for these semi-skilled operatives is different in a factory operating with *Jidoka* as compared with more traditional forms of machine automation used in comparable Western plants. Machine minding is obviated as it is considered a cost which does not add value to the production process. The TPS is aimed at cost reduction in contrast with Western practices.

> An operator is not needed whilst the machine is working normally. Only when the machine stops because of an abnormal situation does it get human attention. As a result, one worker can attend several machines, making it possible to reduce the number of operators and increase production efficiency... The key is to give human intelligence to the machine and, at the same time, to adapt the simple movement of the human operator to the autonomous machines. (Ibid.: 7)

To operate such a system workers must be free to move from one job or task to another, as such Toyota call their workers 'multi-functional' workers. In the gear manufacturing shop for example, each worker attends 16 machines at one time, many of which perform different operations such as grinding or cutting (Mondon, 1993). The worker moves sequentially around the machines unloading and loading each one in turn and starting each machine cycle after loading.

In place of the rigid job designations of conventional systems, the Toyota Production System is predicated on employee flexibility in acquiring multiple skills. And where conventional systems had the schedule for many tasks with so-called reserve time, Toyota's system is oriented toward eliminating every second that is not absolutely necessary to change value. (Ibid.: 7)

The implementation of *Jidoka*, and just-in-time created a flexible workforce and the necessary conditions for the easy introduction of other techniques aimed at removing highly skilled workers from the production process.

THE TRADITIONAL PRESS SHOP UNDER THE TPS

The development of the TPS radically transformed the operation of the press shop and the organization of workers. In the 1950s, Toyota faced severe capital shortage which constrained the ability to purchase additional production equipment to keep pace with the fast growing domestic demand for passenger cars.

Previously when faced with capacity constraints the option chosen by Western vehicle assemblers has been to increase the size of their press shops. This was not a significant problem for Western vehicle producers in the post-war era when they were relatively cash-rich and market projections indicated increased sales. However, Toyota was not in this cash-rich position. As Toyota tried to increase both the volume of output and the range of models it produced the problem of press shop capacity was intensified. The problem affected the press shop in particular, as press machines are amongst the most expensive items in a car manufacturing plant. Management therefore had to resolve the problem of an effective lack of presses to meet the demand for pressed panels.

After analysis Toyota concluded that the problem actually lay in the inefficient use of press machines. In particular the poor rate of utilization or up-time was highlighted. This was due to the extensive periods that the presses were not working due to slow change-over times of about one entire shift. The engineer charged with the responsibility of dealing with this problem of poor machine utilization was Shigeo Shingo. He managed to decrease change over times from the 'standard' period of one shift to less than 15 minutes per line. The system he adopted he named SMED (the Single Minute Exchange of Dies). The SMED system was based on two principles: first, technical changes to the dies and the presses; and second, organizational changes to the labour processes involved in die changing.

The technical changes to a large extent enabled the changes in the organizational process. The technical changes were centred around standardization, the fragmenting of work tasks and the re-allocation of the simplified tasks. However what Shingo did was to analyse the process of die change and apply Taylorist principles combined with some simple engineering techniques in an authoritarian manner and impose the changes on the workforce without consultation or negotiation. Shingo was a dedicated follower of the work of Taylor and the application of his principles to industrial engineering and this had a profound influence on his thinking and production organization.

> Shortly after graduating from college, I read a book by F W Taylor. I felt enlightened and was introduced to the world of industrial engineering. (Shingo 1988, endnote)

One of the first problems Shingo had to solve was that the dies were often of different dimensions. From early this century cutting tools such as drill and milling cutters had been standardized with taper fits so that tool change was a relatively quick matter. However, standardization principles had not been applied to forming tools such as press dies. This was because dies were expensive items made out of very large iron castings. Standardization of the dimensions of the castings would have been very expensive and cumbersome. It would have meant that absurdly large and expensive castings would be necessary for dies for the production of relatively small parts.

The variability of die external dimensions was considered by Shingo to be one of the main barriers to efficiency. When dies of different dimension are placed into a press the shut height must be re-set very accurately, also the dies must be accurately positioned (centred) on the bed and the ram and then bolted in place with a large number of bolts. Shingo analysed the problems and came up with the following solutions. The variability in die heights which necessitated accurate re-setting of the press ram shut heights was overcome by the use of metal packing pieces, or shims, to the die tops. The dies could not be completely standardized, but they could be grouped into standardized families of dies. Each press line would then be associated with specific families.

Another time consuming practice was the bolting of the dies to the press rams and beds. The problem was associated with the use of a large number of bolts. Previously, the bolts and their heads had been of many different sizes, necessitating different spanners to perform the operation. Shingo firstly standardized the bolt head sizes so that only one spanner was needed. This could then be left clipped to the press machine. Shingo had found that a lot of time in the set up operations was accounted for by workers going to the stores to get additional bolts or correctly sized spanners during the die change operations, while the machine was not running. By organizing housekeeping operations, the correct bolts were then always stored with the die sets, and improvement was obtained at a minimal cost. Shingo went a stage further and started to use quick-action clamps or bolts. Finally, the number of bolts or clamps was reduced. Shingo realized that, for example, the bottom die weighed a considerable amount and only needed moderate force to hold it in location and so needed less clamping load than was formerly thought necessary.

The problem of accurately centring the dies was overcome by adding automatic centring devices. These could comprise V grooves milled into the die or bed that would mate up with raised Vs. Two grooves at $90°$ provide accurate and easy centring. Also in some cases simply bolted fixed stops would serve the same purpose. What these measures did was to remove the skill content from die change operations so that the skill level went from 'Stradivarian' proportions to at best semi-skilled operations.

A significant amount of time was saved by separating 'internal' from 'external' set up operations. Internal operations are those which can only be done while the press machines are stopped. External set up operations can be done while the machines are running – such as transporting the dies ready for insertion. This was an important conceptual breakthrough because, to maximize capacity utilization, the key was then to externalize as many functions as possible and enable line workers to undertake those functions. Previously, the press line would be stopped and then the die setters would unbolt the dies and move them by crane to the stores and then move in new dies which were inserted by crane. Shingo organized the process so that the replacement dies were brought to the press lines while the other parts were being made. The dies would then be placed on die carts by the side of the presses. The dies would then be prepared, the line stopped, and the old dies transferred onto empty die carts at one side of the press while the new dies were transferred into position from the other side of the press.

By fragmenting the work into logical steps and then removing the skill content of the setters the whole process could then be performed by the machine operators. Table 2 summarizes the effect of the changes on the general skill composition of the press shop.

TABLE 2
THE EFFECTS OF SMED ON THE WORKFORCE

Problem	Solution	Effect
Die dimension	Use dies in families on press lines	Simplification/ rationalization
Shut height	Attach packing blocks	Remove skill
Centring	V groove die backs and press beds in 2 axis (easy, automatic centring)	Remove skill
Bolting	Commonize bolt head sizes, reduce number of bolts, quick acting clamps	Simplification/ rationalization

Thus, the route chosen by Toyota in solving a shortage of press capacity was to focus on unproductive downtime. It also had the consequence of reducing the skill content and the head count in the press shop. The workers were then re-organized around the capital equipment in order to use the machines more fully. Once change-over times were reduced through SMED, Toyota could then work out how to use the minimum of labour to operate the machines and changeovers. In the TPS, indirect workers are not visible on the shop floor. The skills of the setters have wherever possible been embodied in the machine tools themselves. Once Toyota had standardized or commonized its dies by common bolting, sleeves and packing, and automatic centring, it could then specify the standardized die heights and bed dimensions for its future models – thus ensuring the possibility of quick changeovers.

The interesting aspect of this embodiment of skills into machinery is the way in which it was achieved. The solution proposed by Shingo did not involve much in the way of new technology or revolutionary manufacturing techniques. Furthermore, there is very little that would appear to be unusual to Henry Ford, who also realized the importance of set-up time reduction and developed multi-fixtures and 'one touch' clamps of his own. Similarly fixed stops have been around since the industrial revolution and played an important part in the mechanization of cotton and woollen cloth production in the textile mills of Lancashire and Yorkshire. Ford would also have recognized the autocratic way the Shingo solution was imposed on the workforce following, in effect, a classic time and motion study of the production process. In other words, shopfloor workers had no input into or control over the reorganization of the workplace – the principle of continuous improvement via shopfloor-based innovations was only relevant after management had decreed the basic framework within which work was organized.

Allied to the organizational principles of *Jidoka* and just-in-time manufacturing, the effect of SMED as the cornerstone of the TPS in the press shop was to provide the structure within which a redefinition of skills and tasks was achieved. The power of SMED as an engineering philosophy was increased when it was combined with *Jidoka* and just-in-time.

CHANGING TECHNOLOGY IN THE PRESS SHOPS

It is interesting to note that there has been a rapid convergence in press shop organization and management across the vehicle producers in recent years. This has come about through the introduction of a new phase of press technology. The modern integrated tri-axis transfer press effectively replaces the traditional tandem line, but can produce parts at a rate of up to 18 per minute – six times that of a traditional un-automated tandem line. Transfer presses are huge, integrated machine tools holding five or six die sets. Parts transfer is internalized to the machine. Automatic bolsters move dies in and out in under five minutes, while sensors automatically detect the dies and set the press accordingly. Thus a modern transfer press is both more flexible than a traditional tandem line and can produce at a substantially faster rate. Even blank de-stacking and the removal of finished parts and their stacking into stillages may be automated. These machines and associated equipment can cost £50m to £100m and as such demand high levels of utilization to be economic. Computerized systems monitor and control the press, integrating functions such as preventative maintenance, process control and dimensional quality.

With a modern, integrated transfer press, workers are transformed into general machine minders. They supply steel blanks to be fed into the machine, they monitor press performance, remove stillages, prepare the for the next die change, perform quality control, and undertake basic preventative maintenance. The organization of the workers is typically to create a team to 'serve' the transfer press, even in press shops that otherwise have a more conventional form of line organization. The majority of the team is effectively multi-semi-skilled: they are qualified to undertake a range of tasks up to certain defined limits, in most cases including the preparation of production schedules on a weekly basis. However, these skills are constrained by being company-specific, or machine specific and limited in scope. It is interesting to note that the form of organization around these machines differs little from vehicle manufacturer to vehicle manufacturer, and so the organization in Nissan or Toyota differs little from that in Mercedes, Citroen or Ford.

The so called 'lean producers' have embraced the transfer press as it goes one step further in increasing the rapid production and smooth flow of parts than the Toyota press shop organization that was developed by Shingo and Ohno. The newer rounds of investment by the Japanese and Western companies in press shops have been almost exclusively for transfer presses. The composition of the workforce of a typical modern press shop (having five transfer presses) is shown in Table 3.

TABLE 3

THE COMPOSITION OF JOBS AND TASKS IN A MODERN TRANSFER
PRESS BASED PRESS SHOP

Job	Tasks	Number per shift
Tool support staff	Inspection and cleaning of dies, fault diagnostics	10
Crane operators	Moving dies and steel coils	2
5 Teams, each per transfer press	Detailed scheduling, De-stacking, stack parts, move parts, die change, preventative maintenance, quality inspection, operative, monitoring, cleaning	6 people per team (i.e. 30 total)
Quality Inspection	Overall shop quality control	4
Management	Overall schedules, training plans	8
Total		44/shift

IS LEAN PRODUCTION SO DIFFERENT?
FLOW MANUFACTURING AND WORKER SKILLS

The TPS, like the Ford system, is based on cost reduction. For example cost reduction exercises enabled Ford to reduce the selling price of the Touring Model T From $850 in 1909 to $350 in 1916 (Williams *et al.:* 1994). The TPS is overtly focused on cost or waste reduction and SMED, *Jidoka*, just-in-time, and Kaizen are all aimed at cost reduction. Toyota (in house publication) states that failure to arrange equipment in accordance with the production sequence results in an awkward flow which in turn leads to the following kinds of waste:

- Work in process accumulates after each machine and process.

- Additional conveyancing between processes is necessary.

- The amount of material handling is two, three, or four times what it should be.

- Grouping equipment separately by process or by kind of machine allows for fast operation at individual stages of production, but it inhibits improvements oriented toward producing the exact items we need exactly when needed and with a minimal number of employees.

- Responsiveness to change in specifications or in products is poor.

- Defective items do not become immediately apparent, and corrective action gets delayed.

- Production lead times are extremely long.

- The work flow and the production sequence cannot be standardized.

These forms of waste were also the focus of Ford's attempt at improving the cost competitiveness of his products. The account by Williams *et al.* (1994) of actual practices in Ford plants illustrates that what has been termed Fordism is really a simplification that does not take account of the true aims of the system and the delicate interplay between capital equipment and labour on the shop floor. We must add that the effect of the market for cars at the time also had an important part in shaping the nature of production. Ford did not need to introduce a great deal of variety into his products because until 1920 he could sell all that he could make in the Highland Park plant.

The Ford system concentrated on flows of products. Production smoothing was achieved whenever possible. The best way of achieving the flow may not necessarily have been to employ Taylorist methods and fragment and deskill the tasks. If a piece of capital equipment (no matter how complex) could be employed more cheaply and reliably then it would be, even if it meant that higher skilled workers were needed to operate them. Ford should not be seen as synonymous with deskilling. Indirectly the Ford Motor Company probably assisted skilling more people than it ever deskilled, for it was the Ford Trade School Apprenticeship System for skilled mechanical engineers (machinists and toolmakers) that was made the standard for all US military and civil production during the Second World War.

Ford also developed special purpose machine tools, and multi-fixtures to reduce set up times prior to Shingo's efforts in Toyota. Quick acting, or 'one touch', clamps were also used to reduce set-up times. This illustrates that Ford, like the Japanese, had fully realized the important financial and logistical implications of having machine downtime. Ford saw under-utilization of machines as wasteful and thus sought to devise a system where machine up-time was being maximized throughout the factory based on smooth consistent flows of parts or products. Williams *et al.* (1994) argue that stock turns in the early Ford plants, a measure of inventory and work in progress, were not too dissimilar for the best practice lean operating companies identified by the IMVP, and were significantly better than most non-Japanese plants and several Japanese plants.

> By 1915, Highland Park was running with stock cover of 3–5 days for major components like chassis frames and engines; as early as 1913, buffer stocks between individual production departments were down to a few hours, with zero stocks inside the departments. In the case of quick changeovers and low levels of inventory and fast stock turns Ford's organisation could be said to be on a par with many of the better so called Lean producers. (Williams *et al.*, 1994: 80).

Toyota, by re-arranging machines according to flow as Ford did, greatly reduced parts storage and also laid the foundations for the 'one operator many processes' philosophy (Ohno, 1988b). Ohno concludes that this was also made possible because in Japan there were no functionally oriented unions, the transition of from a single skilled to a multi-skilled operator was possible. The actual level of the skills of Japanese operators is termed 'manufacturing skill' by Ohno. Furthermore, Toyota found that by organizing workers into teams and increasing their generic skill levels on problem solving it was then possible to use the workers to increase the levels of machine, worker and processing efficiency. This allowed Toyota to appropriate the tacit skills of the employees who have performed routine tasks with a variety of machines on a day to day basis. However, the power of the Toyota system stems from its ability to elicit such improvements and then codify and standardize them into the production process as the standard job sheet for each operation. The job sheet would remain the reference until it be bettered, then the new way would be codified and used as the reference.

Our experience of researching in plants in Europe (including Japanese transplants) is that operator skills in alleged 'lean producer companies' are seldom up to craft level. Skilled craftsmen (and they are almost invariably male) reside in toolrooms, repair and maintenance departments, and as machine setters. However, in Europe toolroom functions are gradually being externalized and preventative maintenance (Reliability Centred Maintenance, or Total Preventative Maintenance) is being assigned to operators and supervisors, as are the tasks of setting up. In a survey conducted by the authors for the Welsh Development Agency on the training needs of vehicle assemblers and automotive component suppliers the evidence was overwhelming that what volume car manufacturers and their suppliers want are workers with generic, transferable skills such as problem solving, teamwork skills and quality related training. They did not want nor need large numbers of craft skilled workers. The main reason behind this is that on-the-job training was sufficient for operators to be able to use the production machinery. In effect, skill levels for operatives are not particularly demanding and at best may be considered semi skilled.

What the automotive companies sought, for example, were operators who could make sense of the computer-based control systems built into production lines and individual pieces of equipment. If a machine stops due to some irregularity manufacturers want the operator to be the first line technician and to repair or adjust the machine on the spot if possible, and finally to call for assistance promptly if they cannot fix the machine themselves.

In an interview with the Personnel Director of one of Ford's manufacturing plants he made the point that 'we no longer want operators who just push a button all day long. We want them to push a button and do a bit of this and a bit of that as well'. This is quite an accurate reflection of how work is organized under lean production. Ford has recently revised its training programmes to combine many formerly separate trade skills. An example is the 'Mec/Elec' training programme where the mechanical and electrical engineering or maintenance skills are combined into one unit.

The emphasis on the nature of skills required in the automotive industry has changed. Individual worker skills are only part of the necessary skills to run the production line. As most work is now becoming team based it is the skill levels and competencies of the team as a unit that are considered. Not all workers are yet able to set up their machines and the team leaders or supervisor/technicians still have a role to play in many instances. However, the important facet of team working is not that every worker can perform a set of varied tasks, but that the team as a whole can perform all of the necessary tasks. For example, in the press shop of a Japanese transplant factory we visited, team members were located on a simple skills matrix chart. The X axis listed the individual team members (grouped together adjacent to other team members). The Y axis was divided into skills, or more accurately task areas or competencies. Where members had skills or competencies in particular areas they were noted on a nominal scale of 1–5. The training manager and production manager could see at a glance any areas of skill shortage. In general, the aim would be to have at least two members of each team fully competent in the more difficult areas, such as die changes, machine re-configuration while most, if not all, of the team skilled in the more simple areas such as quality control. Thus, it was evident that the company considered the team as the unit that possesses the requisite skills or competencies rather than individuals alone.

It would be difficult to call the workers multi-skilled or 'polyvalent'. Lehndorff (1996) found that although polyvalence took a number of forms in European automotive components companies it really meant a willingness and ability to move between jobs. Furthermore Lehndorff found that job rotation usually only occurs within teams and not across teams. In our investigation of press shops in Europe we found that operatives could move around within press shop operations, but not into other downstream or upstream activities. In effect the workers were 'multi-purpose semi-skilled' able to perform the required tasks for a particular machine. So press shop operatives, even if they could change the dies and service the presses would only be 'skilled' on a narrow range of presses, and would need a reasonable degree of re-training to operate the presses of another manufacturer. Although at an initial glance the worker skills are impressive, in that they seem to run large tri-axis transfer presses autonomously, it must be remembered that many of the skills are very specific – not only to one type of machine, but even to one machine tool manufacturer's machine. This illustrates that skills are not only task specific as highlighted by Garrahan and Stewart (1992), but they are also machine tool manufacturer specific. This restriction of skills or tasks is not as easy to identify in the comparatively low skilled assembly operations, yet it is possible to identify in manufacturing areas.

CONCLUSION

The trend to multi-tasking therefore constitutes a shift within Taylorism in manufacturing areas as well as in assembly areas identified by Schumann (cited in Lehndorff, 1996). Wickens (1993) argues that lean production retains many Tayloristic elements such as the division of labour, standardized operations, the elimination of waste and the 'one best way' of performing operations or tasks. However, Taylorism (like Ford's production at Highland Park and the TPS as practised at its 'showcase' Takaoka plant), is concerned with efficient flows of material. In mass manufacturing the concern of the production or industrial engineer is principally the most efficient use of resources and materials to produce parts or products with a repetitive, reliable system. There was nothing revolutionary about the TPS, individual elements of its building blocks or manufacturing principles can be found in other sectors of the economy in a variety of countries. What was novel was the way they were brought together. Some of the building blocks drew heavily (and explicitly) on the work of Taylor. Furthermore, we consider that Matthews (cited in Wood 1993) is optimistic in his argument that the TPS will lead to highly skilled autonomous workers as a consequence of it being a departure from Taylorism .This is because, as we have argued, the TPS is in fact based on Taylorism and the lessons learnt from Toyota's visits to Ford factories in the 1950s. Moreover, there is no suggestion here of the abdication of management. Quite the contrary, the TPS was clearly imposed by a powerful management, just as the installation of advanced transfer presses have been used by Western manufacturers to impose new job content and working practices in their press shops.

Under such 'lean production' systems many higher level skills are removed from production workers and relocated to (or embodied within) capital equipment. Moreover, skills and knowledge are transferred to the production engineers who effectively 'design' the job tasks, and hence skill levels. Production workers are then given a modest amount of training so that they can then perform a wider variety of semi-skilled tasks. In effect one worker may now perform the work which was formerly carried out by several workers. The founders of the TPS perceived that it made little sense to have someone watch a machine work, as they did not consider this task as one which added value to the product. Instead, they preferred direct workers only to do the tasks that added value or increased the rate of capital utilization. So, workers were used to load and unload parts from machines, and where necessary move the parts between machines, perform (quick) change-overs and setting, with the skill largely 'engineered' out, and to perform preventative maintenance.

Where lean production systems do differ fundamentally from previous 'Fordist' organizations is that they do demand extra skills from workers in the area of problem solving. Workers are then able to make improvements to the work to make it either easier or faster or both. However, this problem solving ability becomes a source for manufacturers to extract the tacit knowledge of workers. These tacit skills generate suggestions for improvement which can then be taken by the manufacturing engineers, and if they benefit capital utilization or make the work more efficient (either quicker or easier) then the suggestions can be re-coded up into the standard job sheet, or the standard operating procedure. The job sheet is a record of how the job or task should be performed correctly and remains the reference until it is improved. What is interesting about multi-locational companies is that they can then use the most efficient job sheet for the sister plants. For example, when Nissan in the UK changes dies on a Hitachi-Zosen press in the UK, if the die change can be performed in a quicker time than in the other plants, it is recorded on video, studied and then used as the reference for other Nissan plants with the same equipment in Japan or North America. Thus the pace of work is no longer controlled and defined on a plant basis but on a global basis.

REFERENCES

Berggren, C (1982) 'New Production Concepts in Final Assembly – the Swedish Experience' in S. Wood (ed) *The Transformation of Work?* (London: Unwin Hyman)

Garrahan, P. and P. Stewart (1992) *The Nissan Enigma* (London: Mansell).

Lehndorff, S. (1996) 'Time Constraints and Autonomous Time Management: The Labour Process in Automotive Component Plants under the Just-in-Time Regime', in P. Broedner, U. Pekruhl, and D. Rehfeld (eds) *Arbeitsteilung ohne Ende.* (Hampp: Muenchen and Mering.

McDuffie, J. (1989) *Worldwide Trends in Production System Management: Work Systems, Factory Practice, and Human Resource Management.* Working paper. IMVP Publication.

Mondon, Y. (1993) *The Toyota Production System.* Second Edition. (Georgia: Norcross).

Ohno, T. (1988a) *Toyota Production System* (Cambridge MA:Productivity Press).

Ohno, T. (1988b) *Workplace Management* (Cambridge MA:Productivity Press).

Shingo, S. (1984) *Non-Stock Production* (Cambridge MA: Productivity Press).

Shingo, S. (1988) *A Revolution in Manufacturing: The SMED System* (Cambridge MA: Productivity Press).

Taylor, F.W. (1947) *Scientific Management.* New York: Harper Bros.

Thompson, P. (1989) *The Nature of Work.* Second Edition. Basingstoke: Macmillan.

Toyota Motor Company (1992) *The Toyota Production System.*

Wickens, P. (1993) 'Lean Production and Beyond: The System, Its Critics and the future'. *Human Resource Management Journal.* Vol 3, No.4. pp.75–90.

Williams, K., C. Haslam, J. Williams, A. Adcroft, and S. Johal (1994) 'The Myth of the Line: Ford's Production of the Model T at Highland Park, 1909–16'. *Business History* Vol.35, No.3, pp.66–87.

Womack, J. D. Jones and D. Roos (1990) *The Machine that Changed the World.* New York: Rawson.

Wood, S. (1991) 'Japanization and/or Toyotaism?'. *Work, Employment and Sociey,.* Vol.5, No.4. pp.567–600.

Wood, S. (1993) 'The Japanisation of Fordism'. *Economic and Industrial Democracy.* Vol.14, pp.535–55.

Index